THE FRACTURED LIFE OF
3743

A JOURNEY TO REDEMPTION

A Memoir by Rob Cabitto

ISBN 13: 971-1-59298-432-9

Library of Congress Catalog Number: 2011936763
Printed in the United States of America
First Printing: 2011
15   14   13   12   11   5   4   3   2   1

Cover and interior design by Alan Pranke

BEAVER'S POND
PRESS

Beaver's Pond Press, Inc.
7104 Ohms Lane, Suite 101
Edina, MN 55439-2129
(952) 829-8818
www.BeaversPondPress.com

To order, visit www.BeaversPondBooks.com or call 1-800-901-3480.
Reseller discounts available.

www.robcabitto.com

3743
INTERACTIVE

Throughout this book you will find QR Codes—short for "quick response" code. Basically by focusing your smartphone on the bar code, you will immediately have access to more information or pictures about that subject. No longer will you have to wonder, "What does his family look like," when you can go to the website to see the photos of that and much more. You will become more intimately connected to the story and to the author's life. If you wish, please share your experience with us on Facebook, Twitter or our blog.

Download a scanner from your favorite app store and join us on 3473's journey.

Follow us on Twitter

Become a Facebook friend

DEDICATION

I want to offer a very special thanks and dedication to my son, Colin. You're an amazing son, and today I listen to the trees clap because of your simple suggestion to "be quiet and listen."

A portion of this book is dedicated to Jennifer, my son's mother, and her new family, husband, Geoffrey, Wyatt, and Cooper, for their ongoing love and support.

I would also like to make a dedication to all those men and women who were courageous enough to tell their stories about survival, loss, pain, hurt, abandonment, and addiction, in order for people like me to find hope and inspiration.

I want to honor Suzanne (Suzy) Green's memory for her support.

DISCLAIMER

Many of the names and places have been
changed to protect their identity.

TABLE OF CONTENTS

Preface

As I tell my story, some of the things I state as "remembering," were in fact things that became clearer to me as an adult.

When I was thirty-eight years old, I reconnected with my biological mother. Frequently we talked about the past, about memories I had from when I was young and still living with my first family. These were not always pleasant memories, for her and for me, but they were our shared memories.

I'd make a statement, and her reply often was: "Ohhhhh, Robbie, I didn't know you remembered that." As a child I recalled things about different incidents, but didn't always understand what they really meant. How could a four-year-old understand violence against his mother, or a father's assault against his own children? How could "little boy" Robbie understand that alcohol and drugs make a man do horrible things to those he is supposed to love? How could a little boy make sense of his mother drinking so much that she'd pass out holding a lit cigarette, thus burning the house down with her children in the house?

After my first mother was diagnosed with cancer, and as her days grew shorter every time we talked, we delved into deeper and deeper regions of our shared life. I'd ask a hard question, which was usually followed by her huge sigh, and then her explanation.

Often her explanation helped me understand about things I had never had closure on—things that had been driving me crazy. I had been holding onto memories that caused me to sleep with a light on all my life. Over the years I had dealt with having "small pieces," and now she was filling in the horrible blanks. Her admissions took away a lot of crazy feelings about certain smells or sounds that flooded my memories.

I am a Karuk Indian from northern California, and my tribe calls the Upper Klamath River home. Karuk (pronounced *Ka-rook*) means "Upriver people." We are a Native tribe with a rich history in basket weaving and fishing. I had nine biological brothers and sisters, and three siblings in my adoptive family, and I was the youngest in both families.

And my roll number, a special appellation given by the state to certain individuals, is 3743. More about that later.

I have been homeless, jobless, and penniless. Spiritually, emotionally, and physically I have been destitute. Over the last several years I have lost family members to suicide, drugs, and, most recently, alcohol. I have been sad, scared, and downright lonely, but I never gave up. The life of 3743 can be summed up as a journey, beginning with tragedy, and culminating in redemption born out of desperation.

And so the story goes. . . .

Acknowledgment

The Fractured Life of 3743 project was based on a collective collaborative effort by so many wonderful and helpful people.

My life experiences have been a gift, and I am grateful to all those who have helped inch my life along, and to those who inspired me to write this book. I much appreciate everyone's spiritual guidance and emotional support during the long process of completing this book. Thanks to all of you for offering to be part of my family—or asking me to be part of yours.

Thanks to all who have become my teachers. Each of you has in some way become a skilled practitioner of your art before you were presented with the gift: a student. Our experience is one of the greatest assets we can offer another human being. Special thanks to Grant, Geno, John, Chris, Cheri, Lonnie and Dan for their loving support.

I want to express my love for all the people that let me sleep on their couches, offered me a warm bed, a job, or food when I was hungry. Each and every one of you has truly been a gift.

To my primary editor, Connie Anderson, Words & Deeds, Inc.: You were a pleasure to work with because of your insight, candor, and responsiveness. Your curiosity changed my thoughts and the very fabric of my book to one I am now most proud of. To all others who helped with various aspects of editing my book: Matt O'Connell, Diane Keyes, and Mandy Marek, thank you for your magnificent craft. Your support, and guidance helped bring my experiences to life on these pages.

Without each of you constantly questioning me about situations, people, and scenarios, I believe the book would lack quality. Your patience, professionalism, and hard work shine in this memoir. As one of my editors put it, "You have your life, and then your book about your life." I have this life because of the people like each of you extending yourself to my life, and to this book about my life.

To my cover designer and book formatter, Alan Pranke: your quiet, consistent, and patient changes gave me a book I am proud of.

Thanks also to my publisher, Beaver's Pond Press, for their expertise and guidance through the final stages of this book, and making it become a reality.

And finally, my eternal love and gratitude goes out to my four-legged friends that have brought so much joy to my life: Nikko, Bear, Nanji, Sujay, Arzu, and Nisha were all special pets that carried and sustained me on days when I thought I could not go on.

PART I:
THE EARLY YEARS

CHAPTER 1

Liquid on My Face

Slippery rocks surrounded me as I sat on the ground next to the rushing stream. The air smelled of fish. Water splashed against the rocks, making a pleasing, comforting sound. Looking up, I saw a round red canister hovering over me. The can had dirt on it. When the cold liquid struck my face and body, I had difficulty breathing, and gasped for air repeatedly while the smell burned my nose.

My brother Greg shouted, "No! No!" as he ran toward me. "What the heck are you doing, Dad?" He screamed again, "No, no!" and pushed my dad, knocking him over. My dad got up and tried to throw a punch at Greg, missing him. It's funny what I remember. Greg was dirty; not the smudge kind of dirt but the hard-core grime that comes from days and weeks of neglect. His hair made him look like a wild man, and his blue jeans and muscle shirt had oil stains. Both he and our dad smelled like sweat.

My mom ran up, sobbing, and screamed at my dad, "What are you doing! What are you doing!" Her long hair blew in the wind, and a brown shawl covered her white shirt. When she picked me up and wiped my hair out of my eyes, I looked at her dark skin, and felt her soft hands and gentle touch. Her breath smelled bad, as it always did when she took a drink out of the big bottle. The odor made me sick to my stomach. As she was carrying me back to the house, tears rolled down her cheek and hit me in the face.

The horrible-smelling liquid my dad had poured on my face and body was gasoline. His sole intention was to set me on fire.

This was 1969—and I was four years old.

CHAPTER 2

From Foster Care to Adoption

The smell of the spaghetti and garlic bread was wonderful. To this day, that simple dish still evokes warm memories and holds a special place in my heart. When I arrived at my new foster family's home in a nearby small northern California town, that's exactly what the place smelled like— spaghetti and garlic bread. I sat down for dinner where I had a clear view of the refrigerator. Incredibly, the refrigerator was packed with food. My first thought was, *Tonight I'm raiding this refrigerator before I go to bed.* That's exactly what I did. I took crackers, cheese, and a piece of fruit to bed that night, but I was too tired to eat it.

The next morning a gentle voice woke me, saying, "Honey, it's time to get up. You have to go to school." I got up, went to the bathroom, and was summoned to come back into the bedroom. The woman with the sweet voice said, "Didn't you get enough to eat last night?"

"Yes, ma'am," I replied, "I had enough to eat. But I wasn't sure when I was going to eat again." Her eyes welled up, and what I now know as pity filled her face.

In my old house, we didn't know when we were going to eat, sleep, or drink water again. Taking a bath was far from a priority for my mom and dad. Many days and nights I did not eat; thus the extraordinary opportunity to take food out of a refrigerator and bring it to bed, eating it on my own time, was a new luxury. The day before moving to my new home, I tried to heat up water for a cup of soup, but I didn't understand how to turn on the gas stove. I'd adjusted every knob on the stovetop, but I couldn't get a flame. I simply poured the water into the cup and ate the crunchy noodles cold.

Living in this new, warm house with a cozy bed, and access to all that food, was like being in heaven. I quickly adjusted to eating every day and night, and my habits became more normal. However, nightmares that I had frequently when living with my biological parents still haunted me at my new house. In one dream, Wes, my biological father, would come home late after a day of drinking. Barely in the door, he'd begin yelling at my mom and my brothers and sisters, putting fear in all of us. With my heart racing, I would try to hide under my covers; I'd even crawl under the bed until my dad calmed down, and I could go back to sleep,

These same nightmares continued at the foster home. I would wake in a sudden panic brought on by nightmares. I would scream for my mom or wake up sweating.

I had three foster siblings, brothers Terry and Roy, and sister, Sally, all older than me. They were kind, sweet, and very giving people when I first met them. In fact, one of my brothers gave me a yellow toy truck.

Over the next several weeks my foster mom, Jessie, made sure I ate well. She came into my room at night and tucked me into bed. It was all so strange because I wasn't used to it. Her breath did not smell from smoke and liquor.

At times, though, I felt like I was on display. Day after day family members and neighbors came over to our house, and Jessie said, "Robbie, come here and meet so-and-so."

When I met the parents of my foster father, RJ, the kids called their grandparents *Nonna* for grandmother and *Nonno* for grandfather in Italian. It was like being back in my biological parents' house. Both looked at me as if I had a disease. Nonna's lips were pursed as she stared at me. She was drinking out of a can that was all too familiar with its white on the outside, a gold top, and on the front, the Olympia Beer waterfall with a horseshoe above it. When she took a big drink, she suddenly started to look like she had to throw up, same as my biological mom when she would drink out of the bottle. Jessie ran into the kitchen, got a pot, and gave it to her. She puked in it. Everyone thought that was funny—everyone but me. When she was finished, she handed the pot to Jessie, looked straight at me, and said, "You're not part of this family. You're not ever going to be part of this family." I suddenly felt chilled, alone, and scared—mostly scared. I felt like running because I wasn't sure what that meant. Did I have to leave again? Didn't they want me here? At that moment I knew I was frightened in a way that was different from any fright I had ever felt before.

Over the next several weeks, the social worker (with a stringy, scraggly mustache and blue polyester pants) came to the house to check on me. He always asked me questions like, "How do you feel? Is everyone treating you well?" and "Do you like being in this house?" or "Do you miss your family?" It was all very confusing. However what was not confusing, were the memories I had of living with my biological family, where almost every day there was yelling, screaming, and my father frequently beating my mother. One day the social worker showed up and asked if I wanted to go back to my mom's.

"No," I said, "I like it here."

"If you stay, will you be a good boy?"

"Yes," I said. "Why are you asking me that?"

"Because if you're not a good boy, we'll have to put you in handcuffs and take you away," he said.

When I asked what handcuffs were, he pulled round silver things off his belt. "These are handcuffs. Stretch your hands out." I did...and *snap!* Those cuffs went around my little hands, and when he tightened the cuffs, I couldn't pull them out. I was frightened, but he just laughed. When I burst out crying, Jessie ran to me, grabbed me, and told him to get the handcuffs off my wrist. He did, and apologized.

After I calmed down, he said, "I have a surprise for you. Two of your brothers are coming to live with you." A few days later a brown station wagon pulled up, and out of the backseat came seven-year-old Ronnie and nine-year-old Matt, dirty as usual, each holding one black trash bag of clothes. I ran outside. Ronnie had this incredible smile, and we hugged and hugged each other. That night we slept in the same bed. It seemed like old times.

The social worker showed up often to check on us, and asked the three of us the same questions. We all said, nearly in unison, "We want to stay. This is great." During one visit he asked us, "Do you want your sister, Marjorie, to join you?" Our excitement and anticipation really began to build. The brown station wagon showed up, bringing Marjorie and her remarkable smile. We hugged her, and again we all slept in the same bed: Ronnie, Matt, Marjorie, and me.

We lived in a small house then, three bedrooms and one bathroom, but we were moving soon. We were building a new house next door. Construction started by removing a foundation left from an old bakery. We lived in a part of town called Tucci Camp, referred to as New Mill, where all the Italians lived.

New Mill was close to the mill where my foster dad worked. He was a workhorse, not missing work for ten years, and was honored for that with a watch. During the day, he'd go to his job, and at night he would work on the bakery foundation next door, using a jackhammer on the foundation, shoveling the remains into his truck, and hauling it to the woods to dump. One day he came home with an orange plastic construction hat for me, and said, "Here, Robbie, wear this when you come next door with me and play with your toy trucks in the sand while I work." He was a good-looking Italian, pretty well-built, and a product of the '50s. He wore jeans with a white T-shirt, his cigarettes rolled up in the sleeve. He styled his hair like a rock star, pompadour and all, accompanied by a beard, mustache, and glasses. I thought he looked like a rebel.

It was great that my foster mom was a stay-at-home mom, but she was on the phone all the time. The yellow phone had a long extension cord so she could do dishes, watch TV, and vacuum, all with the phone pressed to her ear, stretching the cord as far as it could.

Over the next few years, my biological sister Marjorie struggled with our living situation. She fought with my adoptive sister, Sally. They slept in the same room, but didn't care for each other. At one point, my brothers Greg, Matt, and Ronnie, my sister Marjorie, and I all lived with my foster family. But Greg wasn't there very long, and after a while Marjorie became a problem for my foster parents, so she left, but Matt, Ronnie, and I stayed.

After a couple years of work, the new house Dad built with a big backyard was not totally finished, but we moved in anyway. Dad painted, nailed up siding, laid the patio behind the house, and worked on the landscaping at night. He built an eight-foot fence using old burned logs he found for fence posts. The house faced Mt. Shasta, a sacred place that, even as a child, filled me with absolute awe.

We three brothers shared a room facing the front street and train tracks. The carpet in the room the three of us shared was unusual, all these square carpet pieces of different colors and textures put together, creating a psychedelic effect. We had two bunk beds and one small bed, but most of the time we all ended up in the same bed. My adoptive brother Roy stayed in our room with us, bringing in a radio. At night, he turned it on, and we listened to Wolfman Jack, a DJ with a deep, growling voice who occasionally howled like a wolf at the moon, and played one of our favorite groups. It was awesome.

Having my brothers live with me in this great house was ideal, but it lasted only a year. One day Mom came to Ronnie, Matt, and me. She seemed sad when she said, "Your biological mom has cleaned herself up, and is ready to have you return home." Our foster mom knew what kind of situation we came from, and perhaps worried that we'd be returning to the same thing. Now I was puzzled. *Why would I want to go back to that disaster?* Nevertheless, when we were given the choice, the three of us sat down and talked about it. Matt said, "We have to go back home or her feelings will be hurt." At the age of seven, I was the youngest; Ronnie was a year and a half older, and Matt three years my senior. Matt understood better than Ronnie or me what was happening, and he actually wanted to go back home; Ronnie and I wanted to stay.

Matt convinced the two of us to leave. We packed our bags to go back to the reservation. After our bags were packed, Mom came into our room and said, "Robbie, you don't have to go if you don't want to." When they started to foster me, I was the only one from my first family, and quickly had become part of their loving family

The social worker showed up in his familiar brown station wagon, and we got ready to go. I remember looking at Mom, and saw that she was crying. I asked, "Mom, can I talk with you alone?" and we went upstairs to my room.

"Can I really stay?" I asked her.

"Yes," she responded. We went back downstairs, and she told the social worker that I was staying. Matt, Ronnie, and I hugged, and they drove off. Eight-year-old Marjorie had stayed with us two different times, when I was six and again a year later, but she returned to live with our biological mother in between.

When I was about nine years old, I was legally adopted after being their foster child for almost four years. Eventually I began calling them Mom and Dad. When I mention my first parents, I usually identify them as my birth or biological parents.

Biological family pictures

CHAPTER 3

My Second Big Loss— Things Will Never Be the Same

A year or two passed in the new house. In the early '70s, most houses did not have air conditioning. Ours was no different. The day was humid and hot, and I had been playing outside all day. I was tired and decided to take a nap. I climbed into bed, closed my eyes, and quickly nodded off.

I can recall hearing all the commotion downstairs, but I was too tired to get up to see what was happening. Dad had been pouring concrete for the back patio, and he collapsed from heat stroke, suffering from both a seizure and the effects of a blood clot.

This was a life-changing moment for our family.

Before this incident, Dad was funny, brilliant, hard-working—a good man, and a good father to me. Everything changed.

The nearest hospital that could treat a blood clot was in Redding, California, far away from our little town. The doctors determined that they had to do surgery to remove the blood clot from Dad's brain. Unfortunately the surgery affected his brain, meaning he had to learn to walk and talk again. And he kept having seizures. This proud man had much to overcome.

Dad spent many months in the hospital, and was not given much of a chance to live. One side of his body was paralyzed, and he had a hard time talking. On that hot summer day, I lost my adoptive dad. My second dad, as I knew him, was gone, never to be the same again.

While Mom was taking care of her husband, we had to go live with relatives and friends. Terry and Sally went to their grandparents, Roy went to a friend's home, and I went to live with other relatives. Once Dad was out of the hospital, he and Mom went to Redding for the week for treatment, and would come back on the weekends when we all came back home. When Dad was home, all he did was vegetate on the living room couch. His speech was hard to understand, and walking was difficult. He was regressing everyday. His body got older, but his mind got younger, making him say really odd, childish things.

At this point, Dad was totally out of it, and Mom was emotionally unavailable. This went on for about two years. I wonder if she felt RJ abandoned her, like I felt he'd abandoned me.

During these two years, the weekends at home were awesome because I loved my yard, my bed, and being in my own neighborhood. Since we were all staying in different households, we did not see that much of each other. When we were home, we usually slept in the same room, and often the same bed. What great times we all had being together again, on these special weekends.

The loss of my father was when I first became aware there might be a "creative source" interacting with everything. As I look back at the event itself, and my sleeping through it, I didn't have to face the trauma of what was going on. Seeing my dad in that situation would have been even more devastating. From what I understand, water was coming out of his mouth, he couldn't speak, write, or breathe, he was convulsing and experiencing all that comes with having a seizure. Everybody witnessed it but me. Getting up that day, I felt glad that I'd slept, and I felt refreshed. At the time, I thought that was really unusual, and asked myself, *Why did I sleep through that? I don't feel sad or scared like any of these people.*

I still nap like that today, and especially when things get too stressful, taking a nap gives me a completely different perspective.

CHAPTER 4

Back Home with the Boys in the Neighborhood

When RJ and Jessie adopted me, I was adopted into a loving, happy home, with three new adoptive siblings. They wanted the best for all of us. Their hearts were, as people say, "in the right place." Tragedy struck in the form of Dad/RJ's seizure, blood clot, and resulting deterioration, causing Mom to drop into the depth of depression.

They had NOT signed on for this—and neither had I. But reality struck this family in a big way, and each of us had to make our own way the best we could.

The fireplace in our home was built with rocks from Yosemite National Park. This wasn't your normal fireplace. The large, coarse rocks had these amazing swirls in them; some of them seemed alive. The fireplace was the center of the living room, and was so big it covered about half the wall. The sitting area was made of slabs of granite combined with big boulders. To me, it seemed like an altar. I felt connected to that fireplace, and even to this day, I still collect rocks of all sorts. My mom often stood in front of the fireplace in her blue jeans, sweatshirt, and slippers. It was always hot in that house, but she constantly complained of the cold. She rarely cooked dinner and when she ate, she ate by herself upstairs.

The new house had two phones, one in the dining room and one in Mom's bedroom. The dining room phone had a small extension cord, and the bedroom phone upstairs had a longer extension cord. When I went up the stairs, I could hear Mom dialing the phone, constantly calling or getting calls from her sisters or her mom. I thought, *Can't she stay off the phone for five minutes?*

When I was around 11 years old, Mom had totally checked out. Caring for her husband had proved to be too much for her. More and more often she hid in her room. When I came home from school, she was upstairs sleeping. When she got up, her hair was all messy, and her eyes looked tired. On the really bad days, she could be incredibly mean. She even took to "medicating" herself to numb the pain of being left with this unplanned sad twist in her life. She had absolutely nothing left for me.

One year, in fact, I didn't see Mom from Christmas until the spring. She shocked me by showing up at one of my baseball games—I couldn't believe it.

Our home had been a great place, but what was now going on behind the doors was odd. After my dad's stroke, the home became cold and lonely, no longer warm and friendly. Dad was a lump on the couch. He didn't do anything but sit and stare at the TV. Most days I joined friends playing baseball, basketball, and football, at school and afterwards.

Staying away from my house became a priority, as was finding friends' houses where I could hang out. One such house belonged to Ted and Peggy. Ted was a logger and, as is true with many Native Americans, a drinker who did not have much control over his alcohol use.

Ted and Peggy lived right behind us with their daughter, Kelly. She had beautiful curly black hair and big brown eyes. I had a huge crush on her. When I went over to their house, they allowed Kelly and me go into her bedroom, which pleased me no end. Her parents said, "You guys can hang around with each other, but you have to leave the door open."

Every day I went over to their house to see Kelly. Ted took an interest in me and asked me to play catch with the baseball or football, anything athletic. He said to me, "You're a natural. I want you to play Pop Warner football. You can be my quarterback." Ted was a coach for Pop Warner, the local football league. He signed me up, and there I was, playing Pop Warner football, with Kelly as a cheerleader. The uniforms were burnt orange and white, and I wore number 11. Kelly wore this cute little skirt and held pom-poms as she cheered us on. Oh, how I loved her.

The best group of kids lived in our neighborhood, including Donny and Kenny from next door, Ronnie from the alley, the Connor brothers from up the street, and Tom from the hill. We were inseparable. We always found the eighth guy so we could have four-on-four basketball, baseball, and football games. We played from morning 'til night, occasionally coming in the house only to eat. We traded baseball cards and sports memorabilia, and talked for hours about our favorite teams and players.

Every time I had to go stay with other family members or friends, I was sad to leave the boys in my neighborhood. I felt totally fractured, like I couldn't get comfortable—new bed, new rules, new food, and all I wanted was my bed, my friends, and my neighborhood. I was glad when Mom and

Dad were back home, even though it was strange what my mom was going through, and how my dad communicated. I was especially glad to be back with the neighborhood boys.

My Little League baseball team kept me sane. I played on a team of kids that other teams had rejected. Our coach, Curly, was an older Italian guy with a huge belly—and curly hair. His grandson, Mark, and I were the league's two lefties, and two of the best pitchers. Several other guys on the team were having problems at home, and we never wanted to go home. Curly seemed to be aware of that, and every day after practice he'd ask us, "You guys want to hang around a while?" We all sat in the dugout, he cracked open a beer, and started telling dirty jokes. We listening, lying around on our mitts with our hats turned sideways, and laughed until it hurt. The joyful hours were a calm and happy respite for me.

Luckily sports seemed to come naturally for me. I was good at every sport I tried. I was a left-handed pitcher in baseball, a quarterback for football, and the second-best shooting guard on the basketball team. Sports quickly became my outlet, a way to stay away from my family and from Mom's sadness, depression, or whatever it was she was going through. I didn't have to be there because I could be at practice, at Ted's, with friends, or at a game—just not home. I was chosen to do a commercial for Pop Warner football because I was told that I was a good-looking kid with thick hair and a nice smile. It was fun. I met many other young athletes who became both competitors and close friends as the years went on. Being able to hit a padded dummy in football or throw and hit a baseball was a natural outlet for all the anxiety inside me.

The grassy yard behind the house made it easy for all the neighborhood kids to play football. On the side of the house was a dirt strip about twenty feet wide and sixty feet long with a woodpile next to it, and a wooden fence. In the middle of the fence was a square piece of wood that looked like a catcher's mitt, about the same height off the ground as a catcher in the crouch position, ready for a pitch. One day I marked off the distance that a Little League pitcher's mound was from the fence. I used a baseball-sized rubber ball, threw it against the fence day after day for hours at a time, and fantasized that I was a pitcher playing in the Major Leagues. If the ball made it past the cherry tree, it was a home run. I brought a little brown radio outside, set it down where I was pitching, listened to actual professional games, and pitched simultaneously with the pitchers from both teams on the radio. I could escape for hours, even days at a time. I was pleased with my new idea. I thought, *I can practice pitching, be close to home, and not have to see my family at all.*

This makeshift baseball area near the cherry tree and woodpile offered another gift. When Kenny, my next-door neighbor, heard the ball hitting the fence, he came out and sat on the woodpile. I looked forward to him saying, "Hi, Robbie, want to talk?" While I threw the ball, we talked about all kinds of subjects, from baseball to science fiction, from Mark Twain to Archie and the gang. Knocky—that was my name for him—was ten, and I was twelve. He was a skinny kid with a goofy haircut who laughed all the time. He made me laugh because of his laugh.

Each morning I got up, put on my baseball hat, grabbed my glove, and went out to the cherry tree. In a few minutes, Knocky came out and sat on the woodpile and started reading his book while I threw the ball. Knocky read out loud when a part was interesting, and we both commented on the reading. I was excited whenever he had a new book, because it meant hours of mental stimulation. We talked about the characters in the story, and how, if we were them, we would do things differently. We talked as if we were smart and sophisticated, when in reality, we barely knew our butt from a hole in the ground. We skipped the parts we didn't understand, and moved on.

Sometimes Knocky's dad, Dave, came out and said, "Okay, fellas, time to put the books down and get to playin' catch." Knocky jumped off the woodpile, and I climbed the fence into their yard, and we played catch. Before long, all the neighborhood boys came to the yard. These were great times. I felt so stimulated and happy. The other boys went home, but I never wanted to, so I asked them to stay just a little longer. Sometimes they did, but other times I just played by myself.

Many times during the summer, we became bored with reading and playing baseball, so we found other things to entertain us. A tunnel ran under the street by our house. It was for run-off, and was big enough for a five-foot-tall person to walk through. Knocky had a good idea: "Let's get one of Mom's old purses, tie a fishing line to the purse, and put it on the road." Then the fun began. We climbed into the tunnel and waited for cars to pass. When someone stopped to pick up the purse, we jerked the fishing line, and then ran through the tunnel to the other side of the road and down the wash so the driver couldn't catch us. We had so much success doing this that we literally spent our summer mornings entertaining ourselves with this little joke.

Feeling Different

From a very young age, I knew I was different from other people. Whenever I was approaching a situation—or in the middle of one—where I felt anxious, endangered, or vulnerable, I sensed this "vibration" within me. I can't fully explain exactly what it felt like. It wasn't like the feeling you get when your foot or your arm "falls asleep" from being in one place too long. It wasn't the feeling you get when you touch a vibrating washing machine going through the spin cycle. It doesn't feel like anything I can describe, except a hyper-awareness that creates a physical sensation in both my body and mind. Nothing I can do takes these vibrations away for very long.

During the years when I was eleven to thirteen, I found an outlet that took up some of my time, kept me away from home, and changed the vibration inside me. It was the library. All the days that Knocky and I spent reading on the wood pile by the cherry tree had inspired me to continue exploring other books, galaxies, personalities, writings, poems, comic books, and superheroes.

Between the elementary school and the high school, a long road called New Mill Road connected the two schools and both sides of town. This straight, two-lane road had massive pine trees on both sides. Not well lit, it had only two street lamps at either end. At night when the wind blew through the trees, I felt a bit scared to walk down that road.

The library stood about halfway between the two schools. The small, modular gray building had a dirt parking lot that held about three cars. The library had an entry door, an emergency exit door in the back, and two windows. The mid-sixties volunteer librarian had been a librarian at the high school and elementary school. I remember six aisles of books, and several places I could sit and read. An available ladder helped me reach the books on the top shelves, or I sat on the stools to look at the books on the bottom shelves. The library had the best mixture of smells: old paper, leather, and a dusty room.

Walking home after school, I would stop in and looked at the latest comic books and magazines, and occasionally I'd check out a library book. One day I searched for a book on a subject I had seen on TV, called "Chariots of the Gods," written by Eric Von Daniken. Von Daniken postulated that the earth was visited by an alien race in the distant past. This show sparked my interest in ancient history and ancient alien theory. I found some books by J. Alan Heinik and other UFO authors, but not Von Daniken's book. When I asked the librarian about the book and subject matter, she offered to try to find it for me. I left the library with a couple Archie comic books I had checked out. Walking home, I kept hoping that she could get the books I asked for.

Every day after school, I stopped and asked the librarian, "Did my book arrive yet?"

"No, not yet," she responded, as she smiled and pushed her glasses up on her nose.

As I walked home, I'd say to myself, "Maybe tomorrow." After a few days of getting the "No, not today," I didn't stop by the library, and hung out with the neighborhood boys.

Some time had passed, and I had to return my overdue books. I thought I'd see what the library might have on some other subjects. The librarian said, "There's my little friend. Where have you been?" she smiled nicely, and I told her I had been with friends. She said, "I have a surprise for you," and directed me to follow her back to the corner of the library. Wow, there they were: a bunch of books on UFOs, Atlantis, archeology, ancient Egypt, the Mayan civilization, and many more. I was elated.

At that time, the library allowed a person to check out only two books at a time. I read those books, cross-referenced the material in other books, and then requested that the library stock those books as well. I brought bookmarkers along so I could start reading the next books I wanted to check out. I had a great time. Every time I went into this little library, the librarian commented, "Are you thinking about living in the library in order to satisfy your hunger for knowledge?"

At the end of the school day, instead of taking the bus, I would walk home so I could stop by the library. Many times I walked in, took off my coat off, said hello, and disappeared into the back of the library for hours. I sat on a stool and read my books, and listened to the wind blow the pine needles on the huge trees right out back. It was scary and peaceful at the same time. Once in a while, my brother came to get me from the library, asking, "Hey, you coming home? Mom is looking for you." I'd grab my jacket and walked home, listening to the pine trees speak to me.

Pop Warner football Number 11

CHAPTER 5

Hangin' with the Boyz in the 'Hood

One day when I was fourteen, I looked out my second-story window at the neighboring houses. A loud and noisy Spanish-speaking family was moving into the house where Ted and Peggy had lived. I knew them from when they lived up in Old Mill. I thought, *Why the heck are they moving to this side of town?*

Actually, it made sense. The railroad was close to Tucci camp, and all the Mexicans worked on the railroad, and most lived in the trailers at the end of Tucci camp by some cornfields. The town was becoming integrated. I thought, *It's time I investigate and greet the new neighbors.* So, I ventured out through the back fence, down the alley, and through their back gate. There they were, in the basement drinking, smoking, and listening to popular rock groups. I yelled hello to Jose, and he yelled back, "Hey, what's up, Holmes?" I soon learned that calling someone "Holmes" was a sign of affection, belonging, and family.

Jose, about three years my senior, invited me into the basement, motioning toward the guy with his hair slicked back with pomade. "Holmes, this is my uncle Marty," and pointing to the one in the ponytail he added, "and this is our friend Thomas." Both had goatees and were wearing baggy blue jeans and muscle shirts like Jose. Being at Jose's house was great. His mom, Brenda, was beautiful, and his sister Sabrina looked like her mother. Younger brother, Teddy, a skateboarder, was also very cool. Every day I came home from school, pretended to do homework, ate quickly, and announced as I went out the door, "I'm going to a friend's house to practice a sport (or do homework)." I disappeared through the back fence, down the alley, and over to Jose's house. We sneaked down into the basement and sat there for hours, talking, laughing, and listening to popular rock groups. It was great. For me, the basement became a valuable hideout; I felt safe there. Locking the door from the inside, we covered it with some small blankets so that no one could smell the smoke from the bong. We thought we were pretty smart. Jose sent me outside. "Rob, can you hear us when we talk loud?"

I replied to Jose, "No, Holmes, can't hear a thing."

Around nine every night I left, walked up the back alley, came in through the sliding glass door, took my shoes off, quietly walked up the stairs, and went straight to my room and bed.

After several months, Mom caught on. Out her window, she could see the alley and Jose's house, and see us out back, or if she opened the window, she could hear us. Suspicious, she ordered, "Jose and his family are dopers, and I don't want you to hang out with them."

Angry, I ran out of the house. As I often did, I went to the wood mill to calm down because I loved the smell of the wood when it was being processed. When I returned home, I told my mom, "I am not going to stop hanging out with them, so leave me alone." By now, my mom was taking all sorts of prescribed pills like Valium, that put her out for days. Every day she went to the next town, Mt. Shasta, and sometimes she came home all giddy, like a schoolgirl. My older brother Terry said she was seeing some guy there, and that made her so happy.

Sometimes at night, she dressed up and said, "Well, I'm going to meet a girlfriend for dinner. Be back late." Mom was attractive, with curly hair and pretty eyes. People looked at her with the same expression I had when I looked at Kelly, Ted's daughter. Those nights I could go to Jose's house without her bothering me, and be in bed before she got home. The days she was not running off to be with her "friends," she was hiding out in the bedroom with the door shut, listening to soft rock music.

Hanging out at Jose's was entertaining. I watched them tie blue headbands around their heads, wear muscle shirts, and call each other "Vato." Day after day, I watched them smoke weed, drink beer out of a brown paper bag, and listen to tunes on the black eight-track player. All the while, the smell of tortillas filled the air. Their mother was always sweet to me, and I badly wanted her to be my mom. Several times, I wanted to ask her if I could call her "Mom," and she did mother me on many, many occasions. When she yelled at her boys, she'd yell at me, too. One time she said, "If you're going to be here this much, you're going to do chores, too."

"Okay," I agreed. She smiled and hugged me. It felt incredible. Here I was, 14 years old, and this was actually the first time I ever remember anyone hugging me other than my brothers and sister. After that day, I took out the trash, brought in firewood, and did what she told me to do, and with no argument. Brenda never complained about my hanging out there, and because Jose had told her that my home life was messed up, she never hassled me. Being there was much better than being part of what was going on in my house.

This was the year I took my first drink. To this day, the experience is burned into my mind. Marty asked my friend and me, "Hey, guys, want a drink?" My friend took a big drink. Initially I turned him down, and sat there watching the crew drink. I saw how soft their eyes became, and how calm everyone was. I was intrigued, tempted, and wondered: *Could this happen to me?* This stuff, alcohol, seemed to soothe everyone's nerves.

"Give me the bottle, Marty."

"Yeah, you go, Holmes."

The taste was very sweet at first, but going down it burned a little, then became warm and gentle. After a few minutes, I became numb, the anxiety and vibrations went away, and the fear and pain were gone. The song on the eight-track was about coming of age, going from the innocence of childhood to the cynicism of being an adult. After my first drink, I thought, *Wow, I'm in love.* My next thought was, *I'm going to make sure this love is in my life for a long, long time. Is this why all the adults in my life drink—because it kills their pain? Ahhh, I get it!*

Over the next several months our little crew of Jose, Marty, and me, and their friends, Mel and Paul, hung out nearly every day in the basement, smoking off the bong, drinking booze, and listening to music. Weed was such a strong part of our social being. The guys talked about how we were going to get the weed, and when we'd smoke it. Weed was the focus of many deep conversations, and we'd even get books about it. With alcohol we just drank, then we'd laugh about stupid stuff, and get silly.

We worked when we needed money, doing things like mowing lawns, and collecting wood for older neighbors. I believed in working for money I needed, but Jose and the crew had a different way of life. Thus, we also sold weed, and when we didn't have enough money from working, we'd hustle, stealing things like toolboxes, chain saws, and stuff like that out of neighbors' garages.

Mel, a transplant from a nearby town, was like his dad, a loose cannon. School-smart, he could fight like nobody's business. People did not understand him, and he was teased a lot but, inevitably, that person had to deal with Mel's fighting prowess. I was anything but a fighter, and wanted to be friends with everyone, constantly playing both sides of the fence. I was the jock during the day, and at night I went to Jose's and was a stoner. Mel was not like that. With him, what you saw is what you got, and I always envied that.

Paul was exactly the opposite of Mel. Paul's mother was Mexican, and his dad black, making "Big Paul" tall and big, with frizzy hair. He did not smoke weed very often; he drank beer when we smoked weed. Paul was happy and friendly with everyone. The five of us took our weed and booze, and went out into the woods to a lot that was for sale. Once there, we parked on one of the dirt roads, and faced Mt. Shasta. We pulled our bong out, drank our booze, turned the music up loud, and zoned out. In the winter, we sat in the car, rested our heads on the top part of the seats, and watched the snowflakes fall on the windshield while listening to music. The car always smelled like a mixture of gas, bong water, and stale plastic seats. However, after a while the music, booze, and weed no longer calmed my awful fear, pain, and anxiety. Dad could not really communicate, and sat in front of the TV all day, smoking pack after pack of cigarettes. Mom hid in her bedroom. I did my own laundry and, if I needed money, I left a note on the table by the white coffeepot.

Dinner was always ready when I came home. I did not have to talk to anyone, which was good, because I was often stoned. I could eat and go watch TV or go outside and play basketball. I always ate alone. Roy hung out in my mom's room or went to my cousin's house all the time. Terry and Sally, both in their twenties, had jobs in nearby towns, but hardly ever came home for a visit. When Mom wanted to see them, she went to their houses. And since Sally lived in the town where my mom's boyfriend lived, Mom saw them on the same trip.

I always hung out with friends at their houses or a mutual meeting place. I never dared to have anyone over to my house. I thought, *I don't want anybody to find out about our screwed-up family. Dad can't talk. Mom doesn't come out of her room.*

Because I always wore a smile, people thought I was happy-go-lucky. For me, though, it was a way to keep people at a distance. If I wore a frown or acted pissed, I thought that a person might confront me, and I might have to fight, most likely getting beat up.

As a freshman, my search for relief continued: booze, food, getting high through theft, hanging out, smoking weed. Nothing worked to relieve me of the pain and loneliness. One night when the guys and I were drinking rum and coke at a party, I met a schoolmate. Linda had curly blonde hair, the cutest little nose and lips, big boobs, and the most charming smile.

"Robbie, what are you doing?"

"Nothing, just trying to get drunk," was all I could think to say.

She laughed and got into a car with her best friend. Before they left, Linda leaned out the car window and said, "Hey, you're really cute. Why don't you call me?"

I was amazed. This girl liked me, and had flirted with me. I went home, found her number in the phone book, and called. I knew her dad well from baseball.

"Hi Eddie, this is Rob," I said. "Can I speak to Linda?"

"Rob, why are you calling my daughter?" he asked. We laughed as he gave her the phone. The next day Linda and I went to the elementary school behind her house, played basketball, and hit it off. I was into Linda because I knew a little about her reputation: she was one year older, and already having sex. Since I was inexperienced, entering puberty, I wanted a girl who seemed easy. She lived with her father, a single dad who was never home. He was usually off "looking for romance," or working in Mt. Shasta. Since Eddie was often gone, occasionally Linda had a party. Living in a small town, everyone checked on everyone else. It was no big deal that Linda and Cindy, her sister, were often home alone.

After only a few days, Linda and I were having sex. Here I was having sex with an older girl who was on the Pill. We cooked together, cleaned, watched our favorite TV shows, and came and went when we wanted. It was the perfect outlet for all my pain: as much sex as I wanted, and absolutely no supervision. Mom was happy, saying, "I'm glad you quit hanging out with Jose and the crew. I think Linda is good for you." This, in certain respects, was true; the sex was better than the booze and weed, and it made me feel worthwhile inside.

Everyday, I went to school, to sports practice, and then to Linda's. I never had to go home, and no one ever asked where I was or what I was doing. We had parties, hung out with friends, explored sex, and drank when we wanted. This was great. After about six months, she said, "I love you."

For the next two months, we teased each other about being in love. One day she said, "I'm not kidding. I love you."

That was the first time I could ever recall hearing the words. I thought, *It feels great that somebody is falling in love with me—that this relationship has developed to the point into something wonderful and nurturing.* However, I was freaked out and made a joke out of it. *What is wrong with me? What is making me be anything but loving?*

For the next year, we had a volatile relationship. A few of our fights were physical, and many times verbally abusive, yelling and calling each other names.

Finally we broke up before my sophomore year in high school. In this small community, it quickly became known that Linda and I had violent fights. After that, steady girlfriends were hard to find. Even though our relationship had been deteriorating, when it was over I had this sick feeling deep in my stomach. I learned later that's where my emotions were the strongest. It was mixture of embarrassment that people were talking about me in a bad way, and the big question: What did *I do* to make her *leave me?*

However, because I was still the best athlete in my school, my popularity remained high.

During that year, I spent more and more time with Jose and the crew. Mel and I were good friends, but Mom hated him. She felt he was "scummy." His stepmom, Candace, who was much younger than Mel's dad, was a pothead and allowed us to come to their house and smoke weed and listen to their old jukebox. As the year went on, I became more and more isolated. Every day after sports practice I went to Jose's basement to get high. My smoking and drinking became a daily ritual that I built my day around. As my stoner reputation grew, I was invited to fewer parties.

Mom was concerned for me, but it was probably because she was now known as "Rob's mom." My athletic ability began to give her status, and she leveraged that when she could.

Once during a basketball game, when I racked up the most points in that game, I became our school's all-time leading scorer. After I scored the final basket, there was a standing ovation. I looked up in the crowd to see several people hugging my mom, talking with her as she made her way to the middle of a crowd of standing people. As I drew closer, I heard her say, "Yeah, that's my son."

Sports were one of the areas of my life that provided constant positive feedback, even as my feeling of hopelessness grew. I was being touted as one of the best athletes in northern California, but I used my athletic talent to keep people away from me. I remained on all the teams because teachers gave me a free pass academically, allowing me to play whatever sport was in season. I showed up to class, received passing grades, hung out with shady people, and no one questioned me. As long as I could launch a touchdown pass, hit a jump shot, or throw a baseball with real heat, everybody turned their heads the other way.

The summer after my sophomore year, I was fifteen and playing Babe Ruth baseball. I made the all-star team, consisting of the best players from many towns in northern California. It was an opportunity to hang out with other popular athletes and escape from my parents' house on occasional overnight trips. I stayed with other athletes at their houses in nearby towns. Their parents were always nice to me since they hadn't a clue about my growing reputation for being a pothead. I was still recognized as "smiley Rob," who was always easy-going. Even on the all-star team, the coach thought I possessed the best pitching talent and potential. During an all-star tournament match-up, I was in a pitching duel. Scouts from the Dodgers, the Giants, and the A's were in the crowd, and one of the scouts asked, "Who are the lefty's parents?" A parent who knew me, pointed Mom out of the crowd, and the scout went over to her.

"Are you the left-handed pitcher's mother?"

"Yes, I am," Mom responded.

"That kid has the right stuff. Keep after him. With work and discipline, he can make it to the big leagues." After the game, a lot of parents and kids told me what the scout had said to her. When I saw her, she was beaming from ear to ear. I felt proud and amazed by that look. Usually, no matter what I did, she looked disgusted.

That single tournament propelled me into an all-but-legendary status in northern California towns. That summer, everywhere I went people bought me beer, talked to me, and girls giggled and flocked to me. It seemed unreal, all because I could throw a baseball faster than most boys my age. I was running with the most popular athletes in each town. We were the best of the best. When we showed up at a party, other guys stepped aside, and girls gave us that interested look. I always stayed with the guys, but never had them to my house. I did not want anyone to see how I actually lived.

During the summer of my sophomore year when I was fifteen, I spent a lot of time with the pretty, smart, funny, and motivated Megan. People knew we hung out, but not to what extent. My friends and family knew I practiced baseball, basketball, and football whenever possible. Megan often met me at the sports complex late in the afternoon when the sun was behind the grandstands. I brought a large bag of balls, and practiced throwing them against the backstop. She sat in the grass watching as I repeatedly threw the ball. When the ball hit the backstop, it made this loud pop and echo, and Megan said something like, "Good one, 90-mile-an hour fastball."

After a while I took a break. We sat together and picked blades of grass, putting them in our mouths, kissing and trying to trade the blades of grass without stopping kissing. Often we laughed, and never traded the blades of grass.

We lay down in the grass, our heads close, and looked at the grass as the wind blew through the blades. One day I said, "If you think about it, everything is in motion, and we are watching that motion play out in this blade of grass."

Megan replied, "If you think about it, all life is in motion, and we are just part of that."

We bantered as to whether we were here before, and will be here again, entering into a deep discussion about time and its perceived existence. We rolled over onto our backs, and looked at the blue sky. She asked, "What do you think is up there?"

My reply was, "Life, not as we know it, but life."

Often when we hung out at night, I shot baskets for a couple hours at the elementary school's court, with her rebounding the basketball for me. Later we lay on the nearby hill. I remember the smell and look of her shiny brown hair. Once it was dark enough to see the stars, I explained the galaxy, including the Milky Way and the Zodiac. I shared my knowledge about the Egyptian pyramids, South America, time travel, stars, cars, music, and poetry. She asked, "How come you don't let more people know this about you?" I told her that not everyone wants to hear such things. We laughed, and she snuggled up next to me, saying, "More please."

Megan's parents got divorced, and she moved back to San Jose before that school year began. Having Megan gone really made me sad because she had been a most important part of my life. She had taken the time and looked "behind the veil" I had put up. She saw me, not stoner Rob or sports Rob—but ME.

CHAPTER 6

Geographical Change

By the end of the summer before my junior year, Mom was again tired of my behavior, and I had had enough of living in McCloud. We decided a geographical change was needed. She had a friend in Redding, the largest city closest to us. She called the friend and asked Ernie, his oldest son, if it could be worked out so that I could live with him. She offered to pay them $400 or $500 a month.

Ernie was more than willing for me to live with him because he had his own agenda. Redding was a city of about eighty thousand, much bigger than McCloud, with its population of about two thousand. Redding was also more cosmopolitan than McCloud, making it a lot easier to get access to drugs, alcohol, and many types of chemicals I couldn't score in a small town. They had drugs I'd never heard of before: White Cross, acid, and this new-to-me stuff called cocaine.

A movie about the fast times at a high school was out in the theatre, inspiring all the stoners like me to show up at school half-baked. The movie's main character was doing it and getting away with it, so it must be okay. We carried around shoeboxes with our water bongs in them. For me, the fast times would soon be happening at a new high school with about 1,500 students—huge compared to my last school. I could blend in without anyone knowing who I was or what I was doing. Perfect. Lost in the crowd, I could zone out completely or maybe even, as I wished at times, I could slowly die.

The day Mom dropped me off at Ernie's house, I knew she was relieved to see me go. It was the day I first met Ernie and his girlfriend, Yvonne. His house had two bedrooms, a small yard, a pool table, and a nice kitchen. It was at the end of a cul-de-sac and within walking distance of the school. Talk about great timing: Ernie and Yvonne were married the night I came, and I was invited to the wedding. What more could I ask for? I had an ounce of weed, went to the wedding, got stoned, and watched as the bride and groom left on their week-long honeymoon. I had a new house in Redding to myself for the whole week, and could drink and smoke up as much as I wanted.

In addition, a new, all-music cable TV station was playing the latest videos. That night I turned on the tube after smoking a big bowl of Red Hash, and there she was, Martha Quinn. The first song I heard was "I Ran" by A Flock of Seagulls. I thought, *Wow, an all-video channel! I can smoke weed and watch music. This might be the single greatest thing ever.* When Ernie and Yvonne came back from their honeymoon, we all sat down and had dinner.

"I hear you're a stoner," Ernie said. "You can smoke, but don't do it in the house. By the way, can you grow pot?"

I thought, *Yes, this is going to be great.* "Yeah, I do have a pretty good green thumb," I responded.

That night we got busy growing weed with the milk cartons, lights, dirt, and seeds I had brought with me. We set it up in my bedroom closet in case we got busted. Ernie said, "Since you are under eighteen, it would be best if you took the blame—and you won't be arrested. I can claim I was unaware that you were growing weed." I knew if he got busted, the penalty would be big. That plan made complete sense to me. Plus, I could show the plants off to my new stoner friends and gain their acceptance.

Within a few months, Ernie got tired of my friends being there. He felt I was compromising our efforts to grow weed for money, which was true. Therefore, he took the plants and hid them in the attic. I thought he had thrown them away. One day I was in the garage taking a bong hit when I looked up and saw a light coming through the ceiling from the attic above. They were growing lights for about fifty plants, five to six feet high with beautiful green leaves and buds. I thought, *He did it without me, and this makes me angry.*

My stay in Redding gave me the opportunity to smoke weed and drink every day without any supervision. I hid out in my room from the time I arrived home from school until bedtime, when I smoked myself to sleep. I was right back to where I was when I left McCloud.

I was scared, lonely, and filled with anxiety and pain that no drugs or pills could kill. I was an absolute emotional disaster. I was depressed, and was getting bad grades in school. Ernie and Yvonne didn't know how to deal with me. My last day at school in Redding began with a friend and me drinking the morning before finals before the Christmas break, and doing it right in front of the school. I took a big drink out of the bottle; at that same moment, the vice principal saw me through his office window. He knew me well, as a student, and through Ernie's father because they were partners in a local cement business. He came outside and said, "Come with me."

"Mr. M," I said, "this is my last day here. I'm headed back to my old school in McCloud."

"Okay, but you better be gone after today," he said. That was the day I returned to McCloud.

During Christmas vacation of my junior year, I turned seventeen. Over break, I went back to McCloud and stayed with Mom. I acted contrite, as if I had changed, and begged her to let me come home. During that break, I hung out with a few jocks I knew. I hung out with my cousin, Kristy, who was my age. Mom loved her, and figured if I was hanging out with Kristy, I must be better, so she let me move home. I enrolled in school and attended it with a new attitude. I hid my smoking and drinking with Jose from everyone. I showed up sober—not stoned—for parties. Girls were attracted to me again, and I played baseball for my high school that spring, doing very well. However, my feelings of fear, anxiety, and vulnerability were always with me, manifested by the "vibration."

I discovered when I focused on Mt. Shasta, or put my attention on its beauty, I could feel a rhythmic, soft, and peaceful vibration from the mountain. When I was around negative people, or doing something wrong, I could sense a very different vibration—random, strong, and chaotic— making me nervous, excitable, and anxious.

CHAPTER 7

A Line Is Crossed

While my life seemed to be falling apart from the abuse of alcohol and drugs, I hadn't really done anything seriously anti-social. I had been successful at hiding the inner turmoil by keeping my outer façade friendly and happy. Although anger was boiling up inside, and outside with the conflict with my mother, I was able to keep a lid on it. That was about to change.

By the end of my junior year, I had had enough of being parented. I was 17 years old, smoking and drinking every day, and more out of control than ever. Mom was still in her routine of going to see her "friend." I timed how long she was gone to figure how much time I had to get to Jose's, get high, and be home to sober up before she returned. She was reading me the riot act on a daily basis, like, "Rob, you have to have morals, stay straight, and be honest." All the while she was cheating on her husband with doctors, lawyers, and a cop. What a hypocrite. I couldn't put up with any more of her lying.

It was time to move out and become independent. I had a friend from childhood. Mom said, "I don't like him, and I don't want you to hang out with him. He's trouble." LJ was a small blonde-haired kid with a funny personality. Both his parents were nuts. His mom was a good-looking woman; however, she was also a hardcore Bible-beater, a witness of Jehovah's. In a strong southern drawl, she was always asking if people had heard the Good Word.

LJ's dad, Jack, was the local crazy person and town drunk. One time Jack shot his 12-gauge shotgun at the wall inside his own house. Everybody in town pretty much stayed away from him because he was unpredictable. It turned out that LJ was just like his father. When LJ's mom kicked him out of the house that summer, he went to live with his dad in his trailer, a place I eventually called home.

The trailer was parked behind a local bar—in fact, the lone bar in town. It was the hub for the town drunks and people who might politely be termed as being of questionable character. Many of the single parents in town frequented the bar, along with people who sold weed. The bar was off the main highway, in a brown building that looked like an old hunting lodge you might see on the Travel Channel. Inside were a pool table, dance floor, fireplace, and a few tables for rare but hungry, diners. Stuffed deer heads and fish decorated the walls. Once inside, it smelled like cigarette smoke created by the constant blue haze that hung at eye-level throughout the building.

The single woman who owned the lodge dated Jack, LJ's dad, who was a logger and always dressed in black pants and a brown shirt with suspenders. He usually smelled like cheap liquor, gas, and oil. He always looked dirty, his fingernails had dirt under them, and his hands were chapped. She let him drink for free and, after a few drinks, the resulting scene was almost always the same. He insulted the customers, and tried to pick up women in the bar, before going outside to get in his pickup truck. Many nights, but especially during pool or dart tournaments, Jack went out to the parking lot where he'd shoot off his guns, yelling at the top of his lungs. He'd start the truck's engine, rev it up until it was practically screaming, and burn rubber across half the parking lot, fish-tailing most of the way.

The thirty-foot trailer where father and son lived had a very small bedroom in front, and a little kitchen area with a shower in back. The trailer was parked behind the bar, somewhat out of view. LJ and a mutual friend, David, had been living in the trailer together for several months before I realized it. David was a tall, overweight kid with sandy blonde hair. Having trouble at home, he moved into the trailer with LJ. When I visited them one day, I thought, *These guys are having a great deal of fun, with absolutely no supervision.* I asked how they got food, and they said they went into the bar and took food from the kitchen. LJ said at times he went to his mom's to eat. Occasionally they'd do odd jobs for money to buy food. And, they each depended on their girlfriends to pay for food, since both girls had jobs.

One night my mom came home when I was completely stoned; I couldn't even get out of the chair. Jose and I had been smoking weed all night, and I was irritable, restless, and pretty much out-of-sorts. She yelled at me about being high. That's how I wound up living at the trailer.

"Leave me alone, and stop acting like you're such a righteous person when you're always off with one of your boyfriends," I shouted back.

Then she slapped me, and I laughed. She tried to hit me again, but I grabbed her arm and pushed her away. When she said she was going to call the police, I said, "Good. I hope they'll take me to jail so I don't have to live here anymore."

Waking the next morning, I decided that I didn't want to stay in this house anymore, or be around this crazy woman. I left, heading for LJ's trailer to ask them if I could move in. They agreed saying, "That's a great idea. We are going to have a fantastic summer." I moved in that night, and we laughed, drank beer from the bar, and listened to music, finally falling asleep at dawn.

Our first night together was a complete success. In my newfound freedom, I proposed—and they agreed—that we should think about getting a house where we all could live together forever. I had found my new family, and I was as happy as I could be.

The excitement lasted several days, with music, parties, and running around town at all hours. I thought, *This is the greatest decision I had ever made.* The sleeping arrangement was perfect. LJ and I had the upper bunk that faced the street, and David had the couch that turned into a bed. David's girlfriend Sabrina, Jose's sister, often stayed with us, too.

After a few weeks of constant partying, we were ready for a little rest and relaxation. One day, LJ and I were talking when Mark, one of our friends, walked by.

Mark asked, "What are you doing here? Your mom hates these guys."

"I know," I said. "That's why I'm here." And we laughed at my witty response. Mark lived with his grandparents. There were many rumors about his parents not being sober enough to parent Mark. We convinced him to move in with us by selling him on the idea that we had weed, booze, and no supervision—and that we were having more fun than anyone else in town.

Soon our family included LJ, Mark, David's girlfriend, Sabrina, Marie, LJ's girlfriend, and me. Mark, LJ, and I slept in the upper bunk, David and Sabrina, in the lower. This arrangement seemed to be uncomfortably crowded, but for me, having friends that close meant protection from the loneliness.

Night after night, we partied, hung out, and talked until morning. Mark's uncle, who was angry that Mark had moved in with us, came to the trailer one night and told us not to get into any trouble. Of course, we said, "Hey, that's *not* why we were living together. Our parents don't understand us."

After a few weeks, we ran out of alcohol and weed. Because we're bored, we decided to create a little action, fun, and excitement. Mark, LJ, and I decided to go the private social club about a mile or two away. Unlike the bar, this was more of a club with a bar. Serving mainly older retired people, it was located near a campground for folks living in RVs. Dressed in dark clothes, we walked there. Glad to see it was closed, we kicked in the back door, went inside, and played pool for about an hour, making ourselves a few drinks to get a buzz going. We microwaved some bean-and-beef burritos that we found in the refrigerator, turned on the TV, and relaxed. After a few rum and colas, we got a little rambunctious. Searching the bar for money, we found a couple hundred dollars in the till. That made us a little angry. After we took the money, we vandalized the place, using pool sticks and bar stools. Mark even threw a bar stool at the mirror in the back of the bar.

LJ cut his hand on the glass while snagging a few bottles of liquor. On our walk back to our trailer, we decided we needed new clothes and shoes. David had done handyman work in a small clothing store nearby. One day his job required that he have a store key, and he had a duplicate key made at the local hardware store, giving him access to the store. LJ and David used to go to the store after hours and feed themselves at the small restaurant in the store. They stole pants, shirts, and other items they felt they needed. David gave LJ the key to the store that night, and after vandalizing the club, the three of us went there, stole a few pair of Levi 501 jeans, Nike shoes, and the two shirts. Walking home, we were proud of ourselves for having such fashionable taste in clothes. I was excited to wear the jeans and shoes, thinking, *I'll show Mom my clothes to prove how well I am doing living on my own.* LJ did mention that when he and David stole shoes and clothes, they waited a few weeks before wearing them, so nobody became suspicious. I thought, *Screw that, I'm wearing mine. I need a girl, and I want people to be impressed by me, and my new look.*

While we were walking home, Sabrina tracked us down, frantically telling us that David had been kidnapped at gunpoint. We freaked out. We all ran back to the trailer to sit with and console Sabrina, saying repeatedly, "Sabrina, it's going to be okay. We'll get David back."

Sabrina explained to us that she didn't know the person who took David, but she recognized that a car she saw parked out in front of our trailer belonged to a local guy we all knew as Del.

Wanting to be a hero to the girls, I got angry and said, "Okay, we've got to do something here." We decided to take the law into our own hands and deal with this situation like men. At two in the morning, in this sleepy little town, everybody was in bed but the troublemakers. Since none of us had a car, we walked everywhere. Dressed in black, LJ, Mark, and I left the trailer and headed towards Del's house, where Sabrina thought David was being held. We loaded the guns we took from the trailer, and walked down the alley. Del lived with his sister, my old babysitter. His mom worked in the mill in Mt. Shasta, and having a boyfriend there, she did not come home very often, leaving Del and his sister alone. He had many parties at his house, and hung around people who were total stoners and druggies, people who got high even more often than we did, which was not easy to do. "If Del even tries anything stupid, I'm going to shoot his fat butt," Mark bragged.

"Take the safety off, and spread out," LJ whispered, as we crept through the tall grass in front of the house.

The fence between his house and the neighbor's was about six feet high, and weathered from years of neglect. Mark moved to the corner of the house while I went to the side of the fence that faced a pasture behind the house. Neither of us could be seen from the house. LJ went to the sliding glass door at the back. We raised our guns, and LJ knocked on the glass door. When Del opened it, LJ said, "Let David go. If you don't, we're going to start firing into your house."

"What are you idiots doing?" Del asked.

"Let David go!" Mark yelled.

A trucker we all recognized from around town came to the door with a gun to David's head. He said, "Get out of here. This is none of your business."

"It is our business," I said. "You have one of our family members, and we're gonna start shooting if you don't give him back."

"You stupid punks have more nerve than brains," the trucker said. "You're going to get yourselves hurt."

"No, it looks more like you are," LJ responded.

Del closed the door and shut the curtain. After a few minutes, LJ fired a shot in the air, and the door slid back open.

"What are you jerks doing?" Del asked.

The trucker came to the door with David, and said that David could go when he paid him the money he was owed. We were in this standoff for a while. "You guys are all crazy, and this needs to end," the trucker said, pushing David out of the sliding glass door. "We better not catch any of you alone, or you're going to be in more trouble than ever."

We shouted the same threat right back at him.

After the standoff, we all went back to the trailer, had several drinks, smoked a little weed, and bragged about what big men we were. Sabrina was happy to have David home. We all went to sleep happy that night, feeling absolutely heroic. Then I realized, *Without much thought, I had seriously considered shooting and possibly killing another human being.*

Later, noises coming from the dumpster behind the trailer woke us up. The sheriff, *the law* in this little town, was digging around in it. Since the town of 2,000 inhabitants had one trailer of kids living together, It probably didn't take the sheriff long to guess that we were the likely suspects for the robbery and vandalism committed at the club.

The sheriff found our hiding place for the stolen liquor, as well as the shoes and clothes we weren't wearing. He confiscated all the items, wrote each one of us a ticket, and left. We thought we were off the hook, and went outside.

Shortly after this incident, Mark's uncle drove up in his white pickup truck, jumped out, ran over to Mark, punched him in the face, and threw him head first through the fence. He grabbed me by the shirt, and threw me into the fence. He shouted, "I expect LJ and David to be deadbeat troublemakers, but not you two. Go home."

I left the trailer and walked home. Mom opened the door in her red robe. There I stood, outside on the porch in my red Nike shirt, 501s, and Nike shoes that the sheriff never suspected were also stolen. Mom didn't let me in until I explained what happened. Together we went through a laundry list of rules I had to obey if I wanted to move back in. Mom detailed, "No smoking weed, no hanging out with Paul, Mel, Jose, LJ, or David. You have to be home before ten on weeknights and eleven on Saturdays, except when there are dances, when you can stay out until midnight."

After going over the list I said, "I'm going to follow these rules, I'm a changed kid, and I know how much I need you."

She smiled and gave me a hug. "Great," she said, "I have to get ready and go over the hill; I have business to do." Going over the hill is what people said when they were traveling from McCloud to Mt. Shasta on Highway 89. I thought, *Great, I can run over to Jose's, take a quick bong hit, and get attention from his mom, Brenda.*

The word on the street was that Jose's mom was angry that I had been living at the trailer. I had been lying low, trying to stay away from her because I never wanted to do anything to upset her. Because I so badly needed some motherly love, I went to Jose's with my tail between my legs, ready for whatever she might say to me.

Brenda was gentle with me, and fed me a couple fresh tortillas with butter on them. While I sat at the table with her for a few minutes, she said to me, "Rob, it's time to straighten up. You have a chance to make something of yourself." That kind of talk really mattered to me because I didn't want to let her down. She gave me a big hug, and let me go to the basement where I got high with the crew.

"Did my mom yell at you?" Jose asked.

"No, not really," I answered. "I hate it, though, when she gives me that look of disappointment." Marty, Phil, and Jose all laughed.

"Holmes, she cares about you," Marty said. That made me feel both good and guilty, and I took a big draw off the bong. We got loaded and went upstairs to watch MTV. Two of Stevie Nick's videos came on that day. Stoned, I thought her incredible scratchy voice, curly blonde hair, and special brown eyes, had made me fall in love.

Yet, in one night, I thought about what had happened, *I went from that happy-go-lucky kid (on the outside) to a raging criminal, looking to destroy, steal, and possibly kill. Alcohol and drugs finally busted through any inhibitions I might have had about breaking the law or controlling my use.*

CHAPTER 8

Spirituality—Two Versions

The summer of 1983, when I was seventeen, was a strange time for me. I kept hearing that I needed to repent, find God, be with Jesus, maybe do a confession, because the year 2000 was coming, and people like me were going directly to hell. Maybe this is odd thinking for a normal teenager, but I had never really felt "normal." The prophecies of Jesus returning two thousand years after his birth weighed heavy on my mind. I wondered, *Was the world going to end?*

Throughout my high school years, I hung out with some people who were considered stoners and deadbeats. What people didn't realize about us is that we weren't mindlessly doping or getting drunk and laying back. We talked and read about subjects that challenged the status quo, such as police states, surveillance, mind control, the Bermuda Triangle, UFOs, bar codes, RFID chips, and the end of the world. The information in these books was very interesting, and seemed to present a deeper meaning about our society and spirituality.

While Mom was preaching about "The Rapture," and asking me to go see the priest who could help me repent and save my life, I was exploring fascinating subjects that contradicted the Bible teachings. Mom said, "The Bible and Jesus can help your sick state of mind and behavioral problems."

I found my second library during this time. Our high school didn't have the most challenging books. The selections were mainstream, with a large number for school research projects. As with the county library, the high school library carried a section on alternative medicine, history, and science fiction. Here is where I discovered Martin Luther King, Jr. and Malcom X, as well as Chief Joseph, Scarface Charlie, and the Modoc Indians. This small section hidden in the upper left-hand corner of the library could be reached only by ladder, and was for books not checked out often. I stumbled across this section, if you can believe in coincidences. Anyway, I checked out a few of books, brought them to the basement, and we all discussed these fascinating subjects. Later I checked out a few more books, and finally noticed one day a wider selection had been added, which made me happy, and showed that somebody had taken interest in my readings.

During this time, I spent a lot of days in the principal's office because of my behavior as a class clown, or for my tardiness. One day Mr. D. took me to task for being late, talking in class, and screwing around. Just before he let me go, he said, "Rob, don't think I don't know what you're doing."

"What are you talking about, Mr. D.?"

"I know what books you check out, and I know what you're reading. You can play this game with others, but not me."

I smiled and said, "They're just books."

"Maybe, but a kid smoking grass, who is a pretty good athlete, and supposedly a sub-par student, doesn't read those books."

Meanwhile the vibration in me was speeding up and getting stronger, and I was getting high daily to calm the vibration. At times, I felt like I was going to have a heart attack when I was around certain people or certain places. Conversely, when I went to Mt. Shasta or the McCloud River, the vibration's intensity seemed to slow and lessen.

That summer I heard more and more often that in the year 2000, Jesus was coming back to judge sinners and troublemakers like me. The thought of being judged for my sins, and going to hell, made me feel more despondent than ever. One day, frustrated with the feeling that the world was spinning out of control, I asked myself, *Could they be right? Is this it?* I was sad, and thought that these televangelists, priests, and my mom might be right. I was overwhelmed with a sense of fear. Luckily, one of my friends had a little hash, and after I used, the feeling of despair went away for a short time. Each night I had to emerge from Jose's basement to go home for dinner, to another cold, lonely night on Tucci Street.

One evening I was pondering the images of hell-fire, brimstone, bodies being torn apart, no love, and no sex. Anxiety overwhelmed me. This time another friend rescued me with magic mushrooms. I had heard that taking mushrooms could change a person's view of the world, and I was willing to do anything to change mine.

Jose, Marty, Mel, and I went to the basement and eagerly awaited the delivery of the mushrooms. The local drug dealer showed up. This person was new to our small town, a fiftyish hippie right out of the '60s. We smoked a bowl of weed, and took the mushrooms. The hippie told us it would take about an hour for the mushrooms to take full effect. Before my consciousness began to change, we drove to a place with a perfect view of Mt. Shasta. It was still daylight when we parked the car and walked out

Rob before the gas incident

Rob after the gas incident

Randy and Mike

Randy, Mom, and Mike

Rob in the Pop Warner TV commercial

McDaniel Family

Backyard view of Mount Shasta

Rob at fifteen

Rob at Mike's party, 1982

Rob and Tracie, homecoming 1983

*The Strand;
Newport Beach, California*

Just heaven

into the woods among the giant pine trees. The sound of the wind blowing through the needles was breathtaking. The ground was covered in brown, fallen pine needles, and we could hear the peaceful sound of running water in the creek.

Soon we were feeling the effects of the mushrooms "peaking." I picked up a piece of green moss, and we all admired its color, shape, and smell. Looking closer, I discovered that it looked like a web, and instantly felt like I was launched into this piece of moss. We were connected to everything. For the first time in my life, I felt like I was part of the larger picture—that my heart beat along with everything else. The rapid and strong vibration in me that normally drove me crazy, slowed and lessened. I felt as though I was in perfect harmony with all that was around me.

I couldn't believe it. I was part of, not separate from, the whole. How could this be? I had always felt that I did not belong, was not part of anything. That moment I felt smaller than the smallest grain of sand. The feeling was humbling. I was beginning to notice that I could sense or even feel the emotions of the people around me: sadness, anxiety, and fear, all feelings I had within me but now was also feeling it in those around me.

I asked Marty, "Why are you afraid?"

"What if we go to war?" he blurted out. A few months earlier he had entered the military, but I was amazed that he answered me so effortlessly, and without questioning my awareness of his fear.

I did the same thing with Jose. "How come you feel inadequate?"

"Because my dad tells me I'm a bum," he responded. I thought, *Is it possible to read other peoples' minds while on mushrooms, or are we all vibrating at the same wavelength, and all I'm reading is a vibration pattern?* Whatever was happening, it was astonishing to openly communicate. I must have said a thousand times that night, "I got it, I got it, we are all connected. We are all from the same source."

The guys kept saying, "Dude, you're getting weird on us." That piece of moss was a symbol of my new connectedness, and when we left, we took it with us and put the moss around the rearview mirror. Walking back to the car in the dark, the effects of the mushrooms were "peaking" again. The most wonderful thing happened: The Northern Lights started bouncing over this beautiful mountaintop. From the top of the car, we watched this natural phenomenon for about two hours. I was sure there was more to it than natural selection and evolution. The seed was planted in me, but the trip had to end. Back home, I slept for about ten hours, and woke up the next day feeling splendid.

That summer, we sat around, got high, and watched MTV every day. Brenda went to work for her nightly bartending job; we had the house to ourselves. It was great. Every Saturday night MTV had a different concert, and we turned up the volume, played air guitar, and got trashed. One Saturday night, Buddy, one of my baseball friends from Mt. Shasta, came to McCloud looking for me. Mom told him to check Jose's. Buddy knocked on the door, and Jose opened it.

"Hey, is Rob here?" Buddy asked.

"Yeah," Jose said, as I came out of the bathroom where I hid when I'd hear a knock because I was ashamed to be seen with "the stoners," and because my mom did not want me around Jose.

"What's up?" I asked.

"Hey, come on, we're going to the county fair," Buddy responded. I told Jose I needed to go for appearance's sake. He said he understood, but I could see his sadness. Every time another jock or a popular kid called me, I left Jose and the crew to run with that crowd.

Buddy and I drove to the fair in the next community in his great-looking maroon '65 Chevrolet Super Sport. Buddy was like all the Mt. Shasta boys: well-groomed and hip, with a nice car. They shopped for clothes in bigger cities and listened to popular music. In other words, they were very "preppy." We drank beers on the way up to the fair, listened to Rick Springfield, and talked about all the beautiful girls we were going to see there. The Mt. Shasta crew did not smoke dope, nor did they like dopers, so I had to hide that from them. To be part of the Mt. Shasta "in-crowd," I talked as if I hated dopers, and only drank beer.

The baseball players from my all-star team were already at the fair, as were the popular people and girls from the local schools. So many people were coming up to say hi, asking what I had been up to all summer. Of course, I had to lie. Standing at the pitching machine, my next girlfriend walked by. Theresa was beautiful and tall, with black hair and a pretty smile. When we made eye contact, she smiled, and I did, too.

That night we had a lot of fun. It was great seeing the Mt. Shasta crew and hanging out with the popular crowd. Normally when I got home, I'd go to Jose's and talk with him about my great night. *This* night I wanted to keep to myself.

I realized, *I really don't want to smoke weed, and hang out with stoners anymore. I am done with Jose, Paul, Mel, and Marty.*

Toward the middle of that summer before my senior year, I was at the small convenience store when some friends entered. We hugged because we hadn't seen each other most of the summer. One said, "You're not going to believe who is with me." Megan had moved back, and we picked up right where we left off. She was an avid reader, and at night we went to her place and read together, listened to Foreigner on the record player, and cuddled on the couch. Her dad was always gone, which was good for Megan and me. I shared my ideas about vibrations, and told her about a new book, *Nastrodomus*, and she shared Hemmingway and Longfellow.

The balcony off her dad's bedroom faced Mt. Shasta, giving us an awesome view of nature's majestic work of art. Together we sat on the couch on his balcony and watched the night sky get darker and darker until the snowcaps lit up the mountain. Then Megan drew the rock face, snowcaps, ledges, stars, lights, and shadows. To say her drawings were amazing would not do them justice. Together we studied her artwork, and talked about how many millennia those mountains had been there. Megan wanted to go to art school in the Bay Area, but her dad wanted her to do something else, which made her sad.

Later that summer her friend said that Megan really liked me, and I said I really liked her. The friend asked why I didn't ask her out. I said because we already have a good thing. In the coming weeks, she started dating another guy, ending our shared vibration.

Megan was such a positive influence in my life; I've always wondered if I should have taken the risk.

I started reconnecting with Theresa, hanging around with the most popular kids in my school.

The next day, instead of going to Jose's, I went to the football field and ran sprints. August football practice started soon, and I wanted to play well. Back home, I called Ricky, a friend Mom liked very much. We hung out and listened to music for the rest of that day. By the end of the summer, I was hanging out with other athletes, going to Mt. Shasta a lot, playing basketball at night, and working hard at football practice during the day. On Saturday nights, instead of going to Jose's, I went to dances with other athletes. The dances were a big deal in this area of northern California. A man named Girard had been putting dances together since the '70s disco era. Every Saturday night he moved to a different town, set up these big speakers, a disco ball, lights, a dry ice machine to add that smoky/steamy atmosphere, and played popular music. He rotated towns to give everyone a chance to host the dance. As an eighth grader, the music had been mainly disco, but by my junior or senior year, it was wonderful '80s music.

When senior year started, I was seventeen and was named starting quarterback and captain of the football team. Theresa and I were dating. My mom was happy, and I was, too. I was not drinking or smoking weed—and it felt good. I was clear-headed, showed up at school on time, and was developing a few good relationships. The first quarter I achieved my best grades ever: all A's and B's. Mom commented, "Robbie, I am so happy you are getting good grades." The affirmation made me feel good. The entire football team was doing well academically, which was rare. The football coach said, "Hey, this whole team achieved greater than a B average, even Rob!" and everyone laughed.

I suppose it was meant as a friendly joke, but it wasn't funny to me. I thought, *Now I feel ashamed, and angry.* That night I went to Jose's and smoked weed for the first time in a long time.

The next few days I tried to bury myself in Theresa at school, smothering her to make myself feel better. No such luck. Those negative feelings did not go away. Shortly, one of my good friends said, "Rob, Theresa is using you to get back at her ex-boyfriend." I was devastated, and after that, I started back down the rabbit hole. Back to the basement at Jose's, but this time smoking weed didn't feel good; it actually made me sadder and more paranoid. But I found an alternative, and drinking vodka and orange juice tasted good. Booze was my answer because it killed the pain.

Into fall, I drank more, but because I was hanging around popular people, even though she knew what we were doing, my mom didn't say a word. On Friday night, I hung out with the in-crowd from one town, the all-stars and best athletes at their school. The next night I went to Mt. Shasta to hang out with the great athletes and extremely popular kids there. Other times I ended up in the college town and hung out with older guys and their crew. I was all over the place, running with many different groups—*anything so I didn't have to be me.*

I was drinking nearly every day, and feeling more and more isolated. The more I hung around these crews, the lonelier I felt. It was terrifying. By the time football season was over, my grades were back in the tank. For me to play basketball, my teachers had to give me a passing grade. Again, I was staying away from home as much as possible. The different groups bored me because we always talked about the same things: girls, cars, and liquor. I wanted to scream, *Screw you, idiots. There's much more to life than this.* But I knew if I actually said that, they'd label me a freak, like many of the "thinkers" who lived in our town. I couldn't do that because I wanted to be part of something—anything.

Looking closer at this time, the so-called "dopers" had more substance than the athletes or popular people. I wondered why the "good kids" had little to share when it came to spiritual values. The "dopers" gave much more spiritually, and if you needed it, shared the shirt off their back and the food in their refrigerator. I was being told I needed to have "proper" friends because they would help me in life, but in fact it was the "dopers" who really helped me, not the popular people. With the "dopers," I quickly learned that life was like a web, and I was connected to everyone and everything. With the popular people I discovered selfishness, hardness, and me-focused type of behavior.

I walked between these two worlds for many years.

First sign of trouble

CHAPTER 9

My Collision with a Pine Tree

Leading the league in scoring, I could dunk a basketball, which was pretty good for a five-foot-ten kid. I so badly wanted to be or remain part of the "in-crowd" that I was willing to do or say anything. At the age of eighteen we could write our own notes as to why we weren't at school, and the principal couldn't say anything. I could coast through the rest of the school year.

On January 4, 1984, I went to Mac's Drive-In. Built in the 1950s, it was a popular hangout where you pulled up and ordered from the take-out window. Pinball machines and picnic tables stood out front. This place had the best root-beer floats anywhere. It always smelled like hamburgers; the scent gave me a warm feeling whenever I went there.

On that January day, a friend and I were parked out front when Curt, an ex-Marine and one of my Little League coaches, pulled up in his '68 Willy's Jeep. It was painted maroon, had big chrome rims and tires, and a top that was always down. The temperature was around sixty degrees and sunny, unusual for that time of year.

Curt, who had recently mustered out, was about seven years older than me, and had been a popular athlete in high school. We hit it off when I was a young kid.

"Cabitto, is that you?" he asked when he saw me.

"Yep."

"You look good—getting big," he said. A comment like that from Curt meant a lot to me because I respected him growing up.

"Got a game tonight?" Curt asked.

"Yes, can you make it?" I asked, hoping he'd say yes.

"Yeah, for sure," he responded. "I heard you're awesome." What Curt said was very unexpected. "Hey Rob, do you want to come with us before the game? I'll drop you off, and then after the game, pick you up and you can hang out with us."

"Great!" I said, and thought, *Yes! I'm in.*

Later that day when Curt pulled up at my house, I ran and jumped into the Jeep. "We're going to go out with a couple of girls tonight, but first let's go over to my friend's place and say hi," he said.

"Whatever you want to do, man," I responded. "I'm along for the ride." At his friend's house, we all began drinking and smoking weed. I badly wanted to fit in and so I broke my own rule: never to party the night before or on a game day.

Curt's friend passed the joint my way and offered a beer. I said, "Yes."

"Hey, what are you doing?" Curt asked. "You have a game."

"Come on, I'm going to shine like always," I bragged.

He laughed and said, "That-a boy!"

I cracked open a Lucky Lager beer, took a pull off the joint, and started feeling mighty fine. Before long the conversation between these men was about sporting events and things that adults talk about. To be part of the conversation, I started lying about attending a Ken Norton fight. I told them that I was a huge Norton fan, and went to this fight. Unfortunately, I didn't realize that people might want to hear more about what I had done. "Wow," Curt's friend said. "Who did Norton fight the night you saw him?"

I thought, *Busted. Caught lying again!* Because I hadn't been there, all I could think to do was take a hit off the joint and drink another beer. I never even responded. As with most alcoholics who routinely default to dishonesty and lying when we are using, I can look back and smile at how predictable this incident was. At the time, however, I felt damn dumb and embarrassed.

That night, my high school team was playing against the Native American school in our league. These boys were good basketball players, and normally I'd be prepared for this game. However, on that particular night, being accepted was more important.

When I got to the gym for the game, I was high with a good buzz on. I took a shower to refresh myself and get the smell of booze and weed off me. The team had already started warming up, but I didn't feel like playing basketball at all, and it showed. The first half was a disaster, and I scored only four points.

When the buzz finally wore off by the second half, I scored twenty-eight points, completely dominating the floor. Some college scouts came to talk with me after the game. One told me that he would start me at first string my freshmen year if I committed to his school. I said, "That'd be awesome," but arrogantly my real thought was, *I am good enough to play at a higher level.* After the game, Curt picked me up, and we were off to the party. Two girls from out of town, a bottle of booze, a couple joints, and we were good to go. We cruised around town while everybody in the car told me how great I was, and that I was going to be a star in college. I ate it all up and, in somewhat of a chemical fog, I agreed with all they said.

It was either have sex or go home, and since I was not at all attracted to my date, I decided to go home. Curt had his own plans, and said, "Here, take my Jeep to drive home. You can pick me up tomorrow." My thought was, *YES! I can drive the Jeep to school tomorrow. Everyone will see me in his car and be absolutely envious!* I was elated! Picking Curt up after school would solidify my status as being part of the "in-crowd," and I would have a new, older best friend.

How great this was turning out for me, I thought. When I reflect on that time, I was the star of the football team, basketball team, and baseball team, I was named the Carnival King in my senior year, and my name was in the sports section of the paper every week. I was one of the most popular people in my part of northern California. What "in-crowd" *was* I looking for?

As I walked to the Jeep, I was beaming from ear to ear at the prospect of how popular I was going to be. However, my parents had never taught me how to drive, so I was very inexperienced. This was only the second or third time I had been behind the wheel of a car. Jose had let me drive the Ford Fairlane and I drove his mom places a few times. Even though I had been drinking all night, and didn't have a driver's license, I climbed into the Jeep and started it up, popping the clutch. It died. I started it again, slowly let out the clutch, gave it gas, and I was off. What a great moment, driving Curt's Jeep all by myself. The Jeep was very responsive, and when I gave it gas, it sped up fast. It had power steering, which I wasn't used to, and I was all over the road. I drove around the neighborhood a couple of times, and proceeded to go the long way home, by Old Mill Road.

One of the '80s hair bands was playing, and I wanted to jam to it. Leaning toward the radio to turn it up, I took my eyes off the road for a split second, and hit an obstruction in the road. The Jeep lurched off the road, out of control and still speeding, and hit a big pine tree. Without my seatbelt on, the impact threw me part way out of the car. My left leg was caught under the steel steering wheel. I remember hitting the ground, and trying to get up. Collapsing because my leg felt like mush, I had no idea of the amount of damage, but realized it was extensive because I couldn't walk.

I tried to jump into the Jeep, start it up, and drive off, but I couldn't get it started. I climbed back out of the Jeep and fell down. The radio was playing

Neil Young as I laid there in agony, wishing I could die. My body was in pain, and my mind was racing. *Mom will be upset because I drove without a license, and I had been drinking.* I had a random mix of emotions flying around my brain, among them fear. I was bleeding. And oh yes, I thought, *I have badly damaged my friend's Jeep, a friend who asked no questions and had trusted me with his vehicle.* My final thought was: *I am in big trouble!*

Along came a white Chevy Chevette with music blaring and guys screaming and laughing. I whistled as loud as I could, but the car kept going. After a few minutes, the car came back and a guy got out, stepped over to the Jeep, and yelled, "Is anyone there?"

"Yes, please help, I'm hurt," I cried out. Barry was a big guy I played football against from a neighboring town. Dressed in jeans and a red flannel shirt, he smelled like stale beer. He came to the tree where I was lying in the snow with blood all around me. He picked me up like a child, and put me in the front seat of his car. The pain was unbearable. Barry kept reassuring me that I was going to be fine, and asked me for directions to my house. One of the guys in the back said, "I know him, he lives next to Bess," and gave directions to my house. I was crying my eyes out, screaming from the pain.

When he tried to get me out of the car, I yelled at the top of my lungs because the pain was unbelievable. Mom yelled out her window "Shut up, you're gonna wake up the neighborhood! What's your problem, anyway?" Barry and another friend finally got me out of the car and into the house where they put me on the floor in the living room. The neighbor came over, saw me on the floor, and asked, "What happened?"

Barry ripped my pant leg open and shouted, "Oh, oh!" while everybody kept reassuring me I was going to be fine. However I did hear, "He ain't ever gonna walk again. Man, that is screwed up." The ambulance arrived and took me to the hospital. Every time we hit a bump, I thought I was going to die. The pain was horrific. At the emergency room, the doctor came in with the sheriff, and both of them said, "We have a real problem." The doctor was speaking of the leg—and the sheriff was speaking of the alcohol.

Luckily for me, Mom knew the sheriff "pretty well," and convinced him to talk to the California Highway Patrol officer who wanted to give me a blood alcohol test. I was pleading and bargaining inside my head: *IF I get out of this, I'll never again drive when I have been drinking.* Not yet eighteen years old, I was most fortunate not to be charged for driving while under the influence.

The doctor told me that I had fractured my femur, a most dangerous bone to break. He drilled a few holes in my leg, put it in traction, and began the process of rebuilding me. "When can I go home, and when will I be able to walk again?" I asked.

He looked at me, dead serious. "Rob," he said, "you shattered your femur and did extensive damage to your body. Be grateful you're alive. Let's not worry about walking today." The familiar feeling came over me: Hopelessness. I thought, *Why didn't I just die right then and there?*

The doctor explained, "I will make an incision in your left buttock, and open up the femur at the top of your left hip, then hammer a steel rod down your femur, and put two screws in your leg above the knee, and one in your left hip to hold the rod in place." He added, "More than likely, you'll never walk the same again." My feeling of futility was quickly turning into despair. All I wanted to do was to medicate, but there was no way I could smoke weed in the hospital. Fortunately, the hospital was giving me heavy doses of morphine.

During my hospital stay, visitors came from all the surrounding towns where I hung out or played sports. I was shocked. Since the hospital was in Mt. Shasta, those guys often visited, as did a lot of other people. The hospital said that I was their most popular patient, and at one point, started limiting the number of people in my room at any one time.

Are these people here to see other friends or family? This couldn't be for me. One of the nurses told me that she felt like she was taking care of a rock star. I loved all the attention, especially from the girls. Every day I woke up and made sure I looked presentable before the visitors arrived.

One visitor was Sheila, a beautiful Italian girl with shoulder-length black hair, brown eyes, and a great smile. She was popular, a part of the "in-crowd." We really hit it off. Every day Sheila brought food and music, and hung out. After an extensive stay in the hospital, I finally went home. I almost did not want to leave the hospital because I was getting high on morphine daily.

I was home schooled because I couldn't walk without crutches, and was weak because I had lost a lot of weight during the hospital stay. I couldn't stand for more than a few minutes at a time. This was the beginning of almost a year using crutches. On the plus side, I had a steady supply of pain pills, and took them freely without Mom saying anything.

I was no longer smoking weed because the painkillers were much better, and the effect lasted longer. I passed out painkillers to Jose, Paul, Mel and Marty, and anyone else who asked. Often we watched TV, and got stoned on the painkillers.

As Sheila and I continued our relationship, her family grew to accept me. They accommodated my special needs, and gave me a place to stay, food, and attention. Her mom was growing more aware that my home life was messed up. Sheila was the first girl that I ever took home to meet Mom and Dad, and the first girl I was ever comfortable hanging out with at my house. She caught on to Mom's unusual behavior, and my unhappy life. Sheila's parents trusted her to drive over to my place, pick me up, and go to all the parties together in the area. It was great being seen with Sheila because she had a good reputation, compared to mine. The mere fact that I was dating Sheila elevated my reputation and my status in the nearby towns.

Sheila's mom, Dottie, looked a lot like her daughter except for her beautiful long straight black hair and big glasses. She was young and very pretty. When we went out together, people thought Dottie was Sheila's older sister. After her divorce, Dottie had married a great guy named Rex, who was from a family that had money and status. Maybe because he was much younger than Dottie, they were a bit more open with their ideas about relationships.

Early in my relationship with Sheila, her mom, Dottie, talked with my mom. After that, Dottie, who was very intelligent, felt it might be a good idea if Sheila and I spent most of our time at their house. Later Dottie told me, "Your mom said many negative things about you. That made me feel that you are not getting the love you need at home." All I knew is that I had a place to stay where I could eat good food, watch TV, and sleep in a warm bed.

Over the next several months, Dottie and my mom talked more and more, which convinced her that I should stay with them. Rex spoiled Dottie, and she loved it. He, too, was very smart and took care to dress well. This was foreign to me, and I felt inferior. In fact, many times, I tried to break up with Sheila, and purposefully acted immature when I was around Rex and Dottie. But they were always forgiving and accepting. Dottie said, "Rob you're smart, handsome, and you will be successful someday." At times like that I thought, *Yeah, she doesn't know me at all.*

In late winter of my senior year, after I had been out of the hospital a short time, my classmates elected me Carnival King, one of the two big honors at our school; the other was Homecoming King and Queen. Each class voted on who would represent the class during halftime of the homecoming football game, and halftime of the biggest basketball game against our main rivals. Like most things in high school, the winner was based on popularity. I was excited and honored.

The night before the crowning ceremony, I was hanging with friends who decided to go to a party that was serving mixed drinks. All the usual suspects were there. In this small town, the same crowd ran together, smoked together, and partied together, and I was part of that "in-crowd." One of the residents of the apartments was a girl I had had a crush on when I was younger. Looking at my crutches, she asked, "How are you? How is your leg?"

"Good and getting better," I responded.

"Do you want a drink?" she asked.

"Yes," was my quick answer.

The guys I was with said to me, "What are you doing?"

"Nothing," I responded. "Come one, it's just one drink." One led to two, and before long I was plastered. My friends drove me home, and I stumbled to the door through the snow. Crutches aren't much help in snow. Once inside, the lights above the stairs came on, and Mom stood there.

"Robbie, are you okay?"

"Yeah," I mumbled. She turned out the lights as I made my way to the couch, more falling into it than lying down. The room was spinning, and I had to throw up. I couldn't make it to the bathroom on my crutches so I vomited onto the coffee table. Mom flipped the light on and came running downstairs, screaming at me.

"What is wrong with you? How can you continue to do these things? You've been in a life-threatening accident because you were drunk, and here you are drunk again!"

"Leave me alone, for Christ's sakes!" I shouted, vomiting again. She grabbed me by the head and face so that I could puke into a towel. Her long fingernails tore into my face, causing blood to run onto my shirt. Angry, I pushed her away yelling, "Look what you did!" She fell and hit her ribs, and hurt her back. The fall must have knocked the wind out of her, too, because she started to gasp for air, like she couldn't breathe. Scared, I tried to get up and help her, but I couldn't quite get to her. I tried to apologize, but I could see she was in no mood to hear that old refrain. She was physically hurt, but she seemed to be more emotionally damaged from the incident. She got up from the floor, and limped up the stairs.

The next night I showed up at the basketball game where the ceremony was to take place with two big cuts on my face. People were asking, "Are you okay? What happened?"

"I fell down on the ice walking on my crutches," I lied, too ashamed to tell the truth. People were loving, compassionate, and wanted to be helpful. Neither Mom nor any of my family showed up, but I figured they were upset about the previous night. It wasn't the first time no one was there from my family to celebrate with me, and it wouldn't be the last time.

Dottie, Rex, Sheila, and I did everything together over the next several months. Mom didn't say much because I was not smoking pot with Jose. Since I was hanging out with Sheila and her parents, she thought I was being supervised. And, most importantly, I was staying out of her hair.

CHAPTER 10

Shots in the Night

The evening of March 4, 1984 began like many others. I came home from Sheila's, ate, and then tried to find somewhere to go. Around eight, I heard Jose's car rumbling by. I thought, *Holmes, I haven't seen him in a while, and I haven't smoked in a long time.* I took my usual path, out the sliding glass door because it was the quietest, through the back gate, down the alley, and in through Jose's side door.

Jose and I were both excited, talking like old friends who had not spoken in years, even though it had been only a few weeks. Jose had good bud (marijuana) and a nice new cassette player in his car, having finally replaced the old eight-track. We drove to our familiar place nearby at the sawmill where we had an almost mystical view of Mt. Shasta.

Parking, we turned the music on, and Jose rolled both of us a joint while we listened to the new Thompson Twins cassette. We had tired of the new '80s music and returned to our old favorite, Super Tramp's "The Logical Song." Stoned out of our minds, with the music blaring, we got out of the car to relieve ourselves. When we heard gunshots, we looked at each other, saying "Who's the dumb jerk shooting off a gun?" We climbed back into the car and listened to more music and smoked a bit more before deciding we were hungry. When we pulled up at Jose's house, LJ was pulling up in his white Ford pickup. He jumped out, looking totally stunned.

"Jose, I think something's happened at the bar."

"What?" Jose and I both asked.

"Not sure," he responded. "There were shots, and a man went down." Now we realized that we had heard gunshots earlier. A few minutes later, Marty, Jose's younger brother, pulled up in a car, jumped out, and said, "Let's go, Jose. Dad's been shot."

We jumped into the car and drove down to the bar where the sheriff's car, an ambulance, and fire trucks were parked. At the entrance, Jose and I saw a white sheet with bloodstains near the head area. Almost at the same time, we asked, "What's going on?"

At that moment, Jose's mom, Brenda, was crying hysterically, and Jose said, "What's going on Mom?"

"Jose, Jack shot your dad." After what seemed like the longest pause ever, where everything went quiet, in shock we heard her say, "He's dead." She continued, "Jack and your dad had started to argue, and when your dad went to leave, Jack came around the side of the bar, pulled out the gun, and shot him in the face. He crossed the street, fired off a some more rounds, screaming, and yelling like a wild man, according to witnesses at the bar."

The night that Jose's dad was murdered was the first night I had seen Mom in a few weeks. When I arrived home, she came to the top of the stairs and asked, "Robbie, are you okay?" I didn't answer, and stood there crying as this was my first experience with death. She was no longer mad at Jose, and after that, when I went over there, she didn't complain.

That first week, Jose, his friends, and I stayed in the basement, plotting ways we could kill Jack, and get away with it. We also smoked a lot of dope, and drank a lot because many people who came by to offer their condolences brought along weed and alcohol.

I remember the day, date, and actual time Jose's dad was murdered in March, all these years later. This man had been an important influence and part of my growing-up years. Although he had been an absent father, when he was with Jose, he was good to him and to me. We all spent a lot of great times together. I was shocked and in a state of numbness, and these emotions lasted until anger and grief set in.

I spent the following weeks with Jose and his family, and was invited by Brenda and Jose to participate in planning the funeral like I was a family member. I did not see my mom again for almost three months, until the day I graduated from high school. I was hardly ever home, and when I was, she was always in her bedroom.

Once I graduated from high school, I moved to Mt. Shasta, the near-by town. The saga of the trial continued for Jose's family, but I no longer had the intense involvement I had before.

CHAPTER 11

Graduating From One High to Another

The end of high school could not come fast enough for me—or for the school. Since I missed a lot of school due to my accident, they allowed me to attend night courses to catch up. I loved night school because I chose the subjects. I took a first aid course where I learned about pressure points on the body, how to bandage a wounded person, CPR, and how to use tourniquets. Until now, I had been looking at knowledge outside me. Here I discovered a course that caused me to look differently at my body, and my accident.

Taking night school classes allowed me to miss more day classes. However, one day I made the mistake of coming late into algebra class. The teacher stopped me before I got to my seat. In front of the entire class, he asked, "Mr. Cabitto, why are you even showing up here?"

"What do you mean?"

"You're not very smart, you're way behind, and if and when you graduate from high school, you won't be able to do anything more than clean up at the local diner." The other students laughed.

I couldn't believe what this teacher said. I thought, *This is the first time I've had you as a teacher, your methodology is elementary, and you're teaching an antiquated subject. You've really never met me, talked with me, listened to me, or participated in my life at all.* For a moment, I considered his comments. They may have had some validity, but they weren't the truth. I struggled in school because the subject matter bored me. With the exception of a couple of teachers, there was no creativity. They all were preoccupied with following the preordained rules in some little handbook.

At a young age, I was self-taught. I chose subjects that interested me, and sought out teachers I thought could help me learn those subjects.

This algebra teacher had no idea that while he was teaching the basics, I was on a personal quest for knowledge, exploring 3.14 *pi*, learning about the mathematics used in the Mayan code to record great cycles of time, and looking at numbers that were the building blocks of the universe.

Luckily, each night I went home to Sheila, Rex and Dottie, positive role models who reinforced the value of all types of education. Rex, one of the smartest guys I've ever known, talked about everything: philosophy, history, plants, animals, and even diet. He was a vegetarian, worldly, and well-educated. His opinions and style of teaching deeply and profoundly affected me. It seemed there was nothing that Rex didn't know, and he was always willing to talk with me.

While taking this first aid course, I had a major wake-up call. To have a normal physical life, it will require strong personal commitment and follow-through. I had to be self-motivated, and invest time and energy into rehabbing my leg. My goal was to walk down the aisle at graduation without crutches. This was as much for me as it was to show others that I could succeed when I put my mind to something. Everyone in my family, and the medical community, had such low expectations that I'd ever walk normally again. Everyone but me. This time I was on a different kind of quest, where I was the one responsible for the outcome.

My mom had purchased a gym set for my brother that sat unused. I began lifting leg weights. Every time I went to physical therapy, my therapist told me I was coming along great. I practiced walking on my crutches without my feet touching the ground to make my arms stronger. Soon I was doing leg lifts and extensions, which increased the size of my damaged leg to nearly the size of the other leg. Pleased with the progress of my healing, my doctor took the rod out of my femur. I was thrilled to hear him say, "I've not seen many cases where a person came back from such a bad injury to live a normal life." I had a shot at doing just that.

My partying life actually escalated, graduating from one high to another. While smoking dope at a friend's house one day, his friend showed up with a bag of coke. Doing cocaine was a daily thing for him. They went into the bedroom, and after a few minutes, started calling other friends in one-by-one before asking me, "Robbie, do you want to try a line?"

"Sure," I said. Using a rolled-up twenty-dollar bill, I snorted a line on a mirror. I didn't plug my one nostril as the others did because I had not yet learned that's what you do to get maximum snorting capacity. The guys laughed, and I giggled it off as well. In a few minutes, a euphoria that I had never experienced before hit me. It was like my version of heaven. Deep in my addled mind, I thought, *Where have you been all my life?*

Today, as I think about how I reacted to my first use of cocaine, I find that there are no surprises in the rest of my story. With that attitude about how wonderful the drug made me feel, it was almost guaranteed that I was headed for all the misery-ladened situations I'd face later. I was entering a relationship with the most powerful lover of all: my addiction.

With this newfound drug, soon-to-be freedom, and a need to be independent, I was more eager than ever to be on my own. My relationship with my mom was tumultuous at best. She had her own demons, desires, and needs, and so did I. At times, our relationship was okay, and other times it was crazy. Because of her fear of my partying, we clashed. This led to long periods when we didn't speak or even interact.

The day I left home my dad was very nice, shook my hand, and wished me the best of luck. As usual, Mom did not even come downstairs. I thought, *Wow, this woman hates me so much that she won't even come say good-bye.* I was leaving, and she was not even willing to come to the door.

This was not the end of my conflicts with Mom, nor my need to have her in my life.

PART II:
THE ODYSSEY BEGINS

CHAPTER 12

College or Party, but Not Both

I moved in with two high school buddies whose apartment was close to my work. Living there gave me the freedom I needed to continue with what turned out to be a long-term love affair with drinking and drugs. I spent the summer days working at a job I found at the forest service, and partying at night. My girlfriend Sheila's mom got wind of my nightly escapades because her boss lived in the apartment below us. She did what mothers do to influence our decisions and course in life. She took a stand.

Dottie decided that if I did not register for college on my own, she'd encourage me. She was adamant. "Rob, I want you to go to college because it will give you choices later on in life." I protested, telling her how dumb I thought school was, and although I wasn't book smart, as reflected in my high school grades, I was smart, and was educating myself. Dottie didn't buy it. She could be forceful, like a mother bear, if need be, and I was afraid of her. I did what she said.

At the end of that summer, I moved into a house with three roommates that Dottie found. She helped me get signed up for the maximum amount of student aid, which allowed me to work part-time, and receive funds I didn't have to re-pay. After I left the forest service job, she helped me get a job at the local pizza parlor. At night I worked there, and went to school during the day.

Howie, Sam, and David, my college roommates, were an odd mix of guys. The four of us had this great house on the outskirts of the city. Our different schedules meant there was no telling who'd be home. My conversations were different with each roommate. Sam was a law major, David was a philosophy major, and Howie was in general studies. I also chose general studies because I had no idea what I wanted to do with my life. We sat up late night after night talking about everything imaginable. I loved it. I slowly began to realize that school wasn't as bad as I'd thought.

Howie became upset because the house was dirty, and posted a note saying, "AA meeting tonight." When we all were home, he announced, "We need to have an Attitude Adjustment meeting tonight." At the AA meeting, he asked each of us to pitch in and clean the house.

As the semester went on, Howie didn't live up to his part of the deal. He didn't clean, was behind in rent, and became a troublemaker. He had parties at our place all the time without checking with us. I was okay with that, but the other guys were not. And Dottie certainly wasn't when she heard what was going on. Soon she had a new solution. One of her employees had a three-bedroom apartment over the bakery, closer to school and work. She needed a roommate.

Carol and I met, the price was right, and the vibe was good, so we decided I could move in. When I asked Carol if she had anyone set up to move into the third room, she said, no. The guys were bummed when I told them I was moving out at the end of the semester. David, in particular, was sad. He and I had grown close over the four months as roommates. He was a very gentle soul, smart, well-read, philosophical, funny, and a good basketball player. David had the same concerns about Howie, and so when I asked if he could live with us, Carol said yes.

It was great having David around. He stayed up studying, and when I got home from my job, we talked late into the night. David shared his love of poetry, art, and math, and I shared my ideas on architecture, time, and ancient technology. Night after night we engaged in this philosophical banter that included sports figures, gods, Greeks, and Egyptians. We had a great friendship. Neither of us had classes in the morning, thus it didn't matter what time we went to sleep.

My first semester in college went well. My grades were good, my friendships were growing, and I loved my living environment. However, my desire to party also grew. It seemed everyone I knew was doing cocaine. Cocaine was about $90 a gram, and my weekend habit was often a gram. Nobody was smoking weed; there was very little drinking, but a lot of cocaine use. Anytime I went to a party, I had a way of zeroing in on the group that was partying harder than everyone else.

The beginning of 1985 brought new opportunities and challenges. David decided he wanted to move onto the campus. This made me sad because he was the last person in my life who had a deeper sense of being. By now Megan was gone, and Jose and the guys were living in another town. I didn't have anyone to talk with about my favorite subjects. After David's departure, I closed the door on everything that was most important to me, and did not open it up again for over ten years.

I was now nineteen in my second semester in college. Without David,

I was bored out of my mind. College was a grind, and not surprising, I became more interested in the nightlife than the day life. By the end of the semester, I was on academic probation, and decided that school was no longer right for me.

I talked with Sheila, my girlfriend, and her parents, Dottie and Rex, about being on academic probation, and they agreed maybe work fit me better. Dottie helped me get a job at a local grocery store.

The one good thing I had going for me was my persistence in rehabbing my leg. I continued to practice basketball, running, jumping, and playing pick-up games at the college campus. That summer the coach invited me to practice with the college team. Happily I was able to compete at a reasonably high level. Even with my injury, I was still considered to be among the best athletes in college. Coach said if I kept "working hard," I probably could earn a starting position on the team. With his comment, my hope to play college sports stayed alive. And I was grateful to have that. Although, I had decided not to stimulate my mind by reading and learning on my own, my body was charged up for this new athletic challenge.

The hours for my new job at the grocery store were from three in the afternoon to midnight. I played ball at the college during the day, and partied all night, sleeping until two in the afternoon, if need be. When one of my coworkers came up with an easy way to steal beer from our employer, I jumped at the chance. I could parlay bringing all this free beer to parties into being liked. Before management busted us, we stole two to three cases a night. At the end of the summer, an audit revealed more alcohol was going out the door than came in. I was fired, the police charged me with theft, and I had to pay a $200 fine.

After I was fired for theft, Sheila's parents forbade me to see her anymore. Just like that, the relationship was over—and all these wonderful people were out of my life. I didn't realize how important these people were until they were gone. Dottie and Rex were surrogate mother and father, accepting and guiding me, appreciating and encouraging me. Most of all, they were there for me, until the moment I lost that right. No way could I blame them for wanting to protect their daughter against a thief, or a guy too stupid to realize that they valued honesty above all. I had slammed that door shut myself! Emotionally I came undone at the seams, partying night and day.

By the end of 1985 I had completely lost my way. I'd quit school, lost a job and girlfriend, damaged many friendships, and been charged with a crime. I asked myself, *How could things have gone this bad this quick? Maybe I need a change of environment.* I called the old friends who'd rescued me from the car accident, and asked them if they could use a roommate. With their nod, I was off to Phoenix, but didn't stay long. I felt totally out of place, missed Sheila, Dottie, and Rex, and wanted to be close to Mt. Shasta, the mountain that could give me solace just by looking at it. I thanked the guys for letting me come, but decided I had unfinished business that needed my attention. I drove home to an unexpectedly warm welcome from my mother and father.

CHAPTER 13

1986–1988: The Couch Years

The start of 1986 offered new promise, I had turned twenty, and Haley's Comet was coming. Mt. Shasta was one of the best sites in the world to view it. I thought, *I have to experience this, and I have to experience this sober.* I had been drinking every night for a long time. I don't mean days, but months, snorting cocaine, doing crystal meth—whatever was available. Days in advance, I stopped using and drinking, so on the night the comet came, I was crystal clear. I drove up to Mt. Shasta alone, as nobody in my life at that time was interested in the comet. It had been cloudy and snowing for days, but that night the sky was filled with stars. I felt lonely until I looked up and saw Haley's Comet. It was stunning!

Seeing the comet was a spiritual happening. Watching its slow, forward movement across the sky gave me a sense of purpose, at least for the hours I watched the comet. *Keep going straight ahead, find a path to follow, and stay on task.* Even though the comet was controlled on its trip through the galaxy, we are all controlled in some way. We need to make the best of it. Most of all, I thought about the millions of other people who were watching the same thing, and realized how we are all connected to each other—and the universe.

Amazing, I thought. *Could this clear sky simply be a coincidence?* The next day it clouded up and snowed like crazy for another six weeks. *There has to be a creative force.*

During this time I thought that, like the "flower children" of the 1960s, I could build a family with people I met in the drug world. I was searching for "my tribe," my family, and was willing to do almost anything to belong, to find a way to be with people and have family and friendships.

To some, what I chose to do during this time was unacceptable, intolerable, and downright insane. The eighties were the "me generation," and I wanted to live like the Woodstock folks. It was a perfect storm. I was still riding my wave of popularity from high school. I had my charm, humor, and most of all, great connections to score drugs. I lived rent-free, and went to every party in the surrounding five communities. Life was good, and I was happy. Several of the guys rented houses and apartments, giving us a place to party and crash—and party we did. I lost my new job at the mill that I had found after I lost the one that Dottie had helped me get at the grocery store, so I was on unemployment. Some guys had money from their parents, and still others worked at their parents' local businesses.

During the day, we swam and hung out at Lake Siskiyou, and partied all night. The music was great, the weather was perfect, and I had near-zero responsibility. As long as I didn't go back to my mom's high or drunk, I could crash there when I felt burned out, or ran out of money from unemployment, whichever came first.

We had a blast. I never wanted it to end. We laughed, sang songs, and told each other that we would be friends for life. I went home with whoever the driver was, and crashed on their couch. The next morning we reminisced about what a great time we had had the night before, laughing at our behavior, and calling each other out for pure stupidity.

I was living my Woodstock dream with my '60s-style eclectic family. The problem was that everyone else was cool with going home, but I wasn't. I didn't want the party to end because I was afraid I'd never see these people again. I was sad, and they weren't, and that didn't make sense to me. I did everything I could think of to keep the party going so I didn't have to go home. I saw these people as my family, my life, and an important part of my well-being. They saw me simply as a good time.

As the summer ended, many of my friends were going to college, others starting careers, and a few joined the military. My only plan was to hang out, travel, and move to Los Angeles and the beach. As my old friends left, I gravitated to a new crew who were a little more hardcore with their partying habits. Just what I liked and wanted.

A friend offered me a job and place to live near Los Angeles. His stepdad had landed a contract to build houses, and needed helpers. Since I didn't have anything going on, I accepted his offer, and moved to Southern California. The stepdad expected us to work hard and party hard, and that is exactly what we did. Night after night we drank, hung out, and had a ball. We showed up for work, smelling like sweat and booze, just like the rest of the crew.

Here I was, joining another family that initially accepted me into their home and life—that is, until their son and I broke their rules. He stayed, and I had this independence I had sought while in high school, thinking it was the answer for me. Now my only companions were drugs and alcohol.

This lifestyle started an odyssey that took me from the beaches of California north to Oregon, and everywhere in between. There seemed to be no stopping this train once it came off the tracks. I followed the next job, party, friend, or relationship, no matter where it took me. I had officially lost my way!

When the train finally reached the end of the line in the spring of 1988, I sought employment at the local beer distributor in Redding for a summer job. In late May of 1988, a friend called, telling me that Scott, a childhood friend, had committed suicide. I fell to the ground, feeling like my heart had stopped. When I was in my early teens, I stayed at his house to get away from mine. His mom fed me and let me hang out for endless hours, and at times, days. Only nineteen years old, he put a shotgun under his chin, and blew his brains out.

The next day, I felt like I wanted to die. To kill the pain, I drank, smoked, and got high on meth. Another friend, also close to our dead friend, picked me up. We scored meth and a case of beer before driving to the ocean. Totally loaded, he was doing about a hundred miles an hour in his white sports car when we went into a spinout. After several violent spins, we came to a dead stop in the middle of the road. On the right was a cliff that went straight down for several hundred feet. Had we spun off the road, we would have gone over the edge. We high-fived each other, cracked open a beer to toast our friend's memory, and headed to the ocean.

Scott's death made me question my choices and examine my life as it was *before* all the insanity began. Night after night I asked someone to go to Whiskeytown Lake and watch the sunset with me. When I wore my Ray Ban sunglasses, the reflection of the setting sun on the lake made the water look like melted gold. Every night we drove up to Whiskeytown, put on our Ray Bans, and honored Scott. After a while, many of my friends started doing this on their own. People sat on the hoods of their cars, waiting for the sunsets. No music, no conversation. We just watched this glorious sunset. This routine became my only solace, a sacred place where I felt connected again to nature, to beauty, and to feelings deep inside. I had always had a closeness, a connectedness to nature, but partying, drugs and alcohol had deadened that desire.

For the next few months I continued to work every day, and do crystal meth nearly every night. I was getting more dope than ever on credit, far more than I could pay for. It became apparent that I needed a change.

In July of 1988, I was approached by a friend who had tickets to the Van Halen's Monsters of Rock tour. I had idolized this band since the days of playing the air guitar, and listening to them in Jose's basement. At this time, my friends were degenerates, working harder on their drug use than personal development, and for the most part, had no plan for tomorrow. I was the only one with a car that could make it from Redding to San Francisco, so I volunteered to drive if they paid for gas, food, and accommodations. The four of us loaded my car with a cooler full of beer; threw our clothes in our duffle bags; purchased bread, peanut butter and jelly for sandwiches, and chips and water; and hit the road for San Francisco. A friend living in Santa Cruz was okay with us staying at his house.

We arrived at Jason's house, unloaded our duffle bags, jumped in the shower to clean up, opened a beer, and barbequed the rest of the evening. Jason had many connections to get weed and crystal meth. His roommates were big drinkers, so there was booze all around us. We went to the concert in San Francisco, which was absolutely a blast. We partied all night, slept all day, and hung out at the beach the following days after the concert. My friends were itching to get back to Redding, but since I had nothing to go home to, I wasn't as excited. Jason said I could hang with him in Santa Cruz for a while, if I wanted, and I decided to stay. The guys that rode with me caught a ride home from some other concertgoers. Everyone was happy.

During my time in Santa Cruz, I learned to enjoy the beach-bum way of life. Hanging out at the beach during the day, bonfires at night, always enjoying the sun, fun, and music. Jason and I went to the beach every day, and soaked up all the energy the ocean had to offer. At that time, there weren't as many surfers as today. Most everyone was skate boarding and doing boogie boards. The serious surfers were not at these particular beaches. I did experience the surfers at parties; they were an interesting group. Like their own tribe, they hung out with each other, spoke their own language, and all had great tans.

My time in Santa Cruz was a fun, calm time with Jason and his friends. By the end of the summer, I decided it was time to get back to Redding as I had left a lot of things unfinished that I needed to deal with. I packed my stuff, thanked Jason, and drove back to Redding.

I had a friend Mary Ann, from Orange County. Mary Ann had bleach-blonde hair, a great smile, and a sense of humor. More importantly, she was a hippy chick. She ate brown rice, was a vegan, and loved Bob Marley.

Mary Ann smoked weed, and lived off the land. She told me how once she and her friends protested some protesters, just to stir things up. Mary Ann offered to let me stay on her couch, as that was a common practice within her community of friends and family. I thought, *Perfect. Finally someone who gets my vibe.* I stayed with Mary Ann when I had nowhere to go, or was burned out from partying too hard. Mary Ann was cool with that, and never asked questions, up until the point that I had stayed with her for weeks.

Mary Ann had heard rumors that big dope dealers were looking for me, making her concerned for her own safety. She asked me what my plan was, without a job, and as usual, I had no plan. Mary Ann was really upset that I was not working or doing anything but lounging around and partying every night. To calm her down, I told her that I had a job, and was going to back to work. She was glad, and things calmed down. Every day I dressed and left in my little Celica, drove to the nearest gas station and waited on the side of the building for Mary Ann to drive by. Then I'd go in and buy beer, drive back to Mary Ann's, and watch TV all day. I did this for several weeks until one day Mary Ann said that the neighbor saw me drive back to the house minutes after she went to work. I was annoyed at the neighbor, but angrier at myself for getting caught, and for being chastised by her. Even when I was wrong, I didn't like being called for my behavior. "I was laid off," I told Mary Ann, "but I'm looking for another job."

"Rob," she said, "you've got to find your way."

CHAPTER 14

Back Home, With No Place to Go

What bad luck I was having since graduating from high school. *What happened to that popular and talented guy? How could my life have become this? How much lower will I have to go, and when will I get a break to help me get out of this situation?* I pondered these questions, but no answers came. Finally, I thought, *I just want to die.*

I started to hope that something would happen so I didn't wake up one morning. By this point, I had to medicate myself every day, no matter what. The vibrations inside were overwhelming. I thought my skin might burst open, laying bare a body that had no soul whatsoever.

After Mary Ann asked me to leave, I lived with my friend David. It wasn't long before he suggested that I find another couch to crash on, and do it quickly because he really could not have me stay there anymore. I called one of my old friends who invited me to come down to Los Angeles. When I asked him to fund my trip, he agreed. Off to Los Angeles I went, arriving there in mid-March of 1989 with a couple hundred dollars and one duffle bag. Mark was happy to see me, and I was happy to see him.

I had arrived in L.A via Greyhound bus. The bus stop at 6th and Los Angeles Boulevard was in a depressed and high drug-use area. I thought, *My kind of people.* When my friend picked me up, we drove out to the south bay to Redondo Beach. He rented a nice place just off of the beach on Torrance Boulevard. Los Angeles became a different experience for me. The weather was incredible, seventy-five degrees during the day, and fifty at night. The palm trees warmed my heart, and the ocean left me in awe whenever I looked at it.

My first day there I rode a bike to the beach where I came upon one of the most serene, peaceful places I've ever experienced: The Strand. This long bicycle path ran from Will Rogers State Beach in the Pacific Palisades to Torrance County Beach at the base of the Palos Verdes Peninsula hills. I pulled up to the beach and looked at The Strand—the beach, the volleyball nets, and people surfing. This amazing scene distracted me, and I hit the corner of a fence, and fell off the bike into the sand. I left the bike and slowly walked through the sand to the beach. I noticed a tanned man with blonde hair standing next to his surfboard. At that very moment I thought, *This is the life I want.* I felt like I had died and gone to heaven. I got so excited I forgot I had a bike, and walked all the way to the ocean's edge. Once I was standing knee deep in the water, I remembered I had left the bike in the middle of The Strand. I quickly returned to park it in the bike rack. Standing again in the water, I watched the "surfer god" get on his board and paddle out into the ocean. My emotions were welling up, and almost instantly the vibration in me became rhythmic.

Every day I went to the beach so I could smell the air, feel the sun, and experience the ocean at a close personal level. I felt alive when I was at the beach. The surfers were nothing short of amazing the way they rode their boards, their language, and their fancy-free attitudes. The whole vibe attracted me. Bonfires, beaches, beers, and blondes were on my mind—just like in Santa Cruz, but magnified a thousand times. My friend had different thoughts, like work, rent, car, and utilities. Our opposite priorities caused friction.

After going to the beach many days in a row, and seeing the same people over and over, I befriended the surfer. When I asked him to teach me how to surf, he agreed, and told me to come back the next day at the same time. The next day when I arrived at the beach, there he was with his board, Body Glove wetsuit, and joint in hand. I greeted him with, "Hey man." He replied, "Dude," and handed me a joint, saying, "Cool buds." I laughed and fell in love with the lingo. He took me out into the ocean until we were about knee deep, and began to explain the direction and height of the waves. He said I should feel the ocean, and become part of it when I surf. He talked about the ocean having a vibration—a life of its own, it being a life force.

I observed these tribal rituals day in and day out, and found myself longing to live this way, walk among them, and be one of them, only to return to my habits and fractured life. I left the beach feeling alive, healthy, and connected. Then I went to where I was staying only to find the guys were smoking crack and drinking beer. I had no resistance, and even though I wanted to say no, I didn't.

One day, surfer dude and I were sitting on our boards in the ocean when I heard the waves hitting the board with the exact same repetitive rhythm. Dude was talking to me, but I didn't hear him. I was listening to the ocean. After a while, it seemed like my heart recalibrated itself to the same beat, and I felt little to no pain or worry. I thought, *This must be what surfer dude meant by 'Be part of ocean.'* Dude snapped his fingers, and I looked up at him. "That's right, Bro," he said, smiling.

This life was going to come to an end. My roommates wanted more from me than I could give. Soon rent, bills, and other things needed to be paid. We also owed the dealer who gave us cocaine on credit, and we owed money to the local bar where we drank beer on credit. This portion of my surfer life was temporarily put on hold because I needed to get straight, find some stability, and hit the restart button.

I did not have the ability to meet my responsibilities, and that landed me out on my behind.

I called the one person I could call when I was truly at the end of my rope—my mom—asking what the chances were of coming home.

"Okay," she responded, "but things have to change."

"Of course they will," I said. "I'm different."

Of course I lied to her, saying that my roommates had not paid the rent, and we had all been evicted without them telling me.

She said, "I'll send you enough money to get on a bus and come home." The first day I was back, I slept and ate like a horse because I had not eaten very well for a while. Dad was still the same, smoking cigarettes, watching TV, and sleeping most of the day. Mom was also unchanged; hanging out in her bedroom, and going over to Mt. Shasta to see her boyfriend whenever she could. I didn't last there long.

Soon I was crashing with another friend. One day he said, "Rob, you're really messed up. Get help."

"Dude," I responded, "I want to kill myself, and as soon as I find a gun, I will."

He shook his head, saying, "I feel bad for you."

Mom and Dad had guns I could use because Dad had been a hunter in his better days. I decided to use as much dope as I could, drive to Mom's, get a gun, and go out to the woods behind the house and blow my brains out.

August 1989. I was ready, and partied as if there was no tomorrow, and was looking forward to my life coming to an end. For the first time, I was actually partying with real relief. The guys even said that I seemed more at ease.

The next day I called and asked Mom if I could come home. When she said yes, I drove to her house. When I got there, the owner of the Volkswagen I had been driving called Mom, telling her she was coming to pick up the car. Upset at seeing it had been damaged, she asked me to pay for it, but I had no money. She took the car and drove off.

"Rob, what is going on?" Mom asked. I looked at her, and all I could think about was getting drunk and high.

One night I was partying with a friend, and we went to score cocaine from Dodd. This friend was into cocaine, and had money. By this time, I was carrying a gun that another hunting friend had given me. Because of all the people I had confrontations with, and all who wanted to collect the money I owed them, I felt like I had to carry a gun. I hoped having a gun might deter people from attacking me. When we got to Dodd's house, I went in alone, the handgun secure in my pocket. I went to pick up a quarter of a gram of cocaine, about $30.

I had other ideas on how much cocaine I was going to pick up. I told Dodd that I needed more than $30 dollars' worth.

"Do you have more money?"

"No," I said, and pulled out the gun. Dodd's eyes got huge.

"What are you doing?"

"I need all the dope you have," I shouted. He jumped up, and pulled a shotgun from his gun cabinet. The gun made this loud sound of steel hitting steel and locking when he slammed the barrels shut. I ran around the corner of the room where Dodd could not see me.

"Get out before you get hurt," he ordered.

"Not without the cocaine."

"Okay," he said. "Put the gun down."

"No," I said. "You first, and get the cocaine." He put the gun down and gave me a package with about a gram of cocaine in it. "Sorry man, I have to get high," I said.

"Please, please leave," he said, looking horrified at what had happened. I took the cocaine and left.

My friend drove off, asking, "What happened?"

"Nothing to worry about," I said. "Let's get high."

I had applied and been accepted at a technical school in Tucson, Arizona. I had money because of my new construction job, I was off crystal meth and coke, and no one in Tucson was looking for me, as far as I knew.

Within a few days, I was on my way to Tucson. Mom and her friend happily took me to the bus stop. Mom said, "Robbie, I hope you take this opportunity to get your life together, and really do something with it."

"I will," I said. "This time I'm going to do great." She gave me the money I had earned from working construction, about $500, and I climbed onto the bus heading to Tucson. This was the night of the big earthquake in San Francisco.

What was I going to do this time to shake up my own life?

The Strand

CHAPTER 15

The Move to Arizona

Getting off the bus in Arizona in late October, I quickly found a bar and had a drink before I went to my assigned apartment complex, set up by the school I was about to attend. I found the complex, signed a six-month lease, and went to my new home, a studio apartment. The complex had a swimming pool in the middle. My apartment smelled like new carpet, had a small dining room table, one end table with a lamp on it, and a futon couch that converted into a bed.

Rent-a-Center was my first call to order a TV and VCR, delivered within a few hours. Feeling pretty good about my new setup, I went outside to orient myself, and see what stores might be close. For a little while, I lay by the pool enjoying my newfound station in life.

Once settled into my apartment, I headed out for the grocery store to get food. A guy with a big Afro looked into cars as they drove by. I thought, *Here's the guy who can help me find what I'm really looking for.* I said, "Hey Bro, what's up?

"Not much," he responded. "Just hanging." People, who are on the "sly," or use drugs or prostitutes, tend to be able to recognize each other no matter what city, state, country, race, or color. When a person like me sees another person like me, we gravitate toward each other. More important is how we can strike up the right conversation to get done what we both want to do. My man and I walked to the store together and made small talk about my move. "Can you score?"

He responded with the standard, "Are you a cop?"

"No." He took me deeper into the neighborhood and scored coke for me. By the end of the night, I had spent every dime my mom had given me, and I was out of cocaine. That's when my new friend decided to go home.

However, I was not quite done. Since I was in a new city, and nobody knew me here, I decided to revisit and rob my newest drug dealer since my now best—and only—friend had showed me where she lived. I put a handkerchief over my mouth and nose like a 1800 bank robber, and walked to the house to rob the people where we had scored the dope. When I knocked, I heard, "Who is it?"

"Jamal," I said, the name used by my new friend, and the dealer opened the door. I ran into the house with a knife in hand, and told her to give me all the cocaine she had. She gave me a little bit, and I ran back to the safety of my new apartment.

I was so proud of myself for such a great score on my first day in town that I proceeded to snort up all the cocaine I stole. I didn't realize this girl would go after Jamal, and that he'd rat me out. Around midnight, I was in the midst of feeling terrific from the cocaine when there was a knock on the door and a very angry male voice said, "Open up, you jerk." I didn't open the door.

"No way," I said. "You're going to hurt me." I stood by the door, clutching it with both hands as he was trying to pick the lock.

The standoff lasted for about two hours. He said he was not leaving without taking a piece of me with him. I was really sweating, crying out to a creator I did not know to save me, and yelling for help.

After a while, the noise stopped. I looked out the window, and he was gone. I opened the door, ran to the pay phone by the office, and called 911. In the meantime, another brother approached me while I was on the phone with the cops, and asked me if I wanted to by some "rock."

"Will you take a TV instead of money?" What was I doing? Ten minutes earlier a person wanted to kill me for stealing cocaine, and here I was negotiating another "score." Lucky for me, he didn't take me up on my bargain.

Finally, the cops showed up, and I told them that a drug dealer was trying to break into my apartment. I said it was a case of "mistaken identity." The cops called the apartment complex's manager, and asked her to get me into another apartment for the night.

The next day Jamal came over and said if I gave the gangsters the TV and VCR I was renting, and a radio I bought elsewhere, they wouldn't do anything else to me. I gladly gave them what they asked for.

When I went to the office, I remember the look on the manager's face. I have seen that look before on the faces of many girlfriends and my mom: She was horrified! I was a mess—sweating, nervous, eyes wide open, and grinding my teeth. When I asked the manager to help, she said, "The help you need is a detox center." She gave me the number, and I called a cab, paid for by the detox center. I was off on another Arizona adventure.

CHAPTER 16

Detox for the First Time

One month after I arrived in Arizona, I entered the detox center with my clothes in a duffle bag. I had to sleep in the intake area with a few homeless people who smelled bad. I thought, *What am I doing here? I'm much better than this.* I was in complete denial!

Detox was interesting because once I decided to stay—*like I had somewhere else to go*—they put me in a housing unit where I got my own bed and three good meals a day. Everything was free: bed, food, and healthcare. More importantly, though, the housing unit was a dorm for men and women, and I was close to horny, emotionally unstable women who were hungry for a fix.

One of the girls in the detox had all the right stuff to make her very attractive to me. Wendy was hot with a great body. She had experienced living on the street and shooting cocaine. She wanted to get high. Wendy, two others, and I hit it off and decided that our experience in this dorm unit would be less stressful if we had a drink or two to take the edge off. One night while the four of us were listening to music and talking on the patio, we decided to go for it. Johnny, who was in detox because he was homeless, scaled the eight-foot wall, running next door to the Safeway store, and stealing two pints of vodka. We drank and laughed. The drunker we got, the louder we were, and the louder we were, the more attention we attracted. Eventually the resident assistant approached us, and when he realized we had been drinking, kicked us out of detox. The four of us formed an alliance, deciding to move to Phoenix, hang out, and live free.

So it was that in early December we left the detox center, and walked to the major freeway running through the city. Sitting on the corner waiting for the next car to hitch a ride from, we discussed where we wanted to go from there. The answer: Florida. We candidly discussed how to get there. I said, "If we do this, we have to stay together, we can't leave each other no matter what." When I explained my experience with being abandoned and not having a family, I learned that each of them had a similar experience—and we all agreed we needed each other. After making our pact, I felt comforted.

Our plan was to hitchhike across the country. About 45 miles out of the city, we stopped at one of the largest truck stops in the world, looking for more alcohol and drugs. There we caught a trucker who was going our way.

However, I discovered that anything built on artificial terms was doomed for failure. Each of us was running from our own life situations, addictions, and ourselves. This so-called family was not going to be successful.

As we talked, I felt a familiar feeling in my stomach: anxiety, fear, butterflies, and the vibration. Like many times before, I ignored the warning. This wasn't the simple difference between right and wrong; it was deeper inside me. Later in my life, in a recovery program this was identified as the "nature of the wrong."

Wendy had experience selling her body for drugs or money, an idea most foreign to me. Wendy told me, "When I was married and living in Flagstaff, Arizona, my husband and I were shooting dope, and we ran out of money. The dealer offered us more drugs if I had sex with him." She continued, "Then later when my husband was in jail, and I needed money, I went to a truck stop and earned $300."

Wendy and the other girl began knocking on the door of each truck until they turned a "trick," earning enough money to get us a hotel room, booze, and food. For about a week we lived like this, until the other guy had a drunken rage one night, and our foursome broke up. Wendy and I decided to continue our quest across the United States. A trucker wanted company while he drove to Florida to drop off a load, and let us ride along. It was a good fit, as he was on crystal meth, too. We drove all night, stopping only once, early in the morning, while we were crossing Texas.

I stayed up to watch the most incredible sunrise. It really affected me in a way I had not felt possible, after all I had been through. It warmed my heart. I prayed that morning for the first time in a long, long time, to the source of our existence to "guide and protect us."

In Florida, we dropped off the load and headed for Tennessee where the trucker lived. He told us he knew a place where we could work, and that he'd help us get on our feet. Everything sounded great, and Wendy and I were happy to get started on our new life in Tennessee. He had to return the truck, and needed to do that by himself, offering to pick us up after he did his paperwork. He dropped us at the nearest truck stop, but he never came back. Everything that meant anything to us was in his truck. He left us stranded at a Tennessee truck stop with no clothes, no money—and nowhere to go.

Reaching out to a few truckers, generous people decided to help us return to Arizona.

PART III:
THE HOMELESS YEARS

CHAPTER 17

1989–1994

Wendy and I ushered in the '90s with a few drinks at a local bar, and when the clock struck twelve, I thought, *Thankfully, the '80s are over.* We began the '90s the same way we ended the '80s—with a drink and cocaine. The one constant throughout all this was Wendy's willingness to work. Our relationship was going well, and I had what I considered the ideal life. I stayed home drinking during the day, watched "Days of Our Lives," took my afternoon nap, and generally was lazy while she went to work and earned us a lot of money.

We started each day by having a couple drinks, eating lunch, and taking a nap before Wendy went to work. Wendy knew about many things, including shooting cocaine and crystal. The first time I shot cocaine with her, I thought, *Wow! What an amazing feeling!* The ringing in my ears sounded like a train racing through a tunnel. It was as spiritual an experience as I had ever had, even though it was artificially induced.

A Night of Fight and Fright
One February night, Wendy and I drank more alcohol than usual, and an insignificant fight turned ugly and dangerous. We argued quite a bit, yelled back and forth, and finally started insulting each other. She got up to go to the bedroom, screaming, "Leave me alone." Following her, I stopped by the closet where the former owner's handgun was, and pulled it out. In the bedroom, we yelled a bit more, and I stepped up to her sitting on the right side of the king-size bed. I pulled the gun around from behind my back. Her blue eyes became huge, and she got quiet. I put the handgun to her head, screaming, "We're both nothing, worthless, and we should perish here."

I backed away from her and lowered the gun down to my side. As I did so, we both heard "POP." In my rage and inexperience, I had pulled the trigger and shot myself in the foot.

We actually started laughing nervously because the gun had had at least one bullet, and it was now in my foot. The mere fact that there were bullets in the gun shocked both of us. She said, "No way, Rob. We've handled the gun before with no idea it was loaded." We had even tried to sell that gun to a dealer for cocaine.

Calmly she said, "Okay, I'll get an ice pack, and let's get rid of the gun."

"I shot myself. We have to call the cops, but before we do, let's get our stories straight," I urged.

Tucson had a lot of gang activity in our area. Our story was that gang members were hanging outside our apartment, and that they all had guns, and we were in fear of our lives. When I grabbed the gun to go to the door, it went off. Once we had our story straight, she called 911, and soon enough the cops and ambulance showed up. They believed our story, and took me to the hospital to have the bullet that had lodged in the bottom of my foot removed.

Over the next several weeks, Wendy and I used cocaine nearly every day. We met Jimmy, a cab driver who was really using the cab as a front for selling cocaine. He had good cocaine, though, and always gave us dope on credit when we didn't have money. Perry, fresh out of prison for attempted murder, moved into our complex. The four of us used cocaine all night long at our apartment. We always had an abundant supply of cocaine and crystal meth because we were in a community of people who based their whole lives around partying and using.

Finally, off the crutches, I had no more excuses for not working. I found a minimum-wage landscaping job where they did not care about my lack of experience or work history. They handed me a shovel and said, "Dig a three-foot-wide, four-foot-deep hole."

I looked at the boss, asking, "Don't you have machines for this?"

"Yeah, you."

Tucson gets warm during the summer, often reaching 100, 110, even 115 degrees. February temperatures were in the mid-'90s, and it was hotter than I could tolerate. Digging one hole took me nearly all day. The boss came by and asked, "Is that it? You should have already dug ten of those holes." I laughed because I thought he was joking. He wasn't, and I was fired.

At home I explained to Wendy what this jerk wanted me to do, and how I was not cut out for that type of work. I was the "creative type," a guy that could "make things happen," more of a manager than a worker. She agreed, and said that because she made a lot of money, it was silly for me to work anyway. I heartily agreed.

In early May the leasing company finally said we had to move because we were too far behind in our rent. Wendy and I choose to get high rather than pay rent, and when we were several weeks behind, we paid as much as we could to get the leasing company off our backs. One day there was a knock on the door. It was the police. I ran to hide because every time the cops came a-knocking, I was in trouble.

A Sad Message is Delivered—and Used to My Advantage

Within a few days of giving my adoptive mother my new address, there was a knock on the door of our room. The officer informed me that my biological brother Ronnie had committed suicide two days before. He had put a handgun to his heart, and pulled the trigger. My knees got weak, and I collapsed. I couldn't believe he had committed suicide. *How could this be?*

Today, while I don't agree with his decision, I understand it better; it makes a kind of tragic sense. He was in immense emotional pain, and had never sought help from anyone.

As the functioning addict I was at the time, I used his suicide as an excuse to ask Wendy to take better care of me while I was in mourning. What I needed was more dope to medicate myself. My thought was, *How could I work after this kind of tragedy?* I tugged at her heartstrings, and she promised to keep us high.

On the Move Again: 1991–1993…Drug Use Destroys Every Hope and Dream

We entered 1991 the same way we left 1990, shooting cocaine. Because Wendy was working at a topless bar, it was easy to find cocaine, and every night she came home with both cocaine and liquor. During the Gulf War, we watched the news, and shot up so much cocaine that our arms were torn up from the needle tracks and bruises. Both of us wore long-sleeve shirts or makeup to hide the telltale marks.

That spring, we moved to a trailer in South Tucson. While we lived at the trailer, Wendy found a job at a bar/dance place I'll call El's. Wendy started out as a server there, earning a good living, which meant we could afford to do drugs, and pay rent.

Early in 1992, we moved into another kitchenette, and Wendy was still making good money working for El's. We were doing crystal meth or cocaine, and drinking about a gallon of vodka per day. One day Wendy came home and said, "My boss fired me. Said that I looked like crap, and can't work there anymore."

"I'm not sure what he's talking about," I said. "You look fine." But I knew. She had needle track marks up and down her arm, and was underweight.

One day in spring, we were moving out of the kitchenette and anxious to get to a dealer's house to score dope when we ran a stop sign, hitting a car that was turning. We didn't have insurance. We thought there might be a warrant for our arrest because the car was not really ours. I faked an injury, and Wendy came with me to the hospital. With nowhere to go after we got out of the hospital, we called a neighbor who picked us up.

We had no job, no car, and we were out of dope. Looking in the paper for any dancer or escort jobs, Wendy found one for a company I'll call "Dancers to Your Door." The owners were the oddest couple. Missy and Rick started the company after she had worked for another company that did bachelor parties and private dances for executives. Wendy called the phone number and that night, they showed up at our trailer. "Wendy, you can make up to a $1,000 a week," they said. The business operated on an on-call basis. Wendy had a pager, and when a customer called, they paged us. A driver showed up and took Wendy to the requested hotel. After she danced, the waiting driver took her home. They said if I drove Wendy, I'd also be paid.

"I don't have a car." I informed them. It was true. In the last accident the car was badly smashed, and I didn't ever save enough money to get it out of the impound lot.

"You can use ours," they said. Wendy and I thought this was a deal we could not pass up: good money, a pager, a car, and the freedom to do dope whenever we wanted without Wendy having to work the streets.

Wendy started working for Dancers to Your Door, and we did make about a $1,000 a week. The working hours were odd because we never knew when they'd call Wendy to dance. For the rest of 1992, we earned more money than either of us had ever imagined possible.. We had parties late at night, and dope dealers were at our place all the time. Dancers to Your Door had many repeat customers. The gifts from these people were incredible. One customer bought us furniture for the trailer; others gave TVs, VCRs, and clothes. It was awesome. Wendy told me that she was only dancing for these people, and not selling her body.

The owners did not want to pick us up anymore, and asked us to move in with them, answer the phones, and become partners. We'd handle all the calls, and split the money. At this point, we could no longer pay rent because we were using so much dope. We accepted their offer. They were disgustingly dirty people. Their house was a disaster, and I thought we might be able to keep the house clean, but realized the situation was not going to work. Quickly we moved in with Lucy, another dancer, and her young daughter, whom we had befriended and who lived nearby in a pay-weekly kitchenette.

Kitchenettes were rooms in very cheap motels that had a small version of a kitchen where we could make meals—if we had money, or the desire to eat. Motels/hotels with kitchenette rooms were filled with many Rob-and-Wendy couples. With similar backgrounds, we all spoke the same language. Many of the couples were mixed-race. New people came; old left. We dressed the same, and most of the young females supported their men by prostitution, working the street, or "dancing." Many of the women were beautiful, but most had been abused. They dressed the same: short shorts/skirt, tight clothes, and of course, big hair.

You could see the girls worked hard to hide their emotions while "on the job," and turned to their men at night to protect them. Their men were there to drink and do drugs within the safety of their room. All the while, everyone was looking for "normalcy," as most had come from fractured family situations. None of us had developed effective coping skills, but we tried to support each other as best we could.

The boyfriend's job was to drive our woman to her job, and rest up while she was gone. One customer actually gave Wendy a 1972 Shelby Mustang in mint condition. The car meant I could drive her to jobs, and make extra money. I walked the dogs every day, usually going to the liquor store on the walk. In the evenings, we drove the girls to dance for men at hotels and homes.

The Underground Connection

Even if a person was newly arrived from a city far away, he or she could find people like us to hook up with, as every city had such an area. We were all part of the "underground" connection. Many were runaways whose parents were looking for them. Maybe you got out of jail recently—whatever the circumstances, you were welcome here, wherever "here" was in a particular city. "Here" is where you could find a person willing to listen to your story, and maybe help.

We had stopped shooting cocaine and crystal meth, and started smoking crack. Once we tried it, we were quickly hooked, and started chasing the crack pipe every day. When Wendy got a call for Dancers to Your Door, we'd use that money to get crack. One day a guy offered us $700 worth of crack for our '72 Shelby Mustang, and we gave him the car. We smoked up that crack in a few hours, went broke, and didn't have a ride home. Wendy called Rick, who picked us up and took us back to his place.

Over the next several months, Wendy and I kept working for Rick, staying with him or with Lucy; and other times we slept out in the desert. Still other times we stayed in different hotels, spending every dime on crack. With our new dog, a black Chow named Nikko, we had three pets.

A few times during 1993, Wendy went home to live with her mom, but after a few weeks she tracked me down and went back to work for Rick. At the end of 1993, we were living out of a hotel in South Tucson. Both of us were emotional disasters, staying up for days on end.

1994—What Will the Next Day, This Next Year Bring?

The year 1994 involved one move after another, and as we settled into each new place, we said to each other, "This is it, we are not moving anymore." Because Wendy knew many different gang members from Mafioso, Crips, and Bloods, we could score dope anywhere. All the time we were getting deeper and deeper in debt, and it seemed we had no way out. Our habit had reached about $1,000 a day, and we were drinking constantly.

Life on the streets was scary. What will the next day bring? One time we didn't score all day, and I was getting sick. Wendy said, "Hold on, I'll go and score, and we'll get you okay again." When she left, I started dry heaving, and coughing hard. A few minutes later, I got sick to my stomach, and started throwing up. Blood flew out of my mouth and splattered all over the hotel ceiling. I had torn my esophagus as a result of coughing so hard because I was in withdrawal.

"I got sick and blew chunks of blood," I told her when she came home. She was concerned, but I was not. I smoked the crack, but I kept getting sicker and sicker, throwing up more and more blood. She called the ambulance, and the doctor said that if I'd lost any more blood, I could have died. They cauterized my esophagus and released me a few days later, telling me not to smoke crack. I made it all the way to the hotel before I did. Wendy went out that night and earned enough money so we had drugs again.

Finally we settled down in the desert, and we were not alone. The cops never came there, and we were worry free. Every few days we rented a hotel room to clean up, but for the most part, we stayed in the desert.

Many times over the years, people have asked how I could possibly handle being homeless, or having a girlfriend that earned money in prostitution. My answer is simple: When I believed my options were limited, I sought what I thought was the best option available. Even though it didn't always feel right, I was willing to accept it because Wendy's job provided, food, shelter, alcohol, and drugs—everything we needed at the time.

Homeless and the desert

CHAPTER 18

A Shot to the Head

That cold day in December 1994 did not start like any other day. I had not showered, kept myself clean, or eaten very well. After living in the desert for a while, we had finally rented a motel room. If I did not have a drink every day, I shook all the time with the DTs (delirium tremors).

Wendy said, "I am tired and want a lifestyle change. I can't live this way anymore."

I was scared, and told her, "Remember, I have had a very lousy life, and because I have no family, and I've lost so many friends to suicide, I cannot be sober. I cannot deal with the pain."

Wendy relented, and agreed to get us more crack and booze to make me feel better. She cleaned up, kissed the pets and me, and said she'd return in a short while with more booze and drugs. Thankful, I finished the last bit of the alcohol, and planned to nap until she got back. If I didn't drink and then nap, I puked my guts up waiting for her.

About thirty seconds after Wendy stepped out of the door, the Mobile Agency Narcotics Task Enforcement Services (MANTES) kicked in the door, strapped in full military gear, facemasks, flak jackets, and guns. Surprise! A Drug Enforcement Agency bust. A smoke bomb went off as they yelled, "Get down on the ground!" I got down on all fours, and looked up as two of our dogs ran out the door. The cop yelled, "Get down!" and kicked me in the left shoulder, breaking my clavicle. I fell face first, grabbed my black Chow by the scruff with my right hand, and held him while he barked. The agent yelled, "Let go of the dog!"

"No," I said, "you'll shoot him." He kicked my hand, breaking my thumb, and my hand flew off Nikko. That moment in time is etched in my brain in slow motion. Everything got quiet. As the cop put his boot on my face, I heard the shot, and watched my dog fall to the ground right next to me. He was trying to breathe, making this incredibly scary, heart-wrenching sound. Every time he tried to catch his breath, blood pumped out of his mouth and into mine.

At that exact moment, I realized what my life had become. I couldn't believe that my own behavior landed me here! When my dog was shot, for the first time I saw my life and actions as they really were. A living being was dying as a direct result of my own selfish desires. After a few minutes that seemed more like an hour, my Nikko died. My first thought was, *I need a drink. I can't handle the pain.* My next thought was, *I wish that cop had shot me instead.*

Wendy and I were arrested and handcuffed, then placed in separate police cars.

Shot in the head video of room 139

Homeless in the Wild West

The Road to Nowhere

Living on the Road to Nowhere

Stand alone beauty

View from the front yard

Morning run

Fall in the wash

Fall tree, palm tree

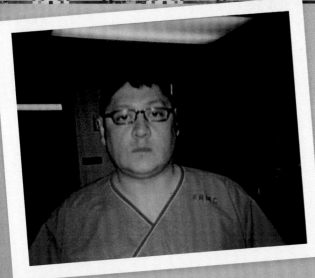

Final Detox

WHEN I'M GONE

*When I come to the end of my journey
And I travel my last weary mile
Just forget if you can, that I ever frowned
And remember only the smile.
Forget unkind words I have spoken;
Remember some good I have done.
Forget that I ever had heartache
And remember I've had loads of fun.
Forget that I've ever stumbled and blundered
And sometimes fell by the way.*

*Remember I have fought some hard battles
And won, ere the close of the day.
Then forget to grieve for my going,
I would not have you sad for a day.
But in the summer just gather some flowers
And remember the place where I lay,
And come in the shade of evening
When the sun paints the sky in the west.
Stand for a few moments beside me
And remember only my best.*

In Loving Memory of

DAVID PRICE OLSON

Born
September 8, 1930

Died
March 22, 2005

Service
Shepherd of the Hills Lutheran Church
500 Blake Road South
Edina, Minnesota

Saturday, March 26, 2005 at 1:30 PM

Officiating
Pastor Daniel Nordin

Organist – Maurice Anderson
Soloist – Celeste Gibson

Entombment
Lakewood Cemetery Mausoleum
Minneapolis, Minnesota

Remembering David

River Road

My Native mother

Rob, alcohol to food; 237 pounds

The Tree of Life

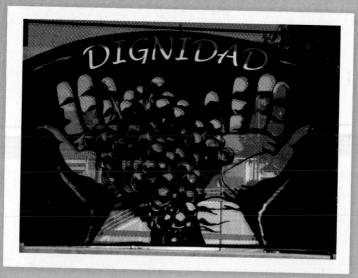

Dignity is restored

CHAPTER 19

Are You Native?

As I reflect on my first night in jail, I must mention the compassion of one person. Upon entering the cell, a large, blue steel door slammed behind me. When I looked up, I saw Will, a huge African-American man sitting by the steel desk with a cup in his hand. He looked at the blood on my face and around my ear and asked, "Are you okay?"

I responded, "Yes," explaining what happened.

Will said, "Bro, that sucks." After I fell lifeless onto the bunk, Will ran warm water over a washcloth, and cleaned the blood from my ear and face. I thought I was going to be beaten and raped, but my experience was the exact opposite: I received care, and compassion.

Wendy and I were both charged with multiple felonies, and we both went to jail. When I arrived on the unit, a part of me was scared and thought, *I am going to be raped or beaten to death.* Another part of me was relieved to be in jail and have that chapter of my life over.

The "not knowing" was causing me tremendous anxiety. And for the first time in a long while, I was not able to use drugs to calm myself down. The vibration inside me was going full-tilt negative. However, that same vibration enabled me to feel the energy of other people.

Many times throughout my life I felt another person's sadness, or glimpsed luminescent energy around people, like blue, white, or lime-green light. I didn't know if anyone else could see the energy, or even if this happened to anyone else. Once when I mentioned it to Wendy, she said, "Please!" with more than a hint of sarcasm. Now in jail, and sober, I could see this light energy around many of the people in there, and I could feel the pain emanating from them. It was extremely difficult and unsettling. There was no way out. This was going to be my home for a while; I was not in control, and I had no idea what was going to happen next.

After a few weeks, a fight broke out on the floor at the jail. It was fascinating. They were like gladiators going at it, throwing punches and kicking each other. I could hear fists hitting men's faces. I was so terrified, all I could do was throw up. The officers yelled, "Lockdown, lockdown

NOW!" and everyone on the floor scattered to their cells. I thought, *What did I get myself into? I had potential. How could I be in jail like this?*

The lockdown lasted for a long time, which caused its own stress since my cellmate and I had to eat, exercise, sleep, and relieve ourselves in the same cell day and night, with absolutely no break. The day-to-day stress of being in that environment causes certain people to go crazy. Many times over the coming months, I saw men fall apart mentally.

The units were set up with four pods facing a central unit. Each day we could look out our three-inch window and see all the other inmates going to the yard, the doctor, or court. One day I realized that a group of people walked to the central unit twice a day at the same time, carrying these blue books. The commanding officer (CO) was walking along the tier one day when I yelled, "What are the guys with blue books doing two times every day?"

"They're in recovery, and they go to meetings at that time."

"You mean to tell me that because they want to quit drinking and using, they get out of their cell twice a day to go a meeting?"

"Yep," he responded, "that's right."

"Well, then," I said to the CO, "I am in recovery, too."

"Shut up and sit down," he said. The next day right before the morning meeting, my door opened, and I was handed a blue book. "Good luck," he said. "I hope this works for you."

The big room that I walked into, it was full of laughter and camaraderie that I had never imagined would exist in a facility like this. I picked up a cup of coffee, took my seat, and said a foxhole prayer, "Great Spirit, if this is what you want for me, then help me to understand it." A tall Native American with great presence, a head of thick black hair, and colorful tattoos on his arms, walked in. When he looked at me, I immediately looked down at the floor because I was too ashamed to make eye contact.

The next thing I knew, he was standing in front of me, his voice booming, "What is your roll number? Are you Native?"

"What?" I asked, totally confused. "I am of the Karuk Tribe."

"Do you know your roll number?" he asked even louder. "Okay, young brother, this is your chance to begin anew." This beautiful guy proceeded to tell his incredible story of survival, molestation, living on a reservation, jail, prostitution, and his rising above the noise and confusion to change his life. I was in awe.

"Our sorrows and wounds are healed
only when we touch them with compassion."
—Buddha

CHAPTER 20

Dishwasher to
Chef-in-Training

I was twenty-nine-years old, and awaiting sentencing. My day of reckoning would come in April 1995. The first judge I was assigned to was considered by many inmates to be lenient on first-time offenders. As with everything else in my life, what I believed was best for me, and what the universe had planned for me were two different things. I thought I was going to get the soft judge, and then a strange twist of fate happened when I went to court. My judge was sick, and in his place was Judge Leslie Miller. She resembled the Wicked Witch of the West from the *Wizard of Oz* and spoke in a scathing way that reminded me of my mom. She read my case and postponed my sentencing, which to an inmate is like putting a knife in our heart, and twisting it.

After the postponement, I arrived back at the jail and went to my pod where other inmates asked, "Well, Holmes, what happened?"

"My case was postponed due to a new judge named Leslie Miller."

Their responses were unilateral, "Oh no, you are so screwed." Apparently Miller's reputation was of being a no-nonsense judge that wanted to make a name for herself, and she sentenced inmates to the maximum.

For a person awaiting sentencing, the not knowing if you're going to prison, jail, or probation, is the worst. The anxiety and fear of the future was overwhelming. I didn't sleep at night, couldn't eat, and I paced in my cell wondering what was going to become of me. I was so angry and resentful of Judge Miller, even though she didn't do anything. I still spent hours planning what I would say to her in court, and what I would do if I ever saw her on the street.

My day in court finally came after much planning, worry, remorse, fear, anger, sleepless nights, and not eating for several days. It was dramatic, and quiet. Then I heard the words that would both piss me off, and leave me relieved and elated. The prosecution had recommended prison, but my public defender asked for credit for time served. Judge Miller said, "This guy is a common drug addict. He doesn't need prison; he needs long-term help."

I was happy that I wasn't going to prison, and applauded that she called me a drug addict. I then thought I was going to beat the system when she gave me four years' probation, one year in jail, and work furlough. She proceeded to verbally strip me down, and looked at me as if she could see right through me. I vowed revenge against this judge, but you will learn later that Judge Miller knew better than I, and a very different outcome happened than the one I planned.

In May of 1995, I was moved over to the work furlough side to complete my sentence. That day was one of the happiest and saddest days of my life. Happy because my sentence was reduced, and I was going to get out of jail to work, and potentially rebuild my life. Sad because they returned my sole possession to me—the room key from the hotel where my dog was shot. My knees got weak, I almost passed out, and I felt overwhelmingly sad, ashamed, and empty.

I put the key in my pocket, and boarded the transport bus to the furlough program. I had no money, no personal clothes, no family, and no idea how to put my life back together. On the furlough side, I was told I needed to have a job, pay rent, and follow the rules, which was very difficult for me.

Work furlough was a strange place. It was like living in a college dorm full of 14-year-olds. Furlough was a big building that looked like a warehouse. It had rows and rows of beds, basketball courts, microwaves, vending machines, TVs, a reading annex, open showers, urinals, bathroom stalls, and washers and dryers. The men of work furlough were really interesting; a few were violent criminals who acted like immature little boys, especially when a female was around. These violent criminals flopped around on the floor, throwing tantrums when they did not get TV time. The guards had to give these people a "time out" when an inmate acted like a child who'd had too much sugar, or was too loud. They were sent to their bunks for a few hours, or even a full day. The problem with these big immature babies was that they could be violent. One minute, people were having fun throwing dice or playing basketball, and the next minute, if an inmate felt like he was being disrespected, a fight broke out. If a person bumped into one of these hot-tempered people, they might start throwing punches. But twenty minutes later the person who had been throwing punches cried and apologized like crazy to the guards. All in all, it was a pretty unstable and emotional group.

Being of Service

While incarcerated, I helped many of the inmates who couldn't read or write. Many struggled to read and understand their cases. When I realized they had a hard time communicating, I decided to read to them or help them read their cases and write letters to their families. In no time, I became a resource for the inmates who needed help, and they seemed to appreciate it.

In jail, non-gang members had to be careful whom they associated with. When helping one gang member, the rest of the inmates associate that person with that particular gang, and if that person were to talk with anyone other than their gang association, they could get in real trouble, like being beat up, raped, or killed. In my case, I helped members from many different gangs. Because I didn't recognize their colors, but honored their humanness, I felt safe.

Job Becomes Available

Chad, another inmate who had heard my story and knew I had no support system while there, became my friend. He was a good-looking body builder, half Mexican and half white, with dark wavy hair. He expressed his concern for me, and asked if he could possibly help. He mentioned that one of his sisters, Tammy, was opening a restaurant and might be willing to hire me. When I called Tammy, she said she'd meet to discuss possible employment. Tammy and her husband owned an auto body shop in Tucson, where we sat down, and I told her my story. Her eyes welled up with tears. She said, "Your life is a tragedy; it's the saddest thing I've ever heard." She decided to put me to work at the restaurant her dad was remodeling.

Back at the jail, I filled out the paperwork, and the following Monday I was released to go work. The restaurant's location required an hour-long bus ride each way. I borrowed bus money from another inmate. Every day I got out of jail to go to work for Tammy, helping remodel the restaurant. It was the first time in years that I felt good about myself and about what I was doing. I felt excited, alive, and grateful. I worked at the restaurant two months while in work furlough.

The mix of people in jail interested me. In my bunk space, on one side was a person who had embezzled from his company, and on the other was a person fresh out of state prison for murder and who was being transitioned back into society. One of the founding fathers of the Mexican Mafia, a true godfather, was in at the same time. One night I got home from work late and we were both doing laundry. We started talking, and he said, "You've been protected here." I asked what he meant.

"You didn't roll over," he responded. Wendy and I had been scoring dope from dealers that were gang-related; we had no idea how connected these people were. Apparently, the Mexican Mafia ran one of those dope houses. When I was arrested, I was asked to show the cops different houses and people, describe scoring activities, and identify certain people. I refused. My lawyer offered me another agreement before I was sentenced, and I refused. I wanted to do time for my own crime. The Mexican Godfather or his crew knew that, and in a way, they protected me. The whole time I was locked up—I now realized—it was no accident that I had never gotten in a single fight or had an issue with anybody.

But gang members were the most fascinating—mostly they were young kids from broken homes with alcoholic and drug-addicted parents. Most of them were funny, and had unexpected sensitivity. It was odd to see Crips and Bloods, Southside Posse, and Mexican Mafioso members all sitting on the couch together, laughing their heads off, and telling war stories, and falling into each other and laughing like family. They told stories describing their shoot-outs, and sometimes they discovered they'd been shooting at each other. At times they stole money from whiteys (white guys scoring dope) at gunpoint. They hugged and sat right next to each other, no matter their gang affiliation. It seemed that they wanted to be loved, to be part of a family. They used the time in jail to relax and take it easy; it was a safe place for them. These people shot at each other in their neighborhoods but when in jail, they were the best of friends and laughed at the situation. But, it could all turn violent in a second!

Out, With My Future in My Hands

In July of 1995, my attorney filed an order to get me an early release because I had done what was called "good time," and I was eligible to come up for early release. I was released in July, but since I had nowhere to go, Tammy and her husband let me stay at their home.

Just like that, my jail stay was over. That night after work, back at Tammy's place, we watched the movie *Forrest Gump*. One scene struck a chord with me, nearly bringing me to tears. When Forrest was running across the country, a guy ran up to him and said, "Hey man, I love what you are doing. I will follow you anywhere." Later, while sitting on a bench, Forrest was telling a woman that for some reason what he was doing gave people hope. Hope was all I'd ever wanted, and at times, it was all I had to hold onto—a hope that some way, somewhere things might get better. That movie touched me deeply, and I thought that if I ever got the chance to carry hope, I wanted to do it, and I would.

When the restaurant finally opened in September 1995, Tammy kept me on as dishwasher. I had bounced around over the years working part-time jobs here and there when I could find them, but I had never really developed a work ethic or skill set. Being a dishwasher was not a bad fit because there was little responsibility, and since I had helped put the restaurant together, I knew all its inner workings. I went to work every day. At first I was filled with gratitude. Nevertheless, I always asked myself, *Is this it? Is this all I have to offer?*

Tammy and I were really getting along, and a mutual attraction developed. Her husband worked at the body shop, and drank every night at a bar until nine, and then he'd come home to bed; a routine he followed for years. Tammy expressed her attraction to me one day while I was washing dishes, and we kissed.

That same day, Tammy took me to the probation office and waited outside. My probation officer was Chuck, a tall African-American who was very serious, and did not think any of my playful jokes were funny. Darvin, his surveillance officer, was white, a big man; balding, with glasses, his face was always red, and he was mean. These two guys questioned me on everything and said things like, "We're going to keep a close eye on you," and "You're the lowest of the low. IPS (Intense Probation Services) is the last stop before prison." They wondered who Tammy was, and why she dropped me off. I explained that she was my boss.

I left the probation office frazzled and scared that these people were either going to pull the plug on my new job, or my relationship with Tammy. Either way my first thought was to run. Tammy told me to calm down. That night we went back to her place, watched a movie, and had sex, and the fear seemed to go away. I stayed with Tammy and her husband for a few more weeks until I had enough money to get my own apartment.

Being on Intense Probation Services meant that I had to follow strict rules. Once a week I had to show up at the probation department to pee in a cup, to ensure that I was not using drugs or drinking. I had to fill out a weekly schedule. The schedule was documentation of where I was going to be every hour of every day of the week. I could leave nothing off, and there was no room for error. If I wrote down on my schedule that I was going to go shopping at 7 p.m. on Wednesday at a certain store, well, I'd better be there at 7 p.m. because the surveillance officer might check up on me. As part of probation, I had to go to two recovery meetings a week, counseling once a week, eight hours of community service per week, and forty hours of work per week. I had to have a telephone, my own apartment, a driver's license and insurance if I had a car, a clean record, and no association with other known felons.

Wendy received almost the identical sentence, but we were not allowed to have a relationship due to our probation restrictions. However, we did have community service at the same place, and we did see each other while at our probation officer's.

My probation officer was not opposed to me dating Tammy, but he thought it was not a good idea until she had final divorce papers. Chuck and Darvin came over to my place at all hours of the night to give me a Breathalyzer test, search my apartment, or, as Darvin put it, "keep me uncomfortable." Chuck was a good person and seemed to think I had a chance to change my life. One day he said to me, "Cabitto, you don't belong here. You're too smart to be wasting your time on drugs, alcohol, and probation." I thought, *Finally a person who knows a great deal about life and who thinks I am smart enough to change my life.* Chuck approved my new apartment, and I moved. I had to tell the apartment complex that I was on probation and why I was on probation before I could rent the place. It was humiliating, going into the office and explaining that I was fresh out of jail, and was a felon on probation. They didn't seem to mind, and went ahead with the rental.

In 1995, for the first time since the end of 1987, I had my own apartment and a job at the same time. In October, walking to work I passed through a car lot. A sales guy approached me and asked, "Hey, have you thought about buying a car?"

"I thought about it but I have bad credit and very little money."

"Let's get you into a credit-rebuild car," he responded.

"Okay," I said, and that day I was approved for a car loan. I went to Chuck and told him the news.

"Great," he said, "get your driver's license." I went to the DMV and got my driver's license. The day of the OJ Simpson verdict, I was driving off a car lot in my 1989 Maroon Chevy Corsica. What an unusual day: I had a job, a car, a driver's license, a furnished apartment, and OJ was found not guilty.

That fall I registered for college again in hopes of getting my degree. My life had greatly changed, and I could not believe what was happening. Drug dealers were not looking for me, and I was eating real food every day. Tammy and I were getting along well, and I loved my apartment. However, I could not help but wonder what was happening with Wendy. And when I thought about my pets, I felt very sad.

Tammy hired three professional chefs to work at the restaurant. François, a few years older than me, was trained in France. Buddy was a short, bald guy, also professionally trained. Daniel was tall like François, and a professional chef, too. Daniel was a cerebral person, very intellectual, and smart. Tammy hired François, and François brought on Daniel and Buddy, who were willing to do this job for minimal pay because they were waiting for another restaurant to be completed.

One day I came into the restaurant and learned that François had fired most of the staff. François told me that instead of washing dishes, he'd teach me how to become a chef. Every day François, Buddy, and Daniel taught me about different wines, foods, sauces, and dishes. It was wonderful. The camaraderie between these people and their skill was most intriguing. In late November, François happened to see my paycheck. He was really upset; I had been earning as much as he was, and he quit on the spot. Later that day Buddy and Daniel quit. Tammy then hired Claude, another chef who was a classic Frenchman, very charming, with a heavy accent, truly a master chef. While I hated to see François, Billy, and Daniel leave, Claude taught me many types of cuisines and cooking styles.

Tammy employed me at the restaurant through the rest of 1995 and early 1996. She had phased herself out of the restaurant, and her dad, who didn't like me, took over. When I caught him stealing, and told her, all hell broke loose—for me.

The writing was on the wall. My relationship with Tammy had come to an end, and my probation officer was keeping a close eye on me. I decided to leave the restaurant and seek employment elsewhere. My relationship with the chefs that trained me, the staff that cared for me, and the job that helped me grow, was over. I was scared, sad, and apprehensive about leaving the restaurant, but knew I needed to move on. I was grateful to Tammy for helping me. I was ready for my next adventure in the world because I felt if I stayed sober, I could do just about anything I put my mind to.

PART IV:
THE AWAKENING

CHAPTER 21

Minnesota Nice—Meeting Jennifer

After my release from jail, I remained on probation with a limited amount of freedom. My probation officer Chuck's seventeen-year-old son had been killed in a car accident, and Chuck was never the same afterwards. Chuck had been good to me, and I was sad to be taken off his caseload because he understood all the nuances of my life. He accepted the fact that I took a nap every day around three, and that I had dated my boss. I was transferred to Gary's caseload because Chuck was moving to regular probation services.

Gary always had this air of sneakiness about him. He constantly demonstrated his control over me with cryptic comments like, "I have the power; don't do anything to mess with me," or when he showed up to check on me at odd times. He loved to show his badge.

Dating was an issue. I could not go to a bar, and I did not have many friends since I'd left the drug community. By February, I was getting lonely and bored with my new life. I felt like I needed a woman to make me complete. Dating at that time was different. Then it meant the newspaper and dating services, which usually cost a lot of money and involved background checks, pretty much eliminating most of my opportunities. One day I looked in the newspaper personals and found a phone dating service where people could call in, fill out a profile, and scroll through the other profiles. If there was a match, they could leave a message in a voicemail box. I tried it, and had decent results. When I was scrolling through the new people, a girl named Jennifer had left her profile in the general mailbox. I called the voicemail box to leave my name and number for her to call me, when lo and behold, a girl picked up the phone—and it was Jennifer who was from Minnesota. We were both surprised because the system was not supposed to work that way. Jennifer was looking for many of the same things I was: companionship, fun, a non-drinker or drug user, a friend to hang with, someone stable. I really thought I fit that description, but most of all we thought it was just meant to be since, because of a fluke in the system, we were talking.

We decided to see a movie, and if things worked out, we'd take it from there. The movie was horrible, and Jennifer fell asleep. However, in the parking lot, we began to hit it off and decided to have a second date. The second date went better. Within two months, we were living together in my apartment, and talking about spending our lives together, even though we really did not know each other very well. My probation officer thought we were nuts, and warned Jennifer of the downfalls of living with a person like me.

After leaving my job at the restaurant, I bounced around trying to stay in the restaurant business, but not having the success I had had at Tammy's restaurant. A new apartment complex was being built close to our residence. Out front was a sign: Hiring. One day, on my way home from the probation department, I pulled in and asked for a job. I told them I was on probation, requiring them to fill out paperwork if they hired me, and that occasionally my probation officer or his surveillance officer might show up to check on me. The construction company didn't care.

When Jennifer moved in with me, all I had to wear were two pairs of jeans, a few socks and shirts, and a pair of shorts. I was broke. She took me shopping before I began construction work, and bought me boots, shoes, pants, everything I needed for my job. I went to work in the hot Tucson sun in May, and the job lasted about two months. The heat was overwhelming, and working from 6 a.m. to 4 p.m., was "hard time" for a guy as lazy as I was. The amount of alcohol these workers drank was unbelievable. And since I couldn't drink, it frustrated me to watch them drink every day after work.

Day after day, I went to work at the construction site, and every morning Jennifer made me breakfast, packed my lunch, and helped me get ready for my day. As I drove to work, I asked myself the same questions, *What am I doing?* and *Is this all there is?* My negative feelings and thoughts were not going away. I had a job that paid well, a beautiful girlfriend, bills paid, good health, and sobriety, and yet I felt as empty at that moment as I did when I was living in the desert.

My vibrations were more overwhelming than ever. If a car drove by at night, I flew out of bed to look out the window. If the neighbor closed her door, I nearly jumped out of my skin. If a door slammed shut, my heart beat like it was going to explode.

In recovery we say, *When things are bad, we drink; when things are good, we drink.* I felt like I had to drink or medicate. I had no idea how to deal with the feelings, nightmares, thoughts, and memories of my past.

I felt like I was living another person's life, as if I did not belong in my head or my skin. The construction workers spoke a language I didn't understand. They joked about their wives, and complained about their tool belts. Their skin was like leather, and many of them smoked constantly. Waiting for me at home at night was this beautiful girl. Jennifer had the apartment clean, dinner ready, and she had already worked out. Depending on her schedule, she might be in her tight, short workout clothes, and I used to think, *This isn't my life.* The construction workers said they had to go home to their fat, complaining wives. That was not what waited for me, and I felt ashamed, like I didn't deserve Jennifer.

When I was working the construction job, I was assigned to a crew made up of people from all over the country, mostly transients, with blisters and callused hands. They smelled like cigarettes, liquor, and sweat, and I was sick to my stomach every day. These people told crazy stories of sleeping in their trucks on job sites. Others spoke about cutting their fingers off with their saws or shooting themselves with nail guns. A few had been in prison riots, and in the most famous prisons in the world. Many of them said to me, "You don't belong here," or "You're smart; you should be doing other things," or "Cabitto, what are you doing? Stop screwing around here at the construction site, and get on with what you're supposed to be doing."

In return, I said, "This is me. I am doing what I'm supposed to be doing," or "I don't know what I'm supposed to be doing." I tried to fit in by telling war stories, and acting as if I did not care about anything. I said things like "my old lady" and "my probation officer isn't going to tell me what to do. If I want a drink, I'll drink." I didn't want Jennifer to ever find out I was talking about her like that. I felt like I didn't belong. I was an outcast; I felt as if I was the person standing outside the dance club watching everyone enter—and I couldn't get in.

Without the medication of booze, crack, or pills, I was dying inside. Life was too real.

A year earlier one of Tammy's sisters had told me I might enjoy a book called *The Celestine Prophecy.* Even though the subject interested me, I had not opened the book. The story was about an ancient manuscript found in Peru that was filled with insights that could help humankind, Yes, the book was right up my alley, but I thought I was too busy to spend time reading. My mind was too consumed thinking about liquor, money, crack, hiding from my probation officer, and generally, focusing on myself all day.

One night I began reading and learning the nine insights. In the acknowledgments, the author, James Redfield, had written in quotation marks, "Why is this happening to me again?" I thought, *What a coincidence! That was exactly what I was thinking.*

The first insight talked about the sense of restlessness, and how people had a "me-first" attitude. That described me perfectly.

The second insight astounded me. My understanding of spirituality was based on religious beliefs that were steeped in method, process, discipline, and the heaven-and-hell concept that frankly scared me. With my belief system, I was going directly to hell because of all the sins I had committed. Thought-provoking ideas from the book were slowly beginning to take root, and hope was welling up inside me.

As I read this book, I experienced very peaceful moments. Here was the answer, the solution; another person knew what I was feeling, and understood. My next thought was fear. *Oh, what if spirituality is a trap?*

I enjoyed the book and continued reading. It filled my time since I could not go anywhere because of probation, and I could not drink.

Insight number three said that the universe is energy, and it responds to our expectations because people are part of the universe. When we have a question, people will show up who have the answer we seek, if we look for them.

The fourth and fifth insights deal with our hidden energy, and how we compete for it, and steal it from each other. This revelation brought me back to my days in jail. That is exactly what was happening inside those walls. I could feel the energy change when a new inmate showed up, and I could feel the sadness of other inmates. This book had a word for what I was feeling, the vibrations: Energy!

One of the most profound moments in my life happened when I read the sixth insight.

Number six says that childhood trauma really blocks our ability to fully experience the mystical. I started having feelings of fear that I had never experienced before; I couldn't breathe. I broke out in a sweat and nearly passed out. Childhood trauma. *Could this be me? Could I actually be operating from a place where my past experiences are dictating who I am today, and what I'm experiencing?* This insight raised all sorts of questions in me.

This book gave me a brand-new look at life, experience, change, and inspiration. I had a clue as to why I thought as I did, and why I felt the way

I did; it was called my childhood. But at this moment, I was not ready to deal with this new insight.

The seventh insight deals with the "evolving self," saying you need to be alert and listen for the answers the universe provides.

Numbers eight and nine show how we can share our own energy by helping others awaken to this new energy. These two insights were a bit puzzling because I was still stuck in the "me-first" drama. Giving things away was not where I was—or had ever been.

Newfound Knowledge, but Without Understanding

I felt energized by reading the book, but did not understand what to do with this newfound hope. I couldn't stand the thoughts, feelings, and nightmares that were arising since I'd read *The Celestine Prophecy*. The book opened a portal into the past where many, many memories had been blocked. Numerous times I thought, *My current circumstance aren't because of my childhood. It's because I always deserved what I got, and what I got was based on my thinking, thus creating my actions.*

The negative feelings and thoughts I had about myself and my past actions were tearing me apart inside. I couldn't stand the memories that were bringing on the pain, and since I didn't have a solution, I returned to a reliable painkiller to medicate myself. After work one day, I stopped at a liquor store and picked up a forty-ounce beer. After drinking it, I felt instant relief. Ah, my familiar friend was back. Jennifer didn't say anything because she was unfamiliar with the consequences of what I was doing. She had no understanding of the disease of addiction.

Booze was my answer to calm the vibration, that energy I was feeling. Drinking daily, I was self-destructing, but I managed not to get caught by my probation officer. One night, however, I drank far more than usual and missed work the next day. My probation officer was livid because I had not shown up for work. Not showing up had been a common theme in my life, and this job was no different. My probation officer said to me, "Living on the streets, you don't show up. Living with this beautiful girl, making good money, you don't show up. Just what is your problem, Cabitto?"

"I wish I knew," I replied. "I should appreciate this life. I can't understand why I blow everything up."

Deb, My Amazing Counselor

Part of my sentencing required me to attend recovery meetings, serve probation, do community service, take counseling, and pay fines. I had no idea how to find a counselor, but my friend Chuck did. Chuck had helped me get a job at the restaurant working for his sister Tammy. I asked Chuck to help me find a counselor. He pointed me to Deb. When I set up an initial appointment with her, I was fully expecting to find a woman who was clinical, dry, and most importantly, who I could manipulate. I needed a counselor to report that I was working to get better in order to get a clean bill of health from the probation department.

I arrived early at Deb's office, and hung out in the parking lot. On the next building a small sign read, "Tiger Messaging." I walked into the office, and this person asked, "Can I help you?"

"What is this business?" I asked.

"A messaging service."

"You guys hiring?" I inquired.

"Ironically, yes, we fired a guy today. Do you have a car that's dependable?"

"Yes, I do." Since being unemployed while on probation is a no-no, I filled out an application, and the next thing I knew I was working in one building, and going to counseling in the next. I thought: *Huh, a coincidence right out of* The Celestine Prophecy.

When I met Deb, I was taken aback first by her beauty and her six-foot stature. She had this peacefulness about her, and her eyes were welcoming. Deb spoke with a soft voice, and she dressed like a hippie I had known when I was young. Deb's office had great Native American art, and dimmed lamps (not fluorescent), which I absolutely loved. Her blue office couch brimmed over with stuffed animals and nice pillows.

Counseling with Deb cost more than the counseling the state recommended, but I was willing to pay for it because she seemed nice, and because her counseling was not at a hospital. My probation officer approved Deb as my counselor, and we agreed upon a fee per session. Therefore, two days a week I went to counseling after work.

Minnesota nice and our home

CHAPTER 22

Finding My Roots, Examining My Life

Deb was the first person who ever asked, "Rob, are your or have you been in touch with your Native roots?"

I said no.

Deb said, "Sometimes when we lose our culture, we lose our identity, and wander aimlessly through life feeling like we are missing something, or are always on the outside."

After our first few sessions, I knew I was *not* going to be able to manipulate this woman. I thought, *I might have to tell the truth, and honestly go through this disaster called my life.* Deb assigned me to do research on my feelings, and gave me articles about Native Americans, and about the prevalence of alcohol and diabetes among Natives. Deb's calm and soothing voice made me want to take a nap after we spoke.

In my early counseling, we spent time covering my life and family stuff, laying out a timeline of events. When we arrived at the age of nine, I clammed up. My head dropped to my chest, and I started to sweat.

"Are you okay?"

"Yes," I said, "but I don't want to do this anymore."

"Rob," she said, "if you don't, the events in your life are going to keep reoccurring because you're pushing the pain back down inside of you."

"Okay," I said. "What do you want to know?

"Tell me about your family." I responded with the ages, gender, and basic information about my adoptive family, almost without emotion. At the time, I was blocking out my biological family. When the session ended, I went to the bathroom to relieve myself because I was nervous and having a difficult time breathing. I thought, *I want to get high.* I began having flashbacks and recalling many things from my childhood I had buried deep down inside. I had done everything I could, like drink and use drugs, to keep them buried.

After the session, I was in emotional pain, based on my thoughts and actions over the past few years and with my childhood memories haunting me. I turned to the only solution I really ever knew that worked 100 percent of the time. In my heart, I did not want to go to the liquor store, and while driving, I banged on the steering wheel and cried out, *"Why, why, am I doing this? I hate liquor, I don't want to go to the store.* The closer I got to the store, the more my heart sank, my hands sweat, and extra saliva built up in my mouth in anticipation. When I pictured Jennifer's face, I lowered my head on the steering wheel in tears. Finally, pulling into the liquor store, I purchased a big bottle of vodka and drank nearly the whole thing. The vodka worked as it had many times before to kill the memories and nightmares I couldn't face. Alcohol or drugs had always been the solution to the pain of my childhood trauma that I still could not really identify, acknowledge, or talk about—even thirty years later in the security of a therapist's office.

Tiger Messaging Met My Needs

When I took the job at Tiger Messaging, I knew I was going to be making less, a step back financially from what I'd been earning at the construction company. But at the same time, I didn't have to be in the hot sun, or in a kitchen on my feet all day. But the real bonus was that I could drive around, and not have to see my probation officer. I felt like I was getting away with things because the probation department didn't know where I was most of the time. That felt good to me. I made $255 a week, paid for gas, drove my car, and listened to music and radio shows.

Ollie and Carol, the husband and wife team who owned Tiger Messaging, cared about the people who worked for them. Both seemed to have had a tough life, but they were very sweet people. They also employed several other people who made up an oddball bunch. Many of them seemed unable to do any other kind of work. This job allowed for flexibility during the day. We picked up mail for mortgage companies, and delivered checks to banks, mortgage companies, and closing companies throughout the day. For a guy as irresponsible as I was, this job was perfect.

My run was along an incredibly beautiful drive that overlooked the city of Tucson. I had to be at work at 8:30 a.m. and I got off at 4:30 p.m. That was fine with me because at midday I got to take a nap over by the Tucson mall. I had a pager so my probation officer knew my route, which forced me to be sort of accountable. Things could not have been better. I thought a few drinks at night might add to my good life.

In September, I was more irritable, restless, and discontent than ever. I had a job that was going well, counseling that was making me dig deeper emotionally and supporting me with real compassion, and a girlfriend who was fabulous. I was frustrated with myself. *How could I be in such a good situation and feel inadequate?* I was ashamed of the things I had done, or had allowed to be done. I felt enormous guilt for not being the man I should have been to Wendy when we were living on the streets. Since I had my probation officer and surveillance officer pegged on the weekends, I decided I needed to kill the pain I was feeling.

Jennifer always was loving, forgiving, and understanding, and never seemed to stop being supportive. However, she did suggest I try participating in my recovery program, rather than just showing up and sitting in the back.

I missed work on a Monday without calling Ollie or Carol. On Tuesday, I explained to them that sometimes I returned to old behaviors even when I don't want to. I told them that I was working with a counselor on some of my issues, and would really try to do better. I was contrite, humble, and meant every word. I did not know the power of my addiction, and that even though I meant all of what I had just said, my addiction had different plans that would overrule. They forgave me, and let me come back to work. I really tried to change, even to the point of not listening to sports talk radio, as all they ever talked about was drinking at the baseball game. That drove me crazy, because I wanted to be the guy who could have "a beer" at a baseball game. Up until this point, I hadn't told Deb when I had used, nor did I tell her that I had been drinking the whole time I was in counseling. Now, telling her I had used was my first real attempt at honesty.

My commitment to this new way of life began with showing up for work on time, and trying to follow directions. Ultimately, of course, I didn't. For example, I didn't deliver the first checks that I was supposed to because I wanted to go have a breakfast burrito at this great Mexican restaurant. I figured that if I did one new thing, that was good enough. As much as I wanted to, I could not maintain that much change at once.

I did listen to different radio stations during the day. That simple change brought a program, and one person in particular, into my life, eventually enriching me more than I could have imagined. When I found Jim Rome on the radio, I'd seen him before on TV. On the night in the Tucson motel before the police had barged in, I had been feeling dejected and scared, as if the world was ending. I had flipped on the TV. There was this frizzy-headed, smart-mouth person with a real edge to him. His show was completely different from anything I had ever seen anywhere. I thought,

What a smart aleck. I love this guy.

Because I moved around much at the time, I saw Jim only once in a while, but when I did, his communication style always resonated with me.

Jim and the Clones, his listeners, brought a twist to events that were, at times, serious, funny, sad, or just plain maddening. The stories were mostly about athletes with huge amounts of money who did one dumb thing after another. I found that I was now excited to go to work because I was able to listen to Jim's show every day for four hours. This was great. Jim was the upstanding man in my life at the time. He was what I aspired to be: honest, decent, an open book—even when it came to mistakes from his past. I could not believe this guy was as smart as he was, as open as he was, and willing to tell it straight, both about himself and others. I made a commitment to listen to Jim's show every day because I could relate to this community of people. I truly started feeling better about myself. I felt like I had made a promise to Jim and his show to do better, and to be better for my community and myself, even though I still did not know how.

Over the next six weeks, I drove my car, delivered mail every day, showed up at recovery meetings, and went to counseling. I did community service at the graveyard, where a number of others from jail met their service requirements on Saturdays. But I was feeling more restless than ever. Even though I had Jennifer, Jim Rome, Ollie and Carol, and Deb, my belief system had not changed.

I drank whenever possible, as it was my only solution to cover the feelings of guilt, shame, and remorse from my past. At least, that's what I believed, and at that time, I had no other solution or way to deal with all the emotional baggage I had accumulated over the years.

CHAPTER 23

Back Behind Bars

I still did not accept that I had a disease or an addiction. I thought, *If I simply stop drinking, that is all it will take. I have a strong self-will, I want to stop, and I have a desire to quit. I have jail time hanging over my head, and could lose my job, not to mention damage my relationship with Jennifer.* To anyone that knows anything about addiction, not surprisingly, I returned to my addictions, and failed a urine analysis given by the probation department.

I was rearrested, arriving back in jail only four short months since my release in October 1996. I was booked, changed into the orange jumpsuit, and called Jennifer to apologize for what had happened. She was supportive, asking what she could do to help me.

"Please come down and put money on my books," I asked her. When I got off the phone, I thought how lucky I was to have a girlfriend like her. My next thought was all too familiar. I fell again into that absolute abyss of feeling hopeless. The day I went to jail was the same day Jennifer and I had decided to move to a nicer, more upscale apartment that was closer to her work. Like many times before, I'd found the perfect time to fall apart.

I spent the first few days in the intake cell where all the drunk, smelly people were waiting to make bail, or be booked for the long haul. Typically, these cells are hot and overcrowded, and if there are too many people, the officers will lay hard, plastic beds in the tiers for inmates to sleep on. I was fortunate, or unfortunate, to get a cell with two other people. The first people in the cell typically get the bunks; the bottom bunk is the bunk of choice. Each cell has a desk with a small round steel seat, and a urinal with running water in the backside. At night the cell gives you a bit more darkness, and is quiet compared to sleeping on the tier along the railing.

My first cellmate, the man with seniority, was a biker gang member and a self-admitted white supremacist. He was a heroin addict who had been using non-stop for five years. The second was an African-American crack addict who had violated probation. The white biker had previously done several years in prison for selling dope. This was his third day without heroin, and the jail had not given him anything to calm him down. He was sweating profusely, in heroin withdrawal, and he was angry. I thought he was going to rip the seat off the bench. The African-American was crying constantly because he was in a lot of pain while in withdrawal. Both of them were throwing up in the toilet. In this small cell, the only place left for me to bed down was next to the toilet. I put my head up toward the bunk and feet toward the urinal. Many times throughout the night when these guys got up to puke, they threw up on my feet and legs, or when they urinated, they missed the urinal and wet my feet under the blue and white bed sheet.

The tension in that cell was intense. Both guys were on the verge of insanity, and talking about how they could end it all. I was simply hoping to survive. I wanted to go home to Jennifer and my warm bed. After a few days in the cell, the air conditioning stopped and the jail cell heated up so much that we were dripping wet with sweat. We could not leave the cell for relief, and we could not sleep because of the heat. Lying on the floor, I prayed to a Creator I did not know or have a relationship with, to get me through this.

Because of a fight the night before I arrived, all the inmates were in lockdown. This meant that we could not shower or eat in the main living area. The three of us were in the cell for a few days before they moved us to our permanent units, where we awaited sentencing. One night, the officers came to transport me to my pod, 2C, a familiar place where I had stayed when I had first gotten into trouble nearly two years earlier.

In 2C we had a bit more freedom, with two guys to a cell, TV, hot water, exercise, and phone access. These cells were clean and much bigger. I arrived with a different outlook and attitude. The first time I had been very green, had no idea what to expect, and I didn't have anyone to put money into my jail account. My time there had been very lonely and scary.

This time, however, I had strength behind me: her name was Jennifer, my rock, who made sure she was home at nine to receive my call before I went to bed. Within a few days, Jennifer drove down to the jail and put a two hundred dollars into my account. "Money on my books" means that a friend has come in and given the cashier money to hold, like a bank. This allowed me to buy food, boxer shorts, T-shirts, and shoes. The jail handed out a statement every Wednesday showing the inmate how much money he could spend at the commissary. With money, one could order food and other items that made the stay in jail easier. If not, one had to eat jail food and wear orange jumpsuits.

It is surprising what can make a man happy when he doesn't have very much. An example of items that an inmate could order might include cups of soup, Velveeta cheese, saltine crackers, and summer sausage. Mix this with hot water, and you have a good bedtime snack. Another item on the list—and what became the most important thing I had—was a radio. The radios, about the size of a man's palm, yellow with a black strip around the middle, picked up a couple of local FM and AM stations. The AM station I could consistently reach on my radio aired the Jim Rome show that came on during the longest, most boring part of the day.

Being locked up in a cell is a painfully difficult thing because there is nothing to do. You cannot come and go at will, and your access to the outside world is limited to radio or television. Day after day, you sit in your cell waiting for food, mail, showers, exercise, and dayroom time. During dayroom time, you could get hot water for soup, talk on the pay phones to your loved ones, watch TV, play cards or dominoes, and talk with other inmates. Jail is a constant assault to your senses. It is loud with all the steel doors shutting, the echoing of voices, and the televisions blaring. And the bright lights are on all the time, making it hard to sleep.

In 1996, the jail started a new policy for "low-risk" inmates. If you were not a threat, you could apply for a move to a minimum-security unit. If a bed was available you could move, and that unit offered more freedom, making doing time less difficult. The jail had built a new work furlough area, and decided to turn the old area into "low-risk" inmate housing. The new minimum-security unit was for inmates who were not troublemakers in the main unit. The officers evaluated an inmate's status, and recommended him to be moved if it was felt he followed the rules and did not cause trouble. I applied for the new housing in hopes of making my stay less stressful while awaiting sentencing. Because of overcrowding, the system took many weeks, months, or years to sentence an inmate, making the stay tough while waiting. Fortunately, I was accepted into the new housing unit.

The Jim Rome show was one of my most important daily rituals. Awaiting sentencing, and having no idea what my jail or prison sentence might be, was as stressful as anything I had ever gone through. The question of how much time I was going to do came up repeatedly. One year? Two years? Five years? My judge had the guidelines, and could sentence me to whatever she felt was appropriate. At 10 o'clock every morning, I went out into the yard, proceeded to the west-end corner for the best reception, turned on my radio, and listened to Jim's show. I took off my orange pullover shirt and my shoes, rolled up my pants, and leaned up against the light-blue twenty-foot-high brick wall. Jim's show was funny, provocative, smart, and witty. I envied his ability, and his willingness to put his own integrity on the line.

Rome never saw himself as better than anyone, but as one who had a responsibility to his listeners and family. I thought, *If I ever sober up, I want to speak authentically like Jim, and make my family and friends proud.* But I didn't know how. My belief system was one of inadequacy, inferiority, rejection, and abandonment. I had to find other options, but I pondered how and what that might be day after day in that jail yard. Many times, I wanted to give up, but I thought of Jim's show, and was inspired to live another day.

Several different aspects of my incarceration were causing me personal pain. First, I was away from Jennifer, and I was afraid she might leave me or give up on me. Second, I worried I might not be able to listen to Jim's show anymore, and that was my daily medicine. Third, I really liked working for Tiger Messaging and Ollie and Carol. The freedom that the courier job gave me was awesome, and I didn't want those aspects of my life to change. After I was arrested, Jennifer called Ollie and Carol to tell them what had happened, and for the time being, Carol committed to saving my job. What a relief. If I didn't have to go to prison, I could return to my old position with Tiger Messaging.

Apologies and Promises

A few days after I was arrested, I walked to the phone to call my employer at least ten times, but I could not pick up the phone because it was too painful. The shame took my breath away, and the phone felt like it weighed a hundred pounds. Finally, after pacing back and forth and back and forth with sweaty hands, I picked up the phone and called my employers and apologized for any inconvenience I had caused them by my relapse and subsequent trip to jail. Carol, always very compassionate, assured me about my job, and even called my probation officer, telling him that if I were to be released, I still had a job with them, which ended up being an important factor in my getting a lesser sentence. Their commitment made me vow to change my ways. *If I get out, I'm not ever messing up again. This time it will be different.*

At the end of October, I was sentenced to eight months in jail; my time was to be served in work furlough. My sentence also included probation, counseling, and recovery meetings two days a week. My first thought was, *Great, no prison.* My second thought was, *I have to be locked up for eight months.* My gratitude left me quickly. I believed I should have been released. Why? Because my thought was always, *I'm a victim of circumstance. It's bad luck or somebody else's fault. I was never the bad guy. I never should have been in the trouble I was in. I didn't deserve it.*

Constantly I compared my circumstances to those of other inmates. It was comparing apples to oranges, as I could not fully know or understand the legal system or another person's situation. Many times when I compared my sentence with others, I didn't take into consideration that many of these inmates had family, homes, and good jobs, and were more stable or had a support system around them. This I did not have. I always thought I knew what was best for me, and at the time, I thought going home and back to my life was best for me. Thank a Universal Consciousness I did not understand that my judge knew more than I did, and had experience with "guys like me."

In early November I moved over to the work furlough side, but before I could go to work, I had to be evaluated and assigned a counselor. The previous time I had been in jail had an effect on my current jail stay. Among the counselors and officers, I had a reputation of being a "manipulator, an inmate that the furlough surveillance officers needed to keep an eye on." When I arrived, I didn't get out right away to go to work because my reputation kept a counselor from taking me onto their caseload. I couldn't believe it; I had a job, I could pay rent, and they didn't let me go to work because none of the counselors gave me a chance. I thought, *This is stupid.*

After a week, one counselor finally took me on. Fred was African-American with big bubble glasses and an Afro. He talked smart-mouth to the inmates all the time, and did not put up with any grief the officers gave him for his methods. Fred was a straight shooter, and he was funny, like TV's Fred Sanford. On more than one occasion, the commanding officer talked to him about his demeanor and his approach. I thought they went after Fred because all the people on his caseload liked him, and did not screw up, out of respect. Not all the counselors could say that.

The first day I met with Fred, he looked at me down his nose over his glasses and said, "Cabitto, back again?"

"Yes, but this is my last time. I've learned my lesson," I said.

He laughed, but a serious look covered his face. "You're right," he said.

"Next time you're going to prison."

A chill ran down my spine. "Fred, I don't think I can handle prison," I complained.

"I know. You're where you're supposed to be." Fred told me none of the counselors wanted to take me. Most of the officers were hoping to catch me doing the wrong thing, and so they could ship me back to the main jail. At that moment, I thought, *What did I get myself into? Here I am again, with others wanting me to fail.*

I said, "Fred, please help me. No one will believe in me, and if I don't get help soon, I'm going to stop believing in myself."

"I'll help you," he said, "but don't mess with me."

"I promise I will do my time quietly and stay off everybody's radar," I said.

Fred wrote my work furlough release plan, a piece of paper that stated I had permission from the work furlough program to be working eight hours a day, five days a week, and had a one-hour drive time each way per day. The next day I was released, and showed up at Tiger Messaging with my tail between my legs. I was welcomed warmly, and put right back to work. I was extremely grateful to have employers who understood, but even more grateful to be able to have a job that allowed me to drive around the city all day. The driving allowed me to listen to Rome's show, and feel free, not trapped in one place. The view I got to enjoy was spectacular. My favorite thing was driving in my new, blue, two-door Ford Ranger, which Jennifer and I bought in December.

The fall months flew by. I was seeing my counselor, Deb, a couple of days a week, going to recovery meetings one night a week, and seeing Jennifer every Sunday night for visitation. Day after day I prayed to a Universal Awareness I didn't fully understand. Nevertheless, things were happening inside me. I was seeing beauty in nature, I was slowing down to let people merge into my driving lane, I was feeling connected to everything. The sunsets and sunrises were spectacular, and I was taking pictures of the moon, blooming trees, and anything else I thought was beautiful. My life at that moment reminded me of being on mushrooms, without the psychedelic trip.

A Moment I'll Never Forget

One day while driving my car up River Road on my delivery route, I had an amazing connected experience. The night before it had snowed in Tucson, and all the mountaintops were covered in snow. I walked out of jail that morning and looked up to white mountaintops, and I became excited. High up on River Road, I looked down over Tucson. All of a sudden, I had this overwhelming feeling of being a tiny particle within a huge universe. I believe I experienced the presence of a Creative source. I stopped the car, climbed out and fell to my knees, and began weeping. It became evident to me that life was precious, and that we all are here having this human experience, none more or less important than the other. I sat on the ground for about 20 or 30 minutes while cars passed, being in awe of all of creation. It was like the universe was inside me, instantaneous, and now, not something billions of light years away. I got off my knees, dusted myself off, and slowly drove down River Road that day. I noticed things I had never seen before. This tree in the middle of a wash had fall colors, another tree with fall colors with a palm tree behind it, which seemed so odd. I was alive, and so was everyone else.

River Road spiritual experience

After that spectacular connection with nature, and that renewed feeling of being alive, I realized how lucky I had been. It made me aware of how close a person can get to fellow inmates, and even the staff. There is a saying in jail, "Do your own time." It's good advice: Jail is full of emotional, immature, sensitive men who act like little boys. Many times, I witnessed one man's struggle becoming the struggle of many men, like when an inmate became emotional when he had an issue with a wife, girlfriend, or family member. Other people tried to console him, and got caught up in the emotion. It was easy to be caught up in another inmate's issues, doing their time rather than your own. It happened to me once. I befriended Jerry, a large, funny, and sensitive black man. Jerry and I found we had a lot in common when we started talking one day after a friendly game of basketball. He and I spent many hours talking late into the night.

Good friends, we introduced our loved ones to each other on visitation nights, and traded phone numbers so we could communicate on the outside. I was always teasing Jerry about his size, the soul food he liked, the tennis shoes he wore, and the music he listened to. He was like a teddy bear with me. He used to say, "Cabitto, you're crazy, and you don't belong here with us." It wasn't the first time I heard that, but coming from him, it went straight to the heart. Around my birthday in December, we talked about the things we would do when we got out of jail, such as barbeque and hang out, that kind of stuff.

The day of Christmas Eve was like any other day. I went to work and came back excited that I had made it through another day without having a drink, and most of all, that the year was ending. Immediately I was escorted to one of offices.

"Cabitto, because you were close with Jerry, it's important that we tell you this."

"What's up? What happened?"

"Jerry died of a heart attack today." My heart dropped; I felt sick to my stomach. He said, "I'm sorry, we all knew that the two of you were close." I thought it was respectful that the officer pulled me aside like that. Jerry's mom and sister were in the waiting area to get his belongings. They came over, and both hugged me and cried. Normally the officers did not allow that to happen, but they let me console Jerry's family for about an hour. I was sad, and for the rest of my stay at the furlough program, I got up every morning and looked at Jerry's empty bed. I said a little prayer and told him I missed him.

I made it through the rest of 1996 without incident. Fred continued to be supportive, saying, "I am very proud of you, Cabitto. Keep plucking away and your perseverance will pay off."

As a result of having Jerry in my life during this time, it was becoming more evident that *everyone* in my life was strategically placed there. Whether my need was food, a job, a place to sleep, or a car, someone helped me. I was aware of the awesome generosity of all the men and women who entered my life.

This new awareness was fully realized in me the night when the Comet Hale-Bopp was visible in the Arizona sky. I had heard that the comet was going to be visible to the naked eye. When I asked Fred if I could stay out of furlough past dark, he said yes. When I asked Ollie to let me leave work early to see the comet, he said yes. And when I asked my surveillance officer to let me drive beyond the city lights to witness this event, he said yes.

That cold winter night I looked up in the sky. There it was, in all its glory:

Comet Hale-Bopp. Again I experienced the "awareness" of the universal intelligence that binds us all together. For the first time in my life, I knelt down and thanked the Source for this day. In my lifetime, I had experienced two comets; both times I was sober and aware.

I let Jerry go that night.

CHAPTER 24

Learning and Growing

Early in 1997, I read the book entitled, *The Bhagavad-Gita* (translated by Barbara Stoler Miller), which became one of the centerpieces of my journey of self-discovery. On page 122, I found this passage: "Know that passion is emotional, born of craving and attachment." That simple passage hit me hard, and at that moment I felt like I was levitating. The hair on the back of my neck stood up as a chill went down my spine. Sitting up in my bunk, this enormous energy surged through my body. Through that reading, I started to understand that my emotional pain was caused by attachment. I was attached to people, places, things, situations, and outcomes, and that all of these "things" were driving my emotional well-being. At that moment, I realized that I was not a victim of circumstance, but rather I was ignorant, and I was addicted to the outcome I thought most suited me.

Sitting on my bed Indian-style, I closed my eyes, and took many deep breaths. After a few minutes, I felt energy surround me. I sensed the energy surround my whole body. I felt myself lifting off the bed, looking down at the other inmates, and when they spoke, it echoed all throughout the dorm. I saw my body quietly and peacefully sitting on the bunk with my legs crossed. I was observing everyone and everything around me. Suddenly my mind/ego became aware that I was no longer in my body, but observing myself from above. Instantly fear took over, and my mind said, *This is not possible.* Immediately I was back in my body, looking around.

My bunkmate next to me asked, "Are you okay?"

"Yeah, I just had a weird experience."

"I know," he said. "Your eyes were glazed over, almost like you weren't here."

"I wasn't." This profound experience reminded me of feeling other people's energy when I was on mushrooms. It was more evidence that we are not only our body, but more is going on in and around each of us, and it wasn't centered on me. I felt relieved that a potential answer had come to me from this book, and from this recent experience. My addiction was in part based on my ego being attached to everything in my life.

On January 30, I experienced another spiritual moment while watching the wind blow blades of grass. I realized how fortunate I was to have jail, the work furlough program, probation, Fred, Deb, Jennifer, my employers, and Judge Miller. The peace I was enjoying was a direct result of the environment I was living in. I asked myself, *Could it be possible that jail was the best thing for me? How could I have gone from having a lot of anger in August to peace in January? Jail is not supposed to be peaceful.* But peace is exactly what I felt. I was slowing down long enough to see the beauty in everyone and everything. That day I also realized I had never pursued my Native American heritage. Deb had said, "Pursuing your heritage will help bring you closer to much of your past, and help you understand yourself and issues of your people better."

That day I picked up the book Deb had given me: *Where White Men Fear to Tread,* by Russell Means. On the front was this big intimidating Indian with a mean look. I thought, *Wow, how great does this guy look, and how crazy that he is willing to dress like an Indian in this day and age?* I was astonished to find a note from Russell on the inside of the front cover. The note said, "Believe me, you will have to begin anew." I thought, *This is exactly what the Indian who spoke at a recovery meeting in 1995 said to me.* Many coincidences were occurring like crazy.

The *Gita* book was revealing my attachments. Deb also introduced me to a Yaki shaman. Recovery was showing me how my ego was controlling my life. All paths were leading to recovery and return to my Native heritage.

A shaman is a man or women who interacts with both the natural world and the spirit world. Shamans are often trained by other shamans on culture, language, customs, spiritual needs, herbs, and natural healing remedies. Often shamans have been through many trials and tribulations themselves. Often flawed in various ways, the shaman transcends negative characteristics and turns them into assets.

In early February 1997, I discovered the importance of living my heritage—or at least finding out who my tribe was, who I am, and what it means to be Native American. I had no idea or understanding of these facts. My life and experiences were in the "white world." At Deb's suggestion, I went to meet with a Yaki medicine man who was a spiritual advisor at the Veteran's Hospital in Tucson and worked with anyone who wanted to learn the Native way. Deb thought that this Yaki shaman might be able to help me rediscover my roots, or at least point me in the right direction. We set up a time to discuss my history, life, and experiences, and see if he could help me or give me advice on how to return to my roots. I told him I could be at the hospital between 8 a.m. and 5 p.m. and that I would appreciate it if he could fit me in around noon. His response was, "Do you know what Native American time means?"

"No."

"This is your first lesson," he said before hanging up. I thought, *What a jerk! What did he mean by "Native American time"? Didn't he have a watch like the rest of us?* Later that day the Yaki shaman left me a voice mail stating that he could visit with me at 7 p.m., and gave me directions to his office.

When a person says "Native time," they mean time that goes beyond a clock or the Gregorian calendar. Many Native Americans operate their ceremonies according to spiritual time, not clock time. A shaman might say, "We will begin the ceremony at 7 p.m." When the clock strikes 7 p.m., the shaman will say, "We will begin the ceremony when the spirit moves upon us," thus delaying the ceremony indefinitely. Many Natives will be respectful of other people's time commitments, but will often do carry out Native activities according to their own spiritual clock.

As I drove to Veteran's Hospital in South Tucson, I realized it had been a while since I had been in my old stomping grounds. Many memories and raw emotions washed over me. I drove down the main boulevard where all the hookers and dealers did their business. I could feel the old emotions engulf me as the memories of smoking crack, sex, hotel rooms, and being high all crossed my mind. I felt scared. My hands were sweating, and I had this sick feeling in my stomach. I felt a strange pull to get out of this part of town. *What am I doing?* I realized how dangerous my addiction was, and how quickly it could overtake me. Instantly, I lost my breath, and started crying. For the rest of my drive to see the shaman, I mentally beat myself up, saying I was wrong and bad for even desiring to smoke crack. I completely forgot that I had made a good decision at that moment, and in my self-loathing, I did not give myself credit for doing the right thing.

Before 7 p.m. I parked in the back of the building, as specified by the shaman. I walked to the side door, and rode the elevator down to the basement. Getting off the elevator, I followed his directions, and walked down a long hall to a group of offices where I found three doors. The shaman's was the first door, where I could smell an aroma that reminded me of marijuana. At the same time, I smelled burning tobacco—not the smell of cigarettes, but natural burning tobacco. Opening the first door, I saw that the room was dark.

I stood in the doorway for a moment, looked around, and couldn't see anyone. When I asked, "Hello? Anyone here?" there was no response.

As I started to leave, his voice rang out, "I'm here, come in." I pushed the door open slightly, but still could not see where the voice was coming from.

"It's me, Rob Cabitto. Deb gave me your name and number. You and I set today at this time for us to meet here."

"Yes," he said, "I remember. You don't have to explain the whole scenario."

"Sorry," I replied. "Since it's dark, I thought you were sleeping or— "

"Come in." Finally a very small lamp went on, giving a dim light. This dark-skinned Native American had a ponytail, and wore cowboy boots and a brown shirt tucked into his jeans. He had a cigarette in his hand and his feet on the desk. All around him were Native American artifacts: dream catchers from many nations around the world, medicine wheels, walking sticks, prayer bows, prayer ties, sage, photos of Native American chiefs, and feathers from eagles, red-tailed hawks, and other sacred birds.

I began making small talk, asking him about the Native American artifacts and about his tribe. The flute music by Native American Kevin Locke was the first music that had spoken to my heart in many years, and it made me feel safe. I felt a vibration I had never felt before. The shaman asked, "When did it happen?"

"What?" I asked, confused.

"When did it happen?" he persisted.

"What are you talking about? Nothing happened," I said, getting a little testy.

"When were you molested?" Shocked, I immediately put up my guard and retreated emotionally into fear, which usually means anger—the way I've always deflected people and questions.

The shaman told me a story about his journey into recovery, his own experience with being molested, and working with other men on this subject. The shaman said I was not alone because molestation happens to many Native Americans. My first thought was, *How could this guy possibly know that I was molested?* My second thought was, *Finally, a person to talk to about the feelings I have been holding in my whole life.* But, shame took over as I shut my emotions down and said nothing.

For the first time in many, many years, those horrible, repressed memories came back. Finally I felt safe enough to talk about the childhood incident that I had stuffed so deep. The next thing I knew, I had started to recount the incident, as if I went back in time over thirty years. My silence, my fear of telling, my knowing in my soul of soul something bad had happened to me—all those memories flooded back like water rushing headlong over a dam.

Share your experience on our blog

Because of my dad's health when I was between and nine and twelve years old, I had been temporarily living with my friend Benny's family. His fifteen-year-old sister asked me to sleep with her. I didn't know if she was afraid of the dark, had nightmares, or what. But I had no problem with her request, nor did I think anything of it.

One night after we had climbed into bed, Barbara put her hand down my underwear. Without completely understanding what was going on, I still got an erection almost instantly. Night after night, she did that, putting my hand on her and pushing my middle finger up into her body. This confused me, no matter how good it felt.

The first few times Benny was there, too. She pretended to be asleep, but put her hand in my underwear—and much more. When the ordeal was over for that night, I felt such relief. She kicked me out of bed, telling me, "Go back to Benny's bed." When I got up, I felt exhausted, but glad she was done with me. Immediately a sense of shame, or wrong, or something I couldn't identify, came over me.

Then one day in sixth grade, we watched a PBS special at school. A Public Service Announcement came on, advising that if someone was touching you inappropriately, it was important to tell a parent or adult.

On the Friday after seeing that announcement, I decided to tell Mom about what was going on. I sat down with her that day and said, "Mom, Benny's sister is touching me and asking me to touch her in the wrong way." I explained to her that I had seen this announcement, and it said it was okay to tell a parent. She took a long, deep breath, her eyes were sunk in her head, and a wrinkle creased between her eyes.

"Don't you ever, *ever* tell anyone that story again!" She *never* explained why.

At that moment, I did not just *feel* shame. I became shame.

My whole body began to sweat, and my ears got hot. I felt so lonely and scared. I kept asking myself, *What did I do wrong? What did I do? At this moment, I feel I can never trust an adult. First my biological parents, and now my adoptive parents, have let me down. I am alone again. Is this what my life is supposed to be?*

The sexual abuse stopped at that point, but Barbara started abusing me emotionally. She was mean to me, saying hateful things. Every time I'd see that girl, I was filled with great anxiety. What had I done wrong that now made *me* feel so awful?

The shaman was compassionate and caring, and offered his experience as a way to let me know that I was not alone.

The shaman seemed to know instinctively that I was not going to move any closer to the truth, and the remainder of our meeting stayed very pedestrian. We agreed to meet a couple of times a week to discuss our Native American culture, and to talk about the ancient ways of our people that had been long forgotten. I left his office that day feeling good, but puzzled. It seemed like he could see right through me, and I felt like I needed to be careful to tell the truth because he could detect if I was lying. I felt good about having a person to talk with about my heritage, and to share the traumas of my childhood. Of course, whether more sharing would ever take place, would depend upon how much I could learn to trust him—and him to trust me.

Over the next few weeks, when I arrived at the shaman's office, the lights were either off or down low. The odor I had mistaken for marijuana was sage, and he burned it every visit. Honoring tradition right from the beginning, he had me bring him tobacco because offering a gift to the medicine man was part of the established Native practice when asking for help. He talked slowly and methodically, and always paused for a long time after I spoke, before he answered. Staring at the dream catchers and medicine wheels, he talked about our land and the "old ways."

Then he explained, "Rob, I feel you are the 'chosen one,' the one picked to break the cycle. Your name has a meaning, and that meaning will become clear later in life."

I was not sure what he meant, and I asked myself, *What cycle?*

Although I was still in work furlough, my time there was becoming more irrelevant, and I was being viewed as less of a problem by the jail staff. In recognition of that, my name came up less and less often, which meant my time became easier to do. Every night when I got back to the jail, I looked up words and phrases the shaman had used that day. I searched for information on my tribe in all the Native American books that Jennifer brought from the library. At night before bed, I read Russell Means's book *Where White Men Fear to Tread*, and was shocked by the information he imparted. I couldn't wait to pick up Means's book every day to read what happened next. Means was another Native American who had gone through what I experienced—stripped of his culture, moved around, molested, and made increasingly angry by the injustice and inhumanity of it all.

One March day, I was reading Means's book when I came across three words that brought me to my knees: "Piute Messiah Wavoka,"—or as Russell put it, "walk and act like an Indian." Those simple words touched my Native soul. In supplication, I prayed to the Creative Source of the Universe whom I did not know or understand. I asked that he bring people into my life who would teach me how to "walk and act like an Indian," and return me to my Native heritage. That night, another inmate came up to me in the dorm and said, "I've been meaning to tell you for a while that your attitude is changing. You don't seem like you're always trying to pull a fast one. You don't belong in this place. You should be teaching or doing different things. This is not your world. It's like you're walking between two worlds." His kind words meant a lot.

CHAPTER 25

First Steps Into the Second World

As I continued to read Means's book, I found another aspect to his journey that fascinated me: the Sundance. Means explained in his book what the Sundance is, what it means to the Lakota people, and how important that ritual is to him and to his sobriety. I was reading the book and hanging on every word. I felt like I wanted to walk, talk, and live like my ancestors, and experience the Sundance, an incredible sacrifice. From that moment on, my prayers shifted from early release from jail to praying to the Great Spirit to show me the way to the Sundance. I believed the sacred dance would help me mature, separate me from my addictions, and connect me with my spiritual being.

I remained in work furlough until May 22, 1997, when I was released from jail to return home to Jennifer. At home after work, I unpacked my stuff, and made love to Jennifer. After a big dinner, we went out to the pool where we lay in the sun and talked for hours. We spent the summer living in an apartment with a nice view, close to her work. Life was good! I was going to work every day, and probation was off my back. Even though I was still on Intense Probation Services, they were not harassing me or even coming to my house to check on me like before.

Twice a week I was going to see the shaman, who shared more about our Native ways. I begin sharing more of my personal life, including the things I was scared to tell him or anyone else. I was ashamed and fearful that people would judge me, not like me, or view me differently. He said, "I know." We talked about his journey through molestation, and how many Natives he knew who had experienced the same thing. He said, "Rob, when you truly reach the point that you are in recovery, you will be able to recognize the same shame in others who have also experienced molestation."

Because I was feeling good about myself, I stopped participating when I went to recovery meetings. I sat in the back of the room, and when it was time, I'd get my paper signed and leave. As the summer wore on, I became more and more irritable, restless, and discontented with my life. I went back to thinking, *I am a victim of circumstance.* When I was in my old neighborhood, the sick feeling that had disappeared for several months, returned when I went to that area to deliver mail or to see the shaman. The attraction to drugs and alcohol was back.

When fall arrived, I was invited to participate in an Inipi ceremony sweat lodge. The shaman said, "Rob, you are far enough along in your learning to participate in this sacred ceremony." I was excited because I had read about these ceremonies, and understood their significance to the Native people, but I had never seen or participated in one. The shaman gave me very specific directions I was to follow leading up to the sweat lodge ceremony. He asked me to buy tobacco, pray for my heart to be open, pray for the loved ones around me, pray for my molester, and fast the day of the ceremony. I was able to follow all his directions except one: I could not pray for my molester. I was very bitter about what she had done, and felt she did not deserve my prayers. On September 22, the day of the sweat lodge ceremony, with over 13 months of sobriety behind me, I felt better than I ever had. I had butterflies, much as I did when I used drugs or drank. This time, though, the butterflies were different; I felt like I was opening my heart to the Great Spirit, and I was not sure what he would see. The sweat lodge ceremony is a sacred ritual where Native tribes create a sacred space called a lodge. A circle is made of branches from a cherry tree or Palo Verde tree, and formed into a dome with deerskin or cloth to cover it. Inside the middle of the lodge is a pit filled with hot lava rocks so the medicine man can pour water on them to create steam, much like a steam bath at a health club. The sweat lodge is strategically positioned with the porthole to the spirit world in whichever direction the tribe feels is important to their culture, and to what they are trying to accomplish. Tobacco, sage, and other sacred herbs are used in the ceremony. When the lodge ceremony is ready to begin, the medicine man places people in specific locations in the lodge, and brings in drummers and others to sing sacred songs.

My heart was racing; I was not sure what to expect. What would happen? What would people think of me, since I was a Native American, but didn't know anything about sweat lodges or my heritage? I felt second rate, like I didn't belong. I worked for a courier service, lived off the reservation, and dated a white woman. I asked myself, *What am I doing walking between these two worlds?* When I arrived at the site of the sweat lodge, there were people like me who had not been to sweat lodges before, and many of them were white. My first thought was, *White people shouldn't participate in these ceremonies.* I didn't understand that these ceremonies where spiritual, and had nothing to do with color or blood.

Outside the sweat lodge were various symbols: poles with red, black, yellow and white ribbons, the skin of a deer, deer horns, and sage. These protections help positive energy flow in, and block negative energy.

Inside the lodge, I was placed next to a drummer. At first, I started to panic because of the heat. After the fire-keeper closed the door, the inside of the lodge was pitch black and hot. Soon the drums began to beat, singers began to sing, and the medicine man put herbs on the hot lava rocks; as he added a little bit of water, the steam made a hissing noise. The extreme heat made my shoulders feel like they were burning. As the drumbeat became harder and louder, my heart's beating matched the drum's rhythm. The singing started echoing, and sounded as though the singers were a mile away. After a few minutes, the sound of the singers and the drumbeat faded in my mind, and I could no longer perceive them. Before me, I saw a super-bright white light that looked like a hole made from a pinprick. After some rounds of singing and drumming, the medicine man opened the door to the lodge, and my heart rate and hearing came back into the moment. After two more rounds of water pours, the sweat lodge hatch was opened again. We all stood by the lava rock fire, put tobacco on the fire, finished our prayers, and climbed out through the hatch.

After the ceremony I was standing alone at the side of the sweat lodge, feeling relief and a sense of accomplishment, when the Yaki shaman came up. Again he said, "Rob, you are chosen to break the cycle." I went home that night feeling as if I had a responsibility to my tribe, my family, and myself to live differently. Jennifer was loving and supportive when I arrived home. That night I realized how much I loved her, but it scared the hell out of me. I was afraid that if I loved a person too much, she or he would go away—or die. I told her that the shaman said I was going to a Sundance, and had been chosen to break the cycle. She looked at me, puzzled.

CHAPTER 26

Stepping Back Into the First World

Over the next months, I spent a lot of time with Jennifer as we exercised, cooked, and lay by the pool together. She became my best friend. Because she was going to take a different job in downtown Tucson, we decided to move. My probation was going to be reduced from intense to regular, which would allow me much more freedom. After we moved to our new house on the east side, we decided to get a dog.

Although I was reluctant to get a dog because I was still in a lot of pain from the death of Nikko, my black Chow, Jennifer felt it might help me recover. Our white Chow was named Nanji, short for Topa Najinwin, which means, "Stands strong in the four winds." He was beautiful. I was making good money at work, and Jennifer and I were doing really well. I was attending recovery meetings, and for the first time in my life, I had no worries. The holiday season was fun, our dog and cats were having fun, and we had a bunch of presents under our Christmas tree. It was great to be alive.

At the beginning of 1998, I was experiencing my great personal growth. Even though many things on the outside were wonderful, I still had the same horrifying dreams and feelings from my childhood. Many times when things were going well in my life, I didn't believe I deserved them, and I sabotaged myself.

My ego started telling me that I was too good to work at Tiger Messaging, and that I should find an employer who valued my skills—even though I had no skills. In February I quit Tiger and went to work for another messaging service that claimed I could make twice the money. What they did not tell me was that I had to work twice as long to earn it. Of course, I viewed this as a personal affront, and decided I had one option open to me.

Why, Oh Why?

Even though I had eighteen months of sobriety, I still had not treated my addiction. Quitting drinking and using is not the same as being in recovery. I had untreated alcoholism that was being covered up by my relationship with Jennifer, money, and glimpses of a peaceful life. As things got better, I became more fearful, just as I did when things got worse. It's a bizarre dichotomy that is easily understood in the rooms of recovery, but perplexing to those who do not suffer from addictions. I ignorantly thought that if I stopped drinking for a period of time, the issues and consequences associated with the behavior would go away. I still believed that I would be able to drink alcohol like a normal person.

With this belief system in mind, I went to a convenience store and picked up two forty-ounce bottles of Old Milwaukee. When Jennifer came home from work, I was sitting on the couch with a forty-ounce bottle next to me. Her look was the saddest thing I have ever seen. I gave her an excuse why I was drinking.

The next few weeks were a whirlwind of drinking, sobering up, covering up, and trying to repair the emotional and mental damage done to both Jennifer and me.

The lengths I would go to in order to get my alcohol were astonishing. I remember one morning waiting for my neighbor to leave for his job. When I saw him, I ran across the street and asked for five dollars. I purchased five forty-ounce bottles of Old Milwaukee. After I finished the five bottles, I found pennies I had saved in a jar, enough to purchase a two more bottles of vodka. The attendant at the drive-through liquor store asked, "Hey Bro, why are you paying with pennies? You drive a really nice car, you look clean cut, what's your problem?"

"My wife left me and took the checkbook, and I'm trying to recover my money." I was too embarrassed to say, "I'm broke, and messed up a really good job and relationship."

I was filled with guilt and shame, and felt extreme despair. I thought, *How can I be in this situation again, with no money and no hope?* Jennifer was my only family, and now I'd disappointed her, and was destroying our relationship. I felt bad for my dog because I couldn't give him the attention he needed. My solution to these feelings and issues? I went home, drank myself to sleep for a few days, and realized that if I did not pick myself up, no one would.

In early March, Jennifer and I moved to a small one-bedroom apartment in one of the most peaceful places I have ever lived. My relationship with Jennifer was better than ever. I was sober and finally going to recovery meetings and participating again. My job was costing me more money than I was making, causing me stress since I couldn't pay my bills. Jennifer had a strict policy of making sure we kept separate bank accounts, equally splitting all bills.

I had met another shaman through a person in recovery. She took me to the Papago reservation where I connected with a shaman who would, for the next year, take me through many ceremonies and many conversations about our Native tribes and ancient way of living.

With all the recent ups and downs, I started to become aware that I had two parts: 1) the *selfish* me that wanted to be medicated, and was willing to do anything to make that happen, and 2) the *selfless* me that was willing to do anything to help another human being. These two worlds were constantly colliding. At times I felt enormous pain and wanted to medicate, and at other times I felt a rhythmic motion and wanted to sit quietly and feel everything. This growing awareness posed some problems. How could I sustain it? What would happen when I lose it?

CHAPTER 27

Moving to Minnesota—and Meeting My Most Influential Teachers

The day we left Tucson to move to Jennifer's home state, it snowed, and I thought that was ironic because we were going to Minnesota where it snowed six months out of the year. For some inexplicable reason, I was ambivalent about leaving Tucson, even though it was where I had experienced very low points in my life. Many times, I didn't believe I would live to see the sun come up. I often prayed for my life to end because I felt hopeless. I couldn't help but recall the enormous pain I had felt when my dog, Nikko, was killed.

I thought about Wendy, my ex-girlfriend of four years, and wondered where she was and what she was doing. I reviewed the years of being homeless, destitute, and in jail. I thought of all the drugs I had done, and the pain I'd gone through during the last ten years. Leaving Tucson should have been a welcome change.

However, I reflected on my growth over the past few years in my sobriety, personal, and professional life. I thought, too, about my growing understanding of Native American teachings, my life with Jennifer, and how grateful I was for every good thing. Before we left, I knelt in our apartment and thanked all the people, animals, and events that had been part of my life for the past ten years. I started to feel really, really sad, to the point of tears. However, I fought the tears off and got up. I grabbed my keys, met Jennifer outside, and we climbed into the car and drove east on I-10.

Arriving in Minnesota in late April of 1999, we decided we wanted to live in the southwest suburbs. Jennifer had a job interview with a health club/spa in that area as a director of fitness. Our plan was that Jennifer would find employment first, and we'd get an apartment close to her work, allowing her to walk Nanji over her lunch break. I'd then find employment after we were settled. Once the health club hired Jennifer, we quickly found an apartment nearby. A temp service had an opening for me in just a few days.

My new job was sorting mail at a large rental car agency. It did not require much thinking. I was surprised that the job paid ten dollars an hour, the same as I had made at my last job. I was impressed with the amount of pay, and thought: *If I am being paid that much, Jennifer and I will quickly get ahead.* I didn't understand that the cost of living and taxes were much higher in Minnesota than in Arizona. The position at the rental car agency was close to our apartment, making it an easy commute. The mailroom was isolated in the basement, away from everything else in the building. The small room had four long tables made into a square, with chairs about two feet apart. In the middle of the four tables were bins and bins stacked on top of each other, full of applications from people replying to a promotion for their special elite membership.

I, along with several other people like me, was hired to open the replies offered to their valued customers. The job was supposed to last several months, and if things went well, they will rehire me to enter those names into a computer. I was enthusiastic about the job since it paid the bills, and it was not too stressful. I figured it was a start, and after I got acquainted with the city, I could find a more suitable job that paid me what I thought I was worth—my ego always assuring me that I was underpaid, no matter what job I had.

After a few weeks of employment, several people quit, didn't show up, or moved into other positions. That created a constant influx of new people; I never knew whom I'd be working with the next day. My goal was to see if I could outlast every other temp they had hired.

Meeting My Most Influential Teacher

The day I met Geno was like any other. I drove to work, checked in, grabbed a pile of mail in the mailroom, and began opening it. Out of ten people from the previous day, I was the only one who showed up. I thought, *Good, I get to work alone and listen to the radio in peace.* In walked this unsmiling guy who looked like a bum. Geno had messy black, wire-like hair, and his skin coloring reminded me of South American Indians I had met. I thought he might be from Costa Rica, Brazil, or another South American country. When he passed close by me, he smelled like cigarette smoke. Although we made eye contact, neither of us said anything at first. After a few moments he said, "What's up?"

"Not much," I responded. As it was many times when I met new people, I started to judge him, comparing my insides to his outsides. I thought,

How did this bum get a job here? This is good money for someone like him. Little did I realize that this guy, younger than me in age, but older than me in spirit, was to become one of my best friends, my most influential teacher, and one of my most important guides to helping me return to the Native spirit.

After a few more weeks of employment, everyone had quit but Geno and me. We were moved into a smaller mailroom where our radio didn't work; all we had left to do was talk. We made small talk about sports teams, players, food, and other mundane things. Soon we were talking about interesting things like the Internet, governments, license plates, and how the government tracks people. I was glad to have a guy to talk with who was interested in these subjects. He mentioned a few books I had never heard of, and I mentioned a couple of authors that were new to him. We delved into subjects like the X-Files, conspiracy theories, alternative history, UFOs, and predictions of the future. At that time, the History Channel, Discovery, and Sci-Fi were airing shows on all my favorite subjects. Through them I was starting to find a temporary outlet for the constant vibration and uneasy feelings that consumed me at times. Geno and I had similar interests, and he had wisdom about subjects that I had dreamed about.

I continued to work at the rental car agency through the summer, growing more and more bored with the job. As the year continued, my anxiety grew worse because we were growing closer to end of the millennium. Prince's song, "1999" was constantly being played on the radio, and that contributed to memories of my childhood pain. My anxiety came from the many times when I was reminded as a kid that I was going to hell, if I didn't repent and change my behavior. Added to that was the constant reminder that the Rapture was coming at the close of 1999. The pain inside me was growing stronger and stronger; I had more negative memories than ever, and more nightmares from my childhood. The old familiar feeling was coming back, making me ask again, *Why do I feel so lonely inside?*

Day after day I woke up wondering why I was here, what I was doing, and why I had to wake up. I felt terrible about myself, and I felt bad for Jennifer because she had to be with me.

CHAPTER 28

Going from a Job to a Career

In September of 1999 I went to a job interview with a company that was in the hottest industry in the world, a large company that powered the backbone of the Internet. Here I met smart and personable Mark, who I considered an "executive." He spoke a language I didn't understand, but one that I was hungry to learn: technology. In the interview, Mark and I talked about my "colorful past." Of course, I sugarcoated it and glossed over being homeless, doing jail time, and the drug years. I charmed him with my humor, and we laughed as if we were old friends. After the interview, I asked him how I had done.

"Excellent," he said. "It was a very good interview."

"Great," I said. "Because I have another interview coming up, and I really want to nail it. It's a job I want."

He looked at me, puzzled. "You mean you don't want this job?"

I didn't say it at the time, but I was thinking, *There is no way in hell this company will hire an inexperienced person like me.*

About a week later, I got the call from the company that I was hired, felony background and all. When I showed up that first day, I was absolutely floored; I had my own desk and a security badge to get into the building. I couldn't believe it. The people were most welcoming, all of them smiling, and nicely dressed. This was way beyond what I thought I deserved. I certainly felt like I didn't belong, as if I was mediocre, inadequate, and in way over my head. I thought, *I should be at the local pizza joint or dry cleaners.* The people I worked with used words like bits and bytes, speeds and feeds, information technology, infrastructure, global presence, and economies of scale. I was high just from listening to these new words. We were told that eventually everything would be wireless and that high-speed Internet would be in homes.

I was ready to explode from all the information, and the prospect of the world not coming to an abrupt end. I was stimulated mentally like never before. I was hungry to learn more about technology and to live a new life in corporate America. There was one problem: I felt inferior, like I did not belong. I was "walking between two worlds again," only now it was my sober life, and life in corporate America.

In November of 1999 I purchased my first pair of khaki pants and a red polo shirt. I was making more money than ever before. The CEO gave a speech one day that gave me hope, true hope. Humble, charismatic, intelligent, and with integrity, he became a new role model. Researching him, I found out where he went to school, what his hobbies were, and how he had risen to this point. I wanted to be just like him! However, I had no education.

I had tried college many times, enrolling, but then quitting. Already I knew that without a degree, I was not going to climb the corporate ladder.

Online schools had caught on. I thought, *Yes, this is the way I can get a college education and do it from home.* Every time I had enrolled to attend actual college classes, I felt that I didn't belong, like I wasn't as smart as the other students. Because of my success on the job, I felt like information technology was a good fit for me. I aspired to be equal to my co-workers: educated, and smart. I wanted to speak the language, and drive a Lexus, everything that would help me be accepted by society (according to my belief system). I thought, *If I wear good clothes, have a good education, drive a good car, and make a lot of money, then I will be accepted.* I had been told my whole life that I was dumb, incapable, and, according to a high school teacher, too stupid to have anything more than a lowly job. The teacher had that said because college was not for me, there was no reason to take the SATs. I believed him. But this time my management team was supportive and complimentary of my efforts; I felt like they believed in me, and that made me believe in myself.

As we got closer to the end of 1999, my anxiety was almost unbearable. I thought, *How sad—what if my life is over at the end of 1999?* I wanted to medicate myself as a solution. I searched for other ways to stimulate my mind. I found that shopping was a good outlet, and I went on a spending spree. Jennifer and I purchased a home, two new Lexus cars, furniture, computers, and all new clothes. Shopping, drugs, alcohol, pills, sex—they always made me feel better for a short time, but I always returned to those same familiar feelings.

Finally, we made it to December 31, 1999. Jennifer and I lay on the couch and watched the clock turn over to January 1, 2000. No Rapture, no computer meltdown, and I did not go to hell. I was very relieved, and I felt like shouting, drinking, or partying. We made it; we were still here.

Immediately hope came back. The next morning, I turned my computer on, and it worked fine.

My life on January 1, 1995 was incredibly different from my life on January 1, 2000. Five years earlier I had been in jail, potentially looking at spending much of my adult life in prison, homeless, jobless, with a girlfriend working the streets, and my life in absolute shambles. Jump ahead five years, and I was enrolled in school, working full-time in corporate America, and I owned my first house. However, something inside me was still not right. The vibration, anxiety, fear, nervousness, and sadness were killing me. No matter where I was, I felt as though I didn't belong.

Are You Rob Cabitto?
One night, Jennifer and I were making dinner when there was a knock on the door. I answered, and it was a law officer. My first thought was, *I've paid restitution, I've done my time, and I have healed most of my past. No worries, unlike the last time the cops knocked on my door.*"

"Are you Rob Cabitto?"

"Yes, I am." At the top of the envelope, it said, "Shasta County Child Support Services." I went back inside and opened the envelope. It said that my girlfriend from 1989 had been busted for selling meth, and her boyfriend was already in jail for tax evasion. Her ten-year-old son Billy, had been put into foster care while they were sorting out the particulars of his parents and grandparents, causing them track down the biological father: ME. The government wanted me to pay back the welfare Lucy had collected, and start paying monthly child support on top of that. When I called Shasta County Child Support Services, I told them I wasn't sure if Billy was mine. They set up a paternity test, and sure enough, he was.

Billy was moved from foster care to living with his grandma while both Lucy and her boyfriend, Brad, were in jail. I called and introduced myself to Billy, asking him what he wanted to do. He told me he was very happy with the father in his life.

"Can I stay here?" he asked. "Brad gets out in a short while."

"Is that what you want?"

"Yes,"

"Okay," I said. I called Brad and told him that Billy wanted to wait for him to get out, rather than coming to Minnesota.

"Is that okay?" Brad asked me.

"Yes," I said. "He wants to be with you."

"I've taken good care of him, and I'll keep taking good care of him," Brad said. "I love him." As angry as I was with Lucy, I knew from my own experience that staying with Brad was the best thing for Billy. I hung up sad and disheartened, knowing that I might never know my son. At the time, the role I was allowed to play in Billy's life was financial, and in fact, I went well beyond the minimal requirements: I purchased a car for his mom, paid the rent, purchased furniture for his family, and paid for sports and extended learning.

I started to build my resume in corporate America, specifically in information technology. That, paired with my new enrollment in college, opened a few doors. My attitude about my prospects was healthy. I was told that since I had worked for such a great company, I could get a job anywhere, which made me feel better about myself. I went to work for a company that did data storage, the "next big thing" in technology. The economy was booming. The dot-com era was opening doors, and venture capital money was pouring in for any idea, as long as it was attached to information technology. I felt like I was part of this special work, and I wanted to tell all my teachers, and my classmates that I was a successful guy in IT.

Over the next several months, I changed jobs two times, feeling like I was "undervalued." The funny thing about people like me is that although we have an inferiority complex, we also have superior egos. My belief system was that I did not deserve the good things in life, and always found a way to sabotage my success. But I also felt that because I made good money, dressed better, and could speak the "technology language," I should be worth more money.

Late in October of 2000, I received a call from a former manager who wanted me to join his team; they were developing the world's first technology of its type. He offered me more money than I had ever thought I could or would make in my lifetime. I was given stock options, a 401k plan, a title, business cards, and an expense account. The night I signed my contract to begin working for the new company, Jennifer and I walked our dog around the neighborhood. I turned to her and said, "Honey, look at me. I have arrived." The comment was right out of my recovery book, but I had not really pay attention to what it meant. She gave me an odd look and responded with, "Okay."

This new technology was a way to move information from a disk on a storage device, over the Internet, to another device; it connected storage equipment to networking equipment. This was the catalyst for the development of my corporate career, and my former employer bought the company.

When I started working for them the second time, I was completely honest about my background. The first time, I had been hired by a temporary agency, and their background check was not thorough. This time the company did its own background check, approving me to be hired. I was happy to be part of the team, working with nice people. I showed up for work and felt as if I really belonged there. For the first time in my life I felt like I was being paid what I was worth, my clothes matched the job, and I was driving a car like many others in the parking lot. My self-esteem was high, and Jennifer and I were getting along. For the first time I was considered an "expert," even though I had limited knowledge about data storage devices.

My new manager, the person who hired me, had a reputation for being cutthroat, mean, intense, uncaring, and vicious. My first several weeks with Jerry were not that way at all. He was kind, caring, and willing to help me get on my feet at work. He included me on conference calls with executives and gave me responsibilities that I had never had at a workplace. Jerry had been in technology his whole career, and had made millions of dollars. I thought, *Wow, how lucky I am to be in this position.*

That all changed. In December, I arrived at work early, and heard yelling in a director's office. One of the engineers stopped me in the hall and asked, "Is Jerry going off again?"

"That couldn't be Jerry yelling," I said.

"Yes it is," he responded. "That guy is a real jerk." Shortly the door opened and out came Jerry and Matt, both red-faced. Matt was the manager who supervised the engineering team that supported the sales department. These were exceptional engineers who actually knew how to sell. Jerry and Mike must have had a royal battle over a technical support issue about the sales team.

Over the next couple of weeks, Jerry's attitude changed toward all of us, and he became completely unpredictable. Everyone was working insane hours in order to get the first product out the door, causing a lot of stress among management and staff. Jerry's yelling compounded the situation and put many people on high alert to keep out of his way. One day he came to my cube and started yelling at me to get a certain paper to him and to make sure that I copied him on every single email I sent. The moment he yelled at me, I felt my face get red. I started to sweat, and my back started aching. The last person who had talked to me like that was my adoptive mom. I got physically ill, nearly throwing up right there. I couldn't believe he was talking to me as if I was worthless, less than him. That day, and for the next several months, Jerry was verbally abusive to me—and to many others.

My self-esteem, which had improved over the last three years, was completely gone. The good feelings I was enjoying were becoming feelings of extreme pessimism and fear. Every day I had to listen to this man verbally assault me, and everyone around me. Memories of my childhood resurfaced immediately during his tirades, and daily, I felt like crying. It didn't make sense, but after I was verbally assaulted at work, I went home and verbally assaulted Jennifer. I felt ashamed, caught in a desperate state.

Once again, I wanted to kill myself because I had no outlet for the pain. I was nearly three years sober, but I was not "in recovery," as I did not attend a recovery program and thus had no way to deal constructively with the pain.

CHAPTER 29

Ahhhh, My First Love Is Back

Even though I had been at my new job just three months, I really needed a vacation. Mostly I needed time away from Jerry. In late November, Jennifer and I had planned a trip to Jamaica for late January. Beginning in early December, I started preparing Jennifer for the real possibility that I might drink again. At first, I was subtle about how I introduced my desire to drink. For example, we watched the show "Cops," and when they chased drug addicts, I admitted to Jennifer that I once did the crazy things the people on TV were doing. I always tried to justify the behavior by reminding her that I'd been a drug addict, and that I now understood the drug addict's bad behavior. However I said I'd never gotten in trouble with alcohol, and couldn't relate to people drinking and driving or anything like that. I thought if I continued to introduce alcohol into our relationship gradually, she might see the point that I was trying to make: I admitted I was a drug addict, but I was *not* an alcoholic.

Jennifer occasionally asked, "Are you saying you're *not* an alcoholic?"

"Absolutely," I told her. "I've never had a drunken driving arrest, I've never gone to jail over alcohol, and my problem was cocaine, not alcohol." She looked puzzled, and most of the time didn't dig any further. I knew exactly what I was doing. If I sold her the lie that I was not an alcoholic, I could drink on the trip to Jamaica. I constantly reminded Jennifer that alcoholics did not make the kind of money I made, drive the kind of car I drove, or have the house or life I had.

Arriving in Jamaica, we took a bus to Ocho Rios. The view and weather were spectacular, the rooms were big and beautiful, and the food and liquor were free. Jennifer was teaching fitness classes while we were there, giving me plenty of time alone. My thought was to wait until she was teaching before I drank, but I really was not very good at keeping secrets, and I could never have only one drink. After a couple of days in Jamaica, I thought, *I am going to explode from this anxiety. I want to drink so badly I can't stand it. I am going to drink, no matter what.* While Jennifer was teaching, I ordered a drink, and when she showed up early at the lunch table, I had a rum and cola. Jennifer knew, but I didn't, that the bar put a red straw in drinks that were alcoholic. When she saw the drink, she grabbed it and smelled it.

"Hello, Mr. Alcohol, what do you think you're doing?"

"Enough," I said, "I'm not an alcoholic. My drug of choice isn't alcohol." After lunch we went to our room and took a nap. Later that night we were getting ready for dinner and she asked, "Are you sure you're not an alcoholic?"

"Jennifer," I responded, "do alcoholics drive a Lexus, live in a beautiful home, and work in information technology?"

"What are you talking about?" she demanded.

"Alcoholics live under bridges."

"Okay," she sighed, "if you think you're okay, go ahead and have a drink."

I ordered a margarita, took one drink, and immediately thought, *Yes, thank you. My first love is back.* Slowly I became numb, and I knew that I did not have to feel the pain anymore. I was very happy. We danced and kissed and talked about marriage, kids, and spending our lives together. Up until this point, I was adamantly opposed to marriage and kids. But now that alcohol was back in my life, and I could loosen up, let my guard down, and talk about all that family, love, and closeness chatter that used to drive me crazy. For the rest of the trip, we both drank, and the last night we were in Jamaica we drank very heavily, throwing up all the way to the airport. In the airport, I had two bloody Marys, but Jennifer did not drink.

When we got home, I was elated because I could drink now. I made a commitment to Jennifer that I would not drink too much, and that I would make sure that it did not get in the way of our relationship. I kept pacifying her by telling her that I was willing to marry her and have kids. Jennifer would get what she wanted—a child, and I got what I wanted—alcohol, my first love.

Once back in Minneapolis, I immediately started planning my next drink. I scoped out the liquor stores in my area. When I quit drinking there had been no Mike's Hard Lemonade or flavored martinis, and I was excited to try these new drinks. On Monday I walked into the lunchroom at work, and one of the women said, "Oh my, Rob, you are glowing like you met the love of your life." My thought was, *Not met—I have rediscovered the love of my life.*

The afternoon of my return, Jerry called me into his office and hollered at me for a mistake that was made in distribution ordering. He said that I was worthless, and that he should never have hired me. I slumped in my chair, started to sweat, and thought, *He's right. I'm in way over my head at this job.* I promised Jerry that I would do better, and not make that mistake again. When I left his office, his administrative assistant asked, "Rob, how do you put up with that verbal abuse?"

"It's part of the job," I responded.

"No, *it's not*," she said firmly.

"Kathy, I'm making more money than ever, and my life is finally stable. I don't want to rock the boat."

That day after work, I went right to the liquor store. I opened the bottle of vodka, took two swigs, and within a few minutes I felt better about myself. The thoughts of Jerry's yelling were gone. I thought, *Yes, alcohol can kill the pain and thoughts of my daily life, and for that, I am grateful.* Jerry's treatment made me feel like I did when my adoptive mother verbally abused me: ashamed, guilty, second-rate, inadequate, and rejected. My negative state of mind returned.

Over the next several months, I was thrilled to have alcohol back in my life. Day after day, I went to the liquor store and bought a pint of vodka and a six-pack of beer. I drank the bottle of vodka on the way home, and then cracked open a beer so Jennifer could not smell the vodka. I drank at night; then I'd get up early, and go to spinning class at the health club. I was elated that I could do all that, and show up for work the next day. Most importantly, I was glad to have an outlet for Jerry's daily verbal assault. Jennifer did not really say much to me because I was functioning and bringing a nice paycheck home. My abusive language had lessened; she was okay with my drinking.

September 11, 2001 was a day I will never forget. Like many people around the world, I was saddened by the tragedy at the World Trade Center in New York City. I sat on my couch downstairs feeling like the world as I knew it, was changed. Things for me were about to take a dramatic turn. I didn't have anyone to turn to for help with my unhealthy state of mind, and the fact that I did not have a relationship with a higher power left me feeling isolated. My Papago medicine man had said, "Rob, you've got to return to your Native American heritage so you can have a constant companion, something to hold you up when things go wrong."

Geno had disappeared from my life, dealing with his own demons. He did that frequently, sometimes for weeks, other times for months. My drinking became progressively worse and the verbal abuse, from Jerry to me, and from me to Jennifer, continued to grow daily. I missed Geno and the conversations we had. Geno always pointed me to books, movies, websites—information that helped stimulate my mind and gave me hope. When that was gone, I felt very alone.

One day that September, human resources approached me, asking me to "share my experience with Jerry," since his attitude toward me and everyone else had changed radically. I figured that HR was checking whether Jerry was creating a hostile work environment. I was going to be their snitch if I told the truth. I felt the kind of fear come over me like when I told my adoptive mother I was being sexually abused. After work, I rushed to the liquor store, picked up a pint, and finished the bottle in about five minutes. The next day I called the human resources director and shared my experiences with Jerry. Within a few days, I was transferred to another department. The human resources person told me that if any repercussions came from Jerry, HR would get involved. I was safe. For many days after that conversation, I couldn't sleep, I was having nightmares of the sexual abuse and of my adoptive grandmother telling me I was not part of the family. Every time a door would close, I would jump, and every loud noise would cause my anxiety to spike.

Those old feelings returned, and I had no tools to deal with the emotions that were becoming part of every day. Many days I thought, *Thankfully, I have alcohol to give me the strength to function on a daily basis.* Jennifer was putting more pressure than ever on me to get married and have kids. She wanted to give birth to a child; I wanted to adopt. I never told Jennifer this, and have not admitted it until writing it on this page: I never wanted to have kids because I knew early in my life that I was a drug addict and an alcoholic. I feared that I would pass the disease on to my child. I did not want to be a father because I thought I would be a bad father as a result of all the stuff that had happened to me as a child. All I wanted to do was kill the pain. The one tool I had was alcohol, and I drank myself into oblivion every day for the last few months of 2001.

CHAPTER 30

Becoming a Frightened Father

The year 2001 had begun with martini in hand, waiting for the liquor store to open. Because I no longer reported to Jerry, I felt a sense of relief at work, and I started to feel better about myself. My new task was to build the global go-to market strategy for the company's reseller program. It stimulated my mind, and was very challenging and fun. My new manager had an MBA, which I really wanted. I was in my second year of college, achieving a 3.85 GPA, and I was feeling incredibly energized by my coursework. School was giving me satisfaction, and was an area where I focused on doing well. I wanted to show the people from my childhood that I was smart enough and good enough to be in school. I often dreamed of the day when I'd receive my diploma. I would return to my high school, visiting the teacher who told me I would amount to nothing, and throw my diploma on the table saying, "Look at me now."

In late February 2002, I was in my home office when Jennifer came downstairs and said, "Look, look! We're going to have a baby!" I remember the look on her face like it was ten minutes ago. She was glowing, pure light. Jennifer was pretty, but this was a beauty I cannot describe. My heart was full, and I welled up with tears. A home, job, family, beautiful wife, dog, nice car. *How can it get any better?* I sought out anyone who would drink with me and make a toast to my new life. Soon bottles of liquor were hidden everywhere: in my car, the garage, my office, and around the home. I always had liquor on hand. Many days I woke up shaking, and could hardly wait for Jennifer to go to work, then I'd crack open a bottle to calm the shakes.

Over the next several months I went to work, the liquor store, and my home office to do my coursework, and then I'd get drunk. Jennifer read books about being a mom, checked out Lamaze classes, researched names, and made sure that our schedules matched, allowing her to keep working, and be a mother too. Her actions and behavior were inspiring. Her enthusiasm was incredible, making me fall in love with her like never before. However, right after the feeling of love, I went to the feeling of fear. *What if she or my child die, or leave me? What will I do?* I was overcome with sadness and anxiety. I had never wanted to be in this situation. I asked myself, *Why did I start drinking again? If I had been sober, I would have never allowed her to get pregnant.*

Jennifer and I went to our Lamaze class together, shopped for baby stuff, and began preparing to bring the baby home. I was scared to death, but also excited. The ultrasound revealed we were having a boy. I immediately looked online for baseball mitts, footballs, jerseys of my favorite players, and information about being a father. I was excited our child was a boy.

When Jennifer and I were doing name searches, we learned that if we were not married, the child would take her last name. Because I did not want that, we were married in May by a justice of the peace. I was late for my wedding because I was having shots of Tequila in my garage with Geno, who was back in my life. I felt bad for Jennifer. Her wedding day was supposed to be one of the best days of her life, but I could not give her what she deserved and wanted. I felt I was defective, not marriage material. I had watched many marriages blow up, and marriage seemed like a union that was doomed to fail. I had yet to reconcile that I was lovable, and that very belief put a wedge between Jennifer and me, and everyone else. It would be years before I would find myself lovable.

The Birth Day

The day Jennifer was in labor, she kept asking me, "Have you had a drink?" Her thoughts detracted from this beautiful moment. I understood her fear, but did not drink through his birth.

Our little boy was born in October 2002. It was truly a miracle to watch my son being born. I saw a special-ness in Jennifer, and I was grateful that she was with me.

However, after the baby was born, I rushed home and celebrated by having a few cocktails. While she was in the hospital, I drank myself into oblivion.

We named our son Colin. His name means "young pup or young soul," a name that fits him as he is a very happy boy. Later I learned from a shaman why we named him that.

We brought Colin home and began our new family life. Even though I had a child, a wife, a dog, a cat, and a home, I was more lonely and scared than ever. I couldn't stand myself. I had no idea how to be a father, and I was afraid that my child might have my putrid genes. I prayed at night that the creator had given my boy Jennifer's good genes, and taken any part of me out of him. Every time I thought about being a dad or about Colin having my disease, my demons caused me to drink more and more. By this time, I was drinking about a half-gallon of vodka a day.

Year 2003 began for me like all the others—martini in hand, and filled with paralyzing fear. I could hardly wait to get to the liquor store to get my fix. My pain was enormous, and my solution was to drink. Most of my days and nights I spent in the office trying to do coursework. At this point, I was working from home, which allowed me to drink without my managers knowing. In addition, Jennifer took Colin along to work, giving me all day to drink, and then sleep it off before they came home.

Early in 2003, Jen and I went on a cruise to Mexico, which was ideal because I could drink myself silly. On the cruise, I drank every day and night, and when we toured the Tequila factories, I drank as much as possible. Jennifer was becoming very concerned. However, I reassured her that I was not an alcoholic, and could stop or control my drinking at any time. When we got home from the cruise, Jennifer asked me to stop drinking because she believed I had a problem. She found a few bottles in my car and one or two in my gym bag. I assured her that I would stop when Colin was older, but not today."

In March, I went to work and learned my company had decided to close the Minneapolis office. I was unemployed; the single best job I ever had was ending. I had a child, expensive cars, a mortgage, and no way to pay for my lifestyle. I was sad that my job was going away, and certain I would never again find such a good job. The job loss created a level of fear I had not felt since my girlfriend and I were living on the streets, moving from place to place while she was a prostituting herself for us.

My drinking actually got to the point I could not go to bed without being drunk, and I could not function in the morning until I had a drink. Jennifer and Colin were going to her parents' nearly every weekend, and she took Colin to daycare every day. Any time I was around him, she stayed close to me to make sure I did not do anything stupid. By late March, my problem was so severe I lay on the couch, took a swig off the bottle, then threw up in my own mouth and swallowed it, not wasting any alcohol. Jennifer came home after one weekend at her parents' and found me on the floor shaking. I had thrown up all over the living room floor, the puke was bile because I had not eaten, and my stomach was filled with acid.

Jennifer called Fairview Riverside Emergency Room, and asked if the detox center could admit me. They said if I was as bad as she said, I needed to go to the emergency room before I went to detox. Jennifer drove me to the hospital. After a few days in the hospital, I was transferred to detox, where I spent a few more days. When I was discharged from detox, Jennifer picked me up. "If you want to live at home, you have to go to a recovery program."

"Yes, for sure," I said, knowing I'd go to a recovery program just to get her off my back.

I was released from detox in time to attend Colin's baptism, which was celebrated with the whole family. Standing next to the preacher, I was thinking, *I need a drink bad!* I was sweating heavily and having panic attacks. Colin's godfather leaned over and asked if I was okay. I said, "Yes, great, thanks for asking." I was a physical, spiritual, and mental disaster. Jennifer knew I was in trouble, and each day she disconnected from me more and more.

Posting my résumé to an online job bank, I received a call from a small technology company. My résumé identified my past employer, which made me a hot commodity in the job market. The company felt that I was the right guy for the position. I applied, interviewed, and within a week was back to work.

Here was my new beginning, away from Jerry, fresh out of detox, with a new outlook on life. I was ready to begin anew. My first thought about working at this company was: *Since I am sober, I will perform as a top employee.* For nearly two months, I showed up on time, did a good job, helped build a revenue stream, and felt comfortable with my fellow employees. In June, Jennifer and I decided that we wanted to move to a bigger house, and we started a search. One of my fellow employees approached me, asking if he could be my real estate agent. Even though I knew that was not a good idea, I said yes because I wanted acceptance. I thought, *If he sells my house, he will tell my fellow employees I'm a good guy.*

Quickly we found a home that suited us. My co-worker/real estate agent put our house on the market, and within eight days, it was sold. Jennifer and I had enough money to make an offer on the house we wanted, and we had a contract to buy a home and sell ours. Our agent was set to make, a large commission—about $25,000—on selling our home and buying the new home. With both the buyers and sellers highly motivated, we committed to buying the new home and selling our home by the end of

June. By August first, we were to be in our new home.

Losing Control Again

Like many times before, when the pressure was on me to perform, make a big decision, or do anything that took me out of my comfort zone, I tried to find a way to medicate. The more I thought about selling my first home, packing, moving Colin, and having to pay for a home that was double the mortgage, the more it frightened me, and the more I needed familiar medication: alcohol. I came home, hid the bottle, and started the barbeque. Jennifer arrived home with the steaks and potatoes, and we began cooking. I took a swig off the bottle, hid it, and ate garlic bread to prevent Jennifer smelling the booze. After a few minutes I started getting that warm feeling, and my communication became more loving, which was a sign to Jennifer that I was drinking. Jennifer caught on: she could smell the alcohol, and knew my behavior was different. She packed up her bags, grabbed Colin, and drove to her parents' home for the Fourth of July weekend. I was drinking again. *What the heck is my problem? The results are the same every time, but I can't stop.* I was so angry at myself.

Drinking Alone—to Being Alone

With them out of the house, I had the freedom to drink all weekend. When Jennifer and Colin came home on Monday and saw I was still drinking, they stayed with friends. I did not show up for work all week. I called in sick Monday and Tuesday, but I did not call the rest of the week. Friday my employer called. I admitted that I had been drinking, was an alcoholic, and that was why I wasn't at work. He said, "Sober up, and come back. You still have a job." I was very relieved; I called Jennifer and told her I still had a job, but needed to go to detox to sober up. Jennifer came home, picked me up, and took me to detox. She sat next to me, crying, while I was laying on the bed in the emergency room. I kept apologizing, saying, "I will never do it again."

I spent the rest of the weekend in the hospital, not detox, because I was in such bad shape. Jennifer picked me up from the hospital and said, "Rob, we can't do this anymore. You have a son."

"You're right," I said. "No way am I doing this again." When Jennifer and I arrived home, I found a recovery meeting and went right to the meeting. At the meeting, I found a mentor. When I got home that night, I told Jennifer that I had a mentor, and was beginning a new life. Jennifer and I decided that the new house was too expensive for us at that time, especially with my drinking, and we decided to stay in our current home. We called my co-worker/real estate agent and told him the bad news about canceling the contract because of my excessive drinking. He called the buyers and sellers and told them we would not be buying or selling. Jennifer and I lost about $10,000 because we had money in escrow. The next day at work, my co-worker gave me that look, the one I had seen many times before in my life: disappointment. He had lost a big commission because of my drinking, and could not wrap his brain around why a person would choose alcohol over a new home or his family.

This time I was really committed to changing my behavior and staying sober, but at the same time, I did not have a solution to this issue called addiction. Jennifer and Colin deserved better. I was not living up to my responsibilities as a father and husband. I was still going to school, close to finishing, but that was not going very well because I did not show up even for an online class. Jennifer helped organize my lessons and folders and kept me focused on school. I remained sober the rest of the summer, and actually went to recovery meetings, but I still felt this tremendous sadness and loneliness inside, and being a father scared me to death.

On Halloween, Jennifer came home to find me smashed. Once again the two of them went to her parents' home. I drank the rest of the weekend, and on Monday did not show up at work. I called work, told them I was sick, and that I wasn't coming in. My manager Mark said, "Okay, feel better." That morning at nine, I drove to the liquor store and picked up two bottles of Bombay Sapphire. Over the next couple of days, when I called in sick, Mark did not say anything other than, "Be well." I was drinking so much that I was puking up blood. My nose was bleeding, and I shook uncontrollably. Jennifer came home a couple of times a day to make sure I was still alive. She called the treatment center, and tried to get me a bed in rehab. No way was I staying sober on my own.

Jennifer Has Had It with Me
November 10, 2003 was the date of the last drink I had at my home, and the last time I lived in the home that I really loved. My family unit as I knew it was over, and I was devastated that I could not keep myself together for my family. Mark picked me up that morning and said, "Rob, this is a chance for you to start over. Take advantage of it." Mark said I would not lose my job. I could not believe that another employer was willing to stand

by me while I sobered up. The company committed to keeping my position open, and when I got out of rehabilitation, I could go back.

You're probably wondering, "Why doesn't this guy get it?" and, "How come these people keep helping him?" I have asked myself these same questions over and over. I now realize I needed every single drink I've ever taken because it brought me to the brink of desperation. One drink too few, I might not have sought help. One too many, I might have been dead. I came to understand that alcohol had never been my problem—it has always been my solution to the problem inside of me. I realized that I don't have a spiritual connection that makes me feel well.

CHAPTER 31

The Treatment Center—"The Mothership"

On November 10, Mark picked me up at my house in Eden Prairie, Minnesota. I gave my son, Jennifer, and our dog a hug, climbed into Mark's red car, and we drove off for the hour-plus drive to the treatment center. I was sad, on the verge of tears, during the drive north. Mark and I listened to Led Zeppelin on the way up, and I kept reflecting on my and Jennifer's favorite Led Zeppelin song, "Rambling Man." The sky was cloudy, and the day was cold; light snow and condensation clung to the window. I was scared out of my mind. Life was going to change dramatically. I did not want to live without alcohol, but at the same time, I knew that *I could not live with it*. For years, alcohol had killed the pain, protected my feelings, and was my familiar friend—always there when I was sad, mad, worried, or depressed.

The treatment center staff was gracious and kind. A staff person walked me to the room where doctors examine new arrivals. The intake person sat me down and said, "You will be okay." The thought of not seeing my family, or being in my own home in my nice warm bed, was overwhelming. When I asked the nurse to help with my pain, she asked, "Where is the pain?"

"In my heart."

Compassionately, she said, "Things will get better." The doctor arrived and prescribed a sedative, and I slept through the next couple of days.

After a few days, I was moved to a special unit where I shared a room with a couple of other guys. The beds were horrible, but the view was incredible. The first time I looked out the window in the back of the facility, I saw a bald eagle flying over the lake. The dramatic sight took my breath away. Again I started to well up; on the verge of tears, I had to work to hold them back. The shame I felt was making me sick, and I wanted to commit suicide. I thought, *How could I have screwed up fatherhood, marriage, more than one job, my home, and all the good things I had going for me? I must be crazy.*

In a short time, I integrated myself into my unit, and discovered that all the men there were in the same pain. I felt secure there. Sharing my feelings, and listening to other men share their pain, was helpful because it gave me a platform to trust others. Men on the unit were at different stages of their recovery. A few of the guys were at the end of their twenty-eight days, and they looked and talked as if they really had everything together. I was amazed, and I wanted what they had. Others were at the same place as me, and I felt good that I had a few people who were going to be with me the whole time I was there. While at the treatment center, I really tried to make the point that I was screwed up in every way; maybe I might be able to get sleeping pills, antidepressants, and any other drug that a doctor was willing to prescribe for me.

About ten days into my stay, I was asked to talk to a psychotherapist who dealt with men and women who had childhood trauma, such as molestation or loss of a loved one. The caveat was that this person worked with men and women who had cultural needs. On my intake papers I had checked the box that said I was Native American, which meant I had cultural needs. On the wall of Don's office was a big wrap of sage used in many Native American cultures for ceremony and purification. Immediately I recognized the sage because many of the medicine men I'd encountered used the herb with me, and in sweat lodge ceremonies.

Don, a Vietnam veteran, had a PhD in psychology. He was enthusiastic about Native Americans and the ancient ways of our people. Talking to me about my heritage, he noticed I was looking at the sage on the wall. He asked, "Do you know what sage is?"

"Yes," I said, "I've been in many ceremonies, but not for several years. I lost my way with the Native American community." He asked me questions about my life, my pain, my habits, and how I arrived at the treatment center. Don came across as a trustworthy guy, and I felt safe, and opened up. Over the next weeks we met every few days to discuss my issues. One day I mentioned to Don that a medicine man in Arizona once told me I should go to Pine Ridge to do a vision quest or the Sundance. While I was telling Don this story, we both saw a bald eagle fly by his office window. Don's face lit up and he yelled, "WOW, that is a sign from the Great Spirit." I agreed with him, and continued telling my story. After I finished, Don said, "I know what I'm supposed to do for you." He wrote the name and number of a Lakota medicine man from Pine Ridge. We both thought it too much of a coincidence to ignore—the bald eagle flying by the window, and the fact that Don worked with a shaman from Pine Ridge.

In addition, Don walked over to the bundle of sage, picked off a piece, and brought it to me. "Rob, you have a great gift and opportunity to start over. Return to your Native American spirit. I want to give you this as a gift, and ask that when you go to Pine Ridge, you bring the sage and burn it in the sweat lodge."

"I appreciate your help, and I would be honored to take the sage to Pine Ridge," I said thankfully. Don had helped me identify an issue that had been plaguing me my whole life when I did not know how to deal with feelings. It was Post Traumatic Stress Disorder, or PTSD, which occurred because of my troubled childhood. The other shaman had mentioned PTSD years earlier, but this guy had examples that made me see the similarity to my experiences. He explained that sometimes people that went to war, or saw heavy trauma, have PTSD. I thought, *This might explain why I used to jump out of bed when I would hear a car engine rev up, or a door slam, or why I wasn't able to sleep with the lights out.* PTSD explained so much.

The treatment center is one of the most beautiful, sacred sites on the planet. The serene lake and rolling hills, coupled with the space to meditate and practice mindfulness, and the ability to get sober, are the most remarkable gifts of the place. I refer to the treatment center as "The Mothership" because of its history of helping people understand their need for a recovery program. This center, one of the first alcohol treatment centers in the country, has become the model for many others. The facility and people truly have a place in my heart, and I am forever grateful for this simple but powerful place.

The second to last day there, I was called into my counselor's office.

"Your wife wants to serve you divorce papers, and wants to do it before you leave the facility," she said. My counselor thought that being served papers before I left here was a good idea, because I could share it with my brothers in recovery, and start my recovery plan with the understanding that I was not going back home. I agreed, and allowed the server to hand me papers.

The finality and consequences of my choices had once again put me in a place where I was alone, struggling to get back on my feet. Jennifer no longer wanted to be married to me, and I wasn't going home to my child. All these thoughts were rushing through my head. *What will happen to my dog? Where will I live? What will I do?* Returning to alcohol would make things worse. I was comforted by the fact that I still had my high-paying job and could get back on my feet quickly.

After I was served the papers, I called my employer, sharing what had happened and asking them to help me find a place to live.

"Yes," they responded, "of course we'll help you. You can stay at the corporate apartment." I was happy I did not have to go to a sober house, since I considered sober housing as the bottom of the barrel. I didn't want to live with a bunch of down-and-out guys, completely forgetting that *I, too, was down and out.*

On December 8, 2003, Jennifer and Colin picked me up and took me home. I gave my child and dog a little love, packed my bags, got in my Lexus, and drove to the corporate condominium. Surprisingly, I was not sad, scared, lonely, or mad; I was actually numb. I arrived at work and was greeted with open arms by my fellow employees and managers. I immediately sat down with the management team and expressed my gratitude, telling them that I would not screw up; their efforts to help me would not be in vain. I assured them that alcohol was behind me, and I was going to do everything possible to make this program work for me. They responded, "Great, let us know how we can help."

I told my employers what my treatment plan was and that I needed a couple days off to set up counseling, recovery meetings, and get my affairs in order. They said, "No problem—whatever you need." I went to the corporate condominium, took a nap, and went shopping for groceries and personal items. When I arrived back at the condominium that afternoon, feeling tired and alone, I took a nap before making any plans. When I awoke, I was angry and lonely, and decided to go to a local restaurant to have dinner. When I arrived, the empty seats were at the bar. Fresh out of treatment, I thought it was not a problem to sit at the bar and eat dinner. I ordered an iced tea, and a plate of spaghetti, and I watched the basketball game. All the while, I was watching men and women drink and having a great time. I wanted to drink and have a great time, too. I threw a twenty-dollar bill on the bar, climbed off my stool, and drove home. That night I was very upset that I could not sit at the bar and drink. Since I could not go back home, who cared if I drank, as long as I went to work in the morning.

But when I awoke the next morning, I was glad I was sober. I knew if I took a drink I'd mess up my job, and my opportunity to go home to see my son. I hurried to work and closed a couple of large deals. I spent the day telling stories about my stay in the treatment center, talking about how bright my future was. Later that afternoon, I went to my home to visit Colin and my dog. Jennifer and I got along well. Things seemed very hopeful for me to put my life back together with my family.

For the next week, I was able to go to work every day, stay sober, and see my family. Things were truly looking up. The night of December 21, I went to my favorite restaurant, where a week ago I had sat at the bar and had dinner. I ordered my iced tea and a plate of spaghetti and watched the game for about twenty minutes before a couple came in and sat next to me. They began laughing, kissing, and holding hands; the more they drank, the happier they got. I thought, *I want that happiness.* I said to the bartender, "One Bombay Sapphire martini, please." The next thing I knew, I was laying on the floor in the condominium with puke everywhere. I had a terrible hangover, and I was supposed to be at work. I immediately called and told Mark I had a bad cold. I showered and shaved to waste time until the liquor store opened.

The cycle began all over again. I stopped showing up for work, and I did not see my son or my dog. Within a couple of days, I was drinking about a liter a night.

To understand how much vodka I drank every day, remember that 1.75 liters equals about fifty-nine ounces or over seven cups. Picture a large plastic bottle of soda that is almost two liters, or eight cups of soda pop. As time went on, I drank a 1.75 liter of vodka by myself, often while in the car at the liquor store parking lot or alone on the sofa.

Recycling the Cycle of Medicating

I called in sick, saying that I had the flu, and was not able to stop the diarrhea. Mark did not believe me, and he and the police showed up at the corporate condominium. I was lying on the floor, passed out with a bottle of Bacardi next to me. The police officer woke me up, saying, "Get up, you're going to detox." He put me in handcuffs and walked me to the door where my employer was standing with a look I've seen many times before: disgust. "Mark, I am very sorry; I will never do this again. Please give me another chance." He said nothing, and I knew my employment was over.

On my birthday, December 23, 2003, I arrived at the Medicine Lake detox center in Plymouth, Minnesota and was told I was on a three-day hold, which took me past Christmas. I was frustrated because I was already in the process of lining up my next relationship. I had gone on a couple dates since getting out. I thought if I could not be with Jennifer, I needed to find another woman quickly to fill that spot.

The detox center had a bunch of beds for men on one side of the hall and for women on the other. There was a main lobby where the residents ate, and a smoking room. With me in detox was a young woman whose husband had cheated on her; she was in pain and she offered to have sex with all the male residents. I gladly accepted her offer. Unfortunately I was number four in line, and she had not showered. *Maybe this isn't such a good idea*, I thought, and told her I was going to pass on the sex. She got angry, and said I must be gay. I didn't care; I wanted alcohol and freedom more than I wanted sex. The detox center had two doors: the front door where police brought in the patients, and the back door for staff. On December 24, I was angry because I was in detox, first on my birthday, and on Christmas. I devised a plan to get out.

I recruited one of the residents to make a commotion. When the nurse clicked the key to leave, he yelled, and I ran for the door. I pushed the nurse out of the way and started running. The temperature was below zero. I did not have shoes on, and I only made it about ten yards when one of the staff tackled me and wrestled me to the ground. Because I was still drunk and had the shakes, I was an easy takedown. He walked me back in the building, and the nurse yelled at me, "If you want to die, do it on your own time, not on ours." I thought, *I wish I could die.* Back in the building, the nurse sat me down, asking, "Don't you understand the serious nature of your disease?"

"Yes," I responded, "but I'm in a lot of pain. I don't know any other way, and I can't stop drinking." I lied, telling her that my family in Arizona was waiting for me to visit over Christmas and that if she let me out, I would quit drinking and get help in Arizona.

"Okay," she said, "let's try to get you out of here Christmas morning so you can go be with your family." Even after I had assaulted a staff member, I was puzzled that they were going to let me go. It finally occurred to me how many people had helped me along my journey. Yet, I kept ending up in the same mess, no matter how much help I received.

On Christmas morning the detox center discharged me and let me go home. The nurse that cared for me said, "Rob, get better. You seem to be one of the smart ones." I felt bad for what I had done, but I did not apologize.

"For sure I will get help and change," I said. Since I didn't have any family, and Jennifer did not realize I was in detox—and wouldn't have come to get me anyway—I called one of my ex-coworkers to pick me up. He showed up and took me to my apartment.

A week earlier, I had decided that if anything happened with my job, it would affect my living arrangements. Thank goodness I had rented an apartment to go to when I left detox, otherwise I would be homeless. My friend came inside with me, and said, "Oh dude, this is so unbelievably sad. You have nothing, not even furniture."

"I know," I said. "I have no idea what I'm going to do." He asked me to spend Christmas with his family, but I declined. Jennifer called and asked me to come over and see my son and my dog. I accepted and, since I had booze in my apartment, I showed up for Christmas, drunk. Jennifer was beyond disgusted.

"This is very sad. Colin will never get to know his dad," she said.

"Yes he will," I said, "I promise. This time I will straighten up." I left that day feeling more lonely and scared than I had ever felt before. For the next week or two, I drank every day and night in my apartment. I did not have a job, and I had no prospects. I was drawing unemployment, and using my credit cards for every purchase. I had no intention of going to see my son and dog. All I wanted to do was drink until I died.

The year 2003 was a tough one. Four detox centers, three job losses, one outpatient treatment, one inpatient treatment, and a divorce. Ringing in the New Year was a blur because I sat alone in my apartment and drank.

In mid-January, Charlie, a friend from the treatment center, called Jennifer looking for me. She told him where I was, and what I was doing. Charlie called my cell phone, saying, "I want to come and visit."

"Okay," I said," but I'm not going to any recovery meetings, and I'm not going back to the treatment center." He and Matt, another brother from treatment, showed up. They persuaded me to stay with Charlie and his family until I sobered up. Because I didn't have any food or furniture, was running low on money, and couldn't see my family, I agreed. For the next couple of days, I thought I was going to die from the shakes and sweats. My skin felt like somebody was poking me with needles, and I could not eat, relieve myself, or sleep. I was in absolute terror!

After a few days, the alcohol withdrawal went away, and my body returned to normal. Within a couple of weeks, once I started to feel better and could drive, I asked Jennifer to let me see Colin and my dog. She agreed, and I saw Colin for the first time in about a month. He was getting big, and I was missing his childhood. Jennifer allowed me to come to our house every day while she took our dog for his morning walk, and got ready for work.

One late February morning, I showed up at our house as usual. Jennifer said she wanted to talk with me. "Rob, I think we should try to work things out, if it's not too late."

"You should have thought about that before," I responded. "It's too late!"

She said okay, and that was it. After I left the house, I did not even think of rehab, counseling, my recovery program, or putting my life back together. I had had a chance to go back home with my family, and I couldn't pull the trigger. I had already started running, and I couldn't stop.

Over the next few weeks, I slowly settled into my apartment, acquiring furniture little by little. Jennifer was kind enough to let me have furniture from our basement. By early March, the apartment felt like home. I began working at a data storage company, and slowly my life was coming together. I was attending recovery meetings, but was not fully participating. I always thought if a person showed up, that was enough to make them healthy. Later I found out this philosophy was inaccurate.

My new employer was paying me a lot of mone, and expected me to produce. I thought I could live on my past, and not have to produce very much at all. When I took this job, I had lied on my résumé. I left out the jobs I lost because of drinking. I thought I could submit a résumé without filling out an application. After I had accepted the job, they actually asked me to fill one out. I wrote all the names of my previous employers down on the application. Their HR people compared the résumé to the application, and found out I had lied on the résumé, but not on the application. Why didn't they fire me?

Learning that the Shaman Was Coming

One Saturday in the middle March, a Native American I knew approached me at a recovery meeting, saying that the treatment center was putting on a seminar given by a Lakota medicine man at the end of March. Immediately I called the treatment center to inquire. They had bed space and a scholarship for me if I wanted to attend. I was excited to see this Lakota medicine man; he was the same man the psychologist Don from the treatment center had asked me to contact when I was a patient there earlier.

When the seminar started, the shaman passed around an eagle feather, used during a ceremony to indicate who has the floor to speak. When the feather came to me, I introduced myself, saying I was at the workshop because Don from the treatment center thought I should meet him. I mentioned that years earlier a shaman from Southern Arizona had said I would be doing a Sundance with a Lakota shaman. I said I didn't know if he was the medicine man the Yaki shaman spoke of, but I thought it was a coincidence that he was here at the treatment center from Pine Ridge, and was a medicine man. That described exactly what the shaman from Arizona had said would happen.

The next day the Lakota shaman pulled me aside and asked me about myself. I told him about my tribe, my journey, my sobriety struggles, my family, and my job situation. The whole time he sat and listened intently, never saying a word. I felt good after I spoke with him because I had been honest. I had not been very good at telling the truth my whole life. After I finished, he said, "Let's talk tonight."

"Okay," I said. "But didn't we just do that?"

He responded gently, saying, "Yes, and we will do more."

That night when I met the shaman in the great room, he asked one of the people sitting with us to burn sage while we were talking. She lit the sage and fanned me with the smoke, using an eagle feather. Burning sage, or smudging, is the common name given to the Sacred Smoke Bowl Blessing, a powerful cleansing technique from the Native American tradition. Smudging calls on the spirits of sacred plants to drive away negative energies, and put a person back into a state of balance. It is the psychic equivalent of washing your hands before eating. After I smudged, the shaman handed me a red felt cloth that was wrapped tightly. I embraced the wrapped bundle as he said, "This is not yours; you're only the keeper."

I said, "Okay," and opened the cloth. I discovered a pipe wrapped in the red felt. It was a ceremonial pipe, often referred to as a "grandfather pipe." I embraced the pipe and was astonished to see it; the bowl was a beautiful red clay with sage stuffed into the ends. I was amazed that he was giving me this special pipe.

"What is this for?" I asked.

"This grandfather pipe is for you to take care of and use at ceremonies," he replied. I was honored, but my heart sank as I thought, *I don't deserve this. I'm not good enough.*

"Thank you," I said to the shaman, "but are you sure you want to give this pipe to me?"

"Yes, it is yours to take care of," he assured me.

I embraced the pipe, got up, hugged him, and told him I would take good care of it.

Over the next several days, I talked with the shaman about what a vision quest was, and how I could participate in a Sundance. I wanted to know when I could get started on these spiritual practices. Luckily for me, the shaman slowed me down, saying, "In time we will get to those things." Funny thing about medicine men: they are never in a hurry. They do not operate on normal calendar time. The shaman invited me to come to Pine Ridge in early June to do a vision quest. Over the next several months, he talked with me frequently to discuss my preparation for the vision quest. The shaman sensed my post-traumatic stress disorder (PTSD). On more than one occasion that weekend, the Lakota Shaman had identified ancient native practices to help me sleep better and be more aware of my "nature." I left the treatment center feeling renewed and hopeful for the first time in a while. I thought, *What is the chance that I will have more than one medicine man in my life?*

Arriving home on Easter Sunday of 2004, I was feeling good about what had happened. I could hardly wait to share my experience. Sadly I had built no lasting relationships, and I had no one to tell about this last weekend's experience. Jennifer was not taking my calls, I had no recovery mentor, I did not care for the people I was working with at the time, and my family relationships—both biological and adopted—were completely severed.

I was angry and frustrated with myself about a lot of things and I wanted to reach out for help, but I had no one because of the isolation I had created for myself. Holding the anger inside, I went to work where I took my anger out on my co-workers. I showed up for work that Monday with a bad attitude. In early May of 2004, my divorce became final. The day I received the paperwork in the mail, I asked myself, *Why do I destroy these relationships with good women?* I was truly puzzled. When I thought about losing my home, and getting limited supervised visitation with my kid, I felt physically sick. I hated my job, I had no friends or family, and I really missed Jennifer. That day, and over the next several weeks, I curled up in a ball on the couch and said to myself, *This is just a bad dream. I will wake up in my bed with Jen, and Colin will be in the other room.*

The pain of my divorce was too much for me, and I asked my doctor to put me on antidepressants. I also asked him for help sleeping, even though I did not necessarily have a problem sleeping—I had a problem with nightmares, but for the most part, I could fall back asleep after one woke me. But I did not like to feel pain, and whenever I could, I found a way to kill the pain by medicating with whatever was available: alcohol, food, women, television, or exercise.

My doctor was not what a person might consider "traditional." "Dr. Dave" spoke slowly, quietly, and methodically. He said things like, "Man, Rob, you are lucky to be a Native American." He had participated in sweat lodges and ceremonies, and was very connected to my heritage, and wanted me to be as well. Being called "special," one part of me wanted to choke Dr. Dave, and another part of me was agreeing with him. I felt like I was tearing a layer of skin off, like snakes that shed their skin.

When I went to his office to ask for antidepressants and sleeping medication, he was reluctant to prescribe them. He said, "I will prescribe these medications temporarily, but they are not a long-term fix for your spiritual issues." Dr. Dave took my blood pressure, which was about 140 over 100, and I weighed in at a bulky 235. My face was red from my high blood pressure, and I was sweating from my anxiety. When I begged Dr. Dave to help me get better, he said, "Your Native traditions have helped me, and they can help you, too."

I thought, *Wow, I have been hearing the same theme over and over. Return to your Native heritage!*

Dr. Dave reluctantly prescribed the medication, then announced that he had accepted a position in another state. Over the years, Dr. Dave and I had had many conversations in his office that lasted an hour or more. I would miss him. He was one of my biggest supporters, helping me work toward good mental, physical, and spiritual health through the Native American traditional ways.

In mid-May of 2004, I began taking the prescribed medication plus a little more at bedtime, and soon started to see the results. I was sleeping nine to ten hours a night and my sexual desires nearly went away, but I felt out of it most of the day. One day when I went to visit Colin I was sitting on the floor, and Jennifer said, "Rob, I'm worried about you."

"Why?" I asked, surprised.

"You're like a zombie. You don't laugh, smile, or have any emotion."

"Isn't that what you wanted?" I asked.

"No," she said, "I wanted you to get better, not disappear emotionally."

She was right—I felt like I did not have any emotions at all. I went home that day and thought about what she had said. I wanted to win my family back, and I wanted to feel better, but I had no idea how to do it.

The Friday before Memorial Day, I showed up for work completely out of it. The night before I had taken extra meds, and I was really groggy, restless, irritable, and discontented. The human resource person pulled me aside, saying, "The company is not very happy with your work, and we want to seek a solution." I emailed the CEO, asking to speak with him directly before the end of the day. That afternoon the CEO repeated that the company was not very happy with me. He said they were willing to overlook the fact that I had lied on my application, and give me a chance. However, they couldn't overlook the fact that I was not performing. He went on to say they would overlook all of the issues if I began to work harder and show up on time. My response was, "What's the alternative?"

"A small severance package."

"I'll take it."

"Okay, good luck." We shook hands, and I was unemployed yet again, following my same pattern: self-destruction.

With only one more class to finish, I was excited about the online school finally wrapping up after nearly four years. I couldn't help but be afraid, though, because I had no idea what to do next. School was fun. The learning stimulated me, and school filled a void that otherwise I would have filled with drinking and using drugs. Jennifer and I had done school together. All in all, I was sad because she was gone, school was coming to an end, and I had essentially been fired from another job. I had nothing left.

Memorial Day weekend I sat in my apartment curled up in front of the television, hoping I was having a nightmare. I fantasized that, at any moment, I was going to wake up back home with Jennifer. As the weekend dragged on, I became more despondent, filled with fear and anxiety. I climbed off the couch, ran down to my car, and drove as fast as I could to the liquor store. About half way down the aisle, I began dry heaving because I badly needed to have a drink. I stepped into a corner aisle and began to throw up behind an unopened box of liquor. After I threw up, I purchased a large bottle of vodka, got in my car, and took a big drink off the bottle. I sat there in the parking lot of the liquor store and nearly began to cry. I thought, *This is it for me—there is no way out of this pain.*

That weekend I was supposed to be preparing to go to Pine Ridge, South Dakota, to the Lakota shaman to do a vision quest. Most medicine men have a strict policy of not doing spiritual work or intense ceremonies with practicing drug addicts and alcoholics. They believe the substance blocks the spirit from entering, and that doing a vision quest while in an altered state of mind could be dangerous. I knew taking that first drink would blow my chance to do a vision quest and would potentially damage the relationship I was developing with the Lakota shaman. However, like many times before, the consequences did not stop me.

The rest of Memorial Day weekend I drank, and I did not make any effort to call Jennifer to see how Colin was, let alone to visit him or my dog. By June 2 or 3, I was a mental, physical, and emotional disaster. I had no friends, and felt there was no way out of my current situation. Unexpectedly, my friend Geno, whom I had not spoken to in quite some time, called me. Jennifer told him of my current state of mind and situation, gave him my phone number, and asked him to see if I was still alive.

Geno called. I picked up the phone, not even saying hi, how are you, or anything else. I said, "Dude I'm completely lost, and I need your help."

"What do you need from me?"

"Can you please come to my place and stay with me until I sober up, then take me to Pine Ridge?"

"Dude," he said, "I'm going on a canoeing trip to Canada with a friend."

"Come on, dude," I said, "I'm an inch short of dying."

"Okay," he said, "I'll be right there." When Geno showed up a few hours later, I asked him to call the shaman and see what he recommended.

"The Lakota shaman?" he asked in total shock.

"Yeah, why?"

"No way," he said. "This is synchronous."

"Why?" I persisted

The Lakota Shaman

"I heard him on National Public Radio (NPR), and I thought I might attempt to find him to see if he would teach me ancient Lakota traditions," Geno said, filled with excitement.

"Here's his number," I said. "Call him and see what he'd like us to do."

Geno called the Lakota shaman, who said, "Come out here to Pine Ridge."
Geno immediately went home, packed his bags, and came back to my place to baby-sit me while I was detoxing from alcohol. Over the next several days, I felt like I was going to die because of the sweats, anxiety, and fear, and the fact that I could not sleep. Geno gave me a bag of ice for my head, ice water to drink, and tried to get me to eat.

CHAPTER 32

The Vision Quest

The Lakota shaman gave us the go-ahead to come to Pine Ridge. The journey was amazing; we read out of Greg Braden's book, *The Isaiah Effect,* and Judith Bluestone's, *The Return of the Children of Light,* and we listened to Bob Marley and The Red Hot Chili Peppers. The ride out to Pine Ridge felt spiritual in itself; we were noticing all the wildlife and the flowing grass on the plains. I had no idea South Dakota was this beautiful. For the first time in months, I felt better about myself and about my life. I had stopped taking the anti-depressants and sleeping pills.

Arriving at the Lakota Reservation in Pine Ridge, I thought I'd have immediate credibility and respect because I was the only other person at the vision quest, besides the Lakota shaman and his family, who were Native American. When people did not pay as much attention and respect to me as I thought I deserved, I kept thinking, *Don't they know who I am? I'm the only other Native person here.* Funny thing about being self-centered: When we don't get our way, we begin to act like children, becoming more frustrated and demanding until we get the attention we think we deserve. That is exactly what happened; I started acting like a little child.

Over the next few days, I participated in a few sweats and talked with a few people who were there to support others doing vision quests. However, I could feel my frustration building. Every time I wanted to talk with the shaman, he was busy. I asked him multiple times to let me go up on the hill and do a vision quest, but he didn't respond. Finally I got to a point where I told myself when this week was over, I wasn't coming back to Pine Ridge, nor was I doing any more of this Native American-ceremony baloney. The Lakota shaman had Geno and me help people carry their gear to a specific area on the property in preparation for their vision quest. I thought this was a way for the Lakota shaman to get me out of his hair, not realizing that escorting people up on the hill to vision quest was an important and admirable thing. During one such journey up the hill to start this man on his vision quest, I was asked to bring prayer ties, which are tobacco bundles that hold prayers with the tobacco. The Lakota word is *chanli apahcha.* The person is asked to say a prayer for what he or she wants when tying each of the dozens of little colored cloth pouches on a piece of sinew. I brought the ties with me to the altar on top of the hill next to the Medicine Wheel, and began to pray as I was asked.

Midway through my prayer, I looked up and noticed a few buffalo on the hill across from me. I took special notice, as buffalo are sacred to the Lakota. After carrying the prayer tie bundle I had created to the altar on top of the hill, I walked back down the hill to the sweat lodge. I felt a sense of peace I had not experienced in a while. I forgot about my petty frustration and began to live in the moment. Suddenly I became aware of the air's sweet smell. I took in what I was seeing with a new sense of appreciation of how pretty the area was and how the teepees below looked ancient, and I noticed the smoke rising from the fire.

I felt like I was propelled back in time to an era long forgotten. The people down below became beautiful to me. I could see all these people working together to make the dinner for the night and to clean up the camp. Feeling a sense of belonging, I wanted to surrender to whatever was to come next. Then I heard, "There he is." The shaman was waving me over. "Get your stuff. You're going to vision quest in another person's altar." Immediately I started questioning him, coming up with excuses as to why I was not ready. He said, "Hurry man, you don't have time for all that chaos in your head." I walked to my tent, grabbed my prayer altar, prayer ties, sacred pipe, and sleeping bag. Geno and I walked up the hill.

The person who is embarking on this sacred activity needs prayer flags that are cut into 2 x 2 inch squares. Tobacco is rolled up inside of it, and tied off with string. The red flannel prayer flags (or ties) are connected in one continuous string to create the altar. If chokecherry is unavailable, any fruit tree will do, but chokecherry trees are preferred because they represent the bittersweet nature of life, the blood of life that ties us together and unifies the world family. The cherry itself actually represents the pituitary gland, which allows us to go from the physical into the spiritual world, and back to the physical world, so that we can walk in a good way where we can help bring peace into our hearts, and help everyone on this planet.

The continuous string of tobacco ties for the vision quest must use specific colors such as red, black, yellow, and white in a special order. After the spirits tell the medicine man what they want, he gives the participant exact instructions. Long before my time at the altar, I was asked to make 1,250 ties, two times, which took me about three months, saying a little prayer for each tie. A lot of people want things, but are not willing to do what is required in order to get them. This requires a very strong commitment.

Other items needed are an eagle feather, a piece of a seashell, and a blanket. In Native culture, the eagle is the one that carries our prayers, soaring to the highest heaven. The eagle can see great distances, and can communicate between the physical and spiritual worlds. The shell represents the ocean, which is the salt of life, our origin. The blanket is for protection. When you go to the hill, all you're left with is yourself, and the blanket is to protect you.

I climbed into the altar area, loaded the pipe with tobacco, and said a prayer. Geno assured me that I'd be fine, and that he'd come and get me when the Great Spirit told the shaman it was time. This freaked me out momentarily; with what I knew about "Native American Time," I figured that could be days. Ultimately I was fairly calm and surrendered to the process, and my anxiety dropped to a much lower level.

South Dakota's night sky is the most incredible sight. The Milky Way is thick with stars, and the sky seemed as though I could see forever. I was in the altar with my pipe, and I started to feel uncomfortable as I realized that all I had was *this very moment*. Then a feeling of peace and calm came over me, and I could sense a presence. I sat there thinking of all the people who had come in and out of my life, and how much help I had received along my journey.

Morning came after I had slept for a few hours. When I looked up five buffalo were on a ridge across from me. They didn't make any noise, they didn't move. They lay under a tree and watched me as I watched them. Occasionally one of the buffalo made a snorting sound, or one got up and bounced around or rolled in the dirt, but they did not leave. I was in awe of the size and beauty of the beasts. I was intimately connected to these buffalo and everything else; I had a sense of belonging, and with it, a growing sense of responsibility.

That day I started truly praying for Jennifer, my son, my dog, and people I had harmed along the way. I realized what happened to me happens to other people as well. A thought came to mind: *Don't deny the miracle*. I felt like crying, but the tears did not come.

I slept part of that day, and when I woke up I felt good, better than I had in a while. The buffalo came back over the ridge, and in the sky, an eagle repeatedly circled me. I said a prayer—*"My life is no longer my life, Great*

Spirit. What will you have me do? Whatever that is, give me the strength to do it. "Later that day, Geno and another man came and retrieved me from the altar. My vision quest was over. When we were breaking my altar down, I looked up and saw the five buffalo stand up, walk over the other side of the ridge, and disappear.

That night I did "a sweat" with the Lakota shaman, and he asked me what I had seen on my vision quest. I explained the Milky Way, the eagle, and the buffalo. I explained the prayer I had made, and he said, "That is significant." The shaman mentioned that working a recovery program would help me clean house emotionally, helping with my PTSD.

For most of my stay in Pine Ridge, the shaman did not want me to leave the property. He felt I needed to slow down and detox. I felt trapped, but I was willing to listen. After the vision, the shaman loosened the rules, and let Geno and me venture off the property. We went to Wounded Knee and the Horse Sanctuary. Many of the sites I was seeing I had read about in Russell Means's book. I had this strange feeling at Wounded Knee that I had been there before. The place seemed familiar. I reflected on the days when I was confined to my bunk space and all I'd had was Russell's book, and my imagination had taken me to Wounded Knee. I had longed to be on this reservation many times during my stay in jail, and here I was.

One of my frequently recurring thoughts was that one of the medicine men in Arizona had told me I would be going to Pine Ridge to do a vision quest. Here I was on Pine Ridge, having completed a vision quest. It was all so surreal. That night Geno and I made our way to a powwow on Pine Ridge. Hundreds of dancers were dressed in many different types of beautiful Native American dresses and dance outfits. The drumbeat was a different rhythm—one I was not familiar with, but could feel deep in my soul. On more than one occasion, the sound of the drums brought me near tears.

The next day Geno and I decided we needed to go home. We sat down with the shaman, who gave us last-minute instructions. Mine were to keep my pipe clean, smoke out of it, stay away from alcohol, make prayer ties a couple times a week, and learn to meditate. I thanked the Lakota shaman for his time, and expressed my gratitude for letting us come. Geno and I left Pine Ridge tremendously grateful; both of us were changed from the experience. The vibration in me had slowed down, and my anxiety was gone.

On the drive home, we listened to Bob Marley all eleven hours of the trip. Excitedly, we shared our experiences in Pine Ridge, and while one of us drove, the other read out of one of the books we had brought along. We drove through the White Clay River area, and we saw wild horses running on the prairie, buffalo near the river, and red-tailed hawks overhead. My connection to nature grew deeper! A sense of humility came over me, the first since the day I'd been on River Road in Tucson, and believed I had experienced the presence of "the Great Spirit."

Back in Minneapolis, Geno unloaded his gear from my SUV. I left all my stuff, went upstairs, and went straight to bed. The next morning, I called Jennifer and went over to her house to see Colin and my dog.

"You look much better," Jennifer said.

"Thank you. I feel better." I told her about our experiences at Pine Ridge. Jennifer and I reflected on my journaling from 1997 when the medicine man in Arizona had told me that I would go to Pine Ridge to do a vision quest and Sundance.

Loneliness Took Over

By the end of June, the natural high of being out in Pine Ridge had worn off, and I found myself all alone in my apartment, with no friends or family around me. The loneliness again took over, and the anxiety that had left me in Pine Ridge was back. I asked myself, *How could this be? I thought I got rid of this feeling for good.* Spirituality requires daily work; it is not a one-time awakening. But at the time, I was frustrated that those old feelings returned. Who could I turn to? Geno was back into his own life, so I couldn't lean on him for moral support. These raw feelings grew more and more each day, until finally, the weekend of the Fourth of July, I could no longer stand the pain. I quickly drove down to the liquor store. The whole time I was beating on the steering wheel, saying to myself, *Why do I have to do this? I don't want to drink anymore.*

Picking up a two bottles of vodka, I drove home. The feeling inside me brought me to the verge of throwing up. Next, I took a deep breath and surrendered to the liquor. Popping the top of one of the bottles, I began drinking as if it were water. Within a few minutes the anxiety, fear, pain, and tension was gone, and my old love was back.

I was in my last college class online, but could barely make my way to the computer to sign on for class, even though it was just twenty feet from the couch on which I had been laying, sleeping, and drinking. I gave my instructor a crazy story as to why I could not sign on, and why I could not complete the last paper. She said I had earned a high enough grade at that point to pass the course. I did not sign on again. I received a D for that class, and graduated with a Bachelors of Science degree in Business Marketing after nearly four years of study. I was happy the last day of class, but also sad because I had no one to help me celebrate my graduation. I was all alone in my little one-bedroom apartment, and I did not have a single friend, other than Geno, to call with the good news.

I spent the next several days drinking and watching television. Occasionally, I sobered up to see Colin and my dog. After visiting them, I raced home and drank again for another three or four days.

CHAPTER 33

Medicating for the Last Time—Then Surrendering

In the middle of July 2004, I was lying on the floor of my apartment in my boxers, fading in and out of consciousness for nearly ten days. I was on a binge, attempting to drink myself to death. I had steadily gained weight, and my blood pressure was too high. I had not showered or shaved for many days, and I was severely constipated. I had no family or friends to rescue me. I was a victim of self-destruction. The trauma of my childhood and past transgressions had finally come to a head.

When I woke up, I was in absolute terror. My heart was pounding, I was sweating profusely, my fingernails were bleeding from picking at them, I smelled terrible, and I felt like I was going to crawl right out of my skin. I looked up from the floor to see a large bottle of Bacardi on my oval coffee table. Grabbing the bottle, I took one big drink, then another. I started to throw up. Not wanting to take a chance of losing any booze, I quickly covered my mouth and nose. I threw up and re-swallowed the booze. This continued until the entire bottle was empty. I was relieved I had finished the bottle, and was waiting for the pain to go away. Twenty minutes, and nothing—the fear and terror were still there. I screamed at the top of my lungs, "Help me, I can't handle this pain anymore." I hunched over, praying, *Please, please Great Spirit, if you're there, let me die.*

Alcohol had always been my solution for killing my pain. However, on this day, alcohol was no longer killing the pain, and had stopped being my solution. I was fearful that no longer could I turn to my first love, my painkiller, my old friend. It was over. I lie back on the floor and made one last plea, *Let me die…or show me a way out.*

Most of my life I spent running from my feelings, the past, relationships, police, drug dealers, people I owed money, creditors, and the Great Spirit. I realized I had nowhere else to run. The movie *Forrest Gump* came to mind, specifically the part when Forrest's mom said, "You got to put your past behind you before you can move on." The day I cried out, I died a death of sorts. I could no longer run, I could no longer hide, and I had nothing left in the tank. I was physically, mentally, and emotionally bankrupt. I had no more to give. I felt myself on the brink of insanity, and for the first time in my life, I truly knew that my sole solution was to go deep inside, and deal with whatever demons waited there.

I did not want to face the pain of my brother's suicide, the sexual molestation I experienced as a child, living on the streets, and how many lives I had endangered because of my way of life. My divorce, not being able to see my sons Billy or Colin, and the shooting of my dog Nikko haunted me. I was overwhelmed with sadness when I thought about facing all of these painful life experiences, but I knew that suicide was not the answer. If the Great Spirit wanted me dead, it could have happened on more than one occasion.

I knew I had to begin anew, and the saying from earlier in my life, "Don't deny the miracle," repeatedly played in my head.

CHAPTER 34

Meeting David—2004

After my prayer to "die or be shown a way out," I fell back to sleep on my living-room floor. When I awoke, the hair on one side of my head was wet from sleeping in this mess, and I smelled of urine and alcohol. Immediately I got sick, throwing up green bile. Watching as the bile dripped down my shirtless chest to my urine-soaked boxers, I was too weak to get up and go to the bathroom. I continued to throw up on the floor in front of me.

After sleeping for a few more hours, I awoke feeling better. I got up from the floor and went to my computer, where I typed into a search engine: "Recovery meetings in Minneapolis." The website listed a meeting close to my apartment. I went to the bathroom, showered, and tried to shave, but I was too shaky. I brushed my teeth for the first time in many days. When I spit out the toothpaste, it was tinted red with blood.

I shook so badly the whole drive to the meeting that I had to pull over and collect myself. I arrived an hour early, and was scared to death to walk into the meeting, or even to be out in public looking and feeling the way I did. The meeting was at a coffeehouse, which I thought was unusual. In my previous recovery experience, most sessions were at churches and other meeting places. I mustered up the courage to go inside and ask the staff if there actually was a meeting there. When no one was at the front counter, I continued into the building until I found a person sitting at a back corner table. This man, probably in his early seventies, was reading a newspaper, and when he saw me walk in, he lowered the newspaper as we briefly made eye contact. He continued reading. I stood there for a moment, deciding whether to leave and get a bottle of vodka, when the newspaper lowered again.

"Can I help you?" asked the man, who later told me his name was David.

"Is there a recovery meeting here?" I asked.

"Yes, there is. Are you all right?"

"No. No sir, I am not."

David stood up and walked toward me, and when he was about three feet away, he said, "It's going to be okay." He put out his arms as if he was going to give me a hug.

I fell into David's arms, saying, "I'm dying, I'm dying, and it's painful."

David and I walked outside to a park bench. I started crying. I have never, ever cried that much. Maybe I had shed a little tear here and there. Maybe I had even cried for a little while. But I had never had tears stream down my face, seeming to never end. David held me in his arms while I cried, rocking me back and forth, telling me he loved me, and that I was going to be fine. I repeated to him, "Sir, I'm dying. I'm without hope, and I can't get sober."

"Sure you can," David said. "You may never have been taught how to get sober, or you weren't ready."

That day at the park bench, I cried for nearly four hours, and David held me in his arms most of the time.

"I begged to the creator to let me die, and he didn't," I told David.

"Maybe someone greater than you has a plan for you."

After several hours of crying, I took my head off David's wet shoulder and said, "What should I do?"

David responded calmly and quietly: "Surrender."

I went home that afternoon, completely exhausted from the outpouring of emotion, and the fact that I had not eaten or slept well in days. Dropping onto my bed, I fell asleep. Those three hours of sleep were the best sleep I had had in many weeks. When I awoke, I stared at the bedroom ceiling thinking, *What now?* I got out of bed and, instead of *getting* up, I dropped to my knees and prayed, *God, I'm really screwed up, scared, and I don't want to live this way anymore. If it is your will, take away this obsession, and show me a way out.*

I drove to the store for cleaning supplies, food, and other necessities. I passed by the liquor store—but I had no compulsion to go in. I drove home without the radio on. Having peace and quiet in my car was unusual; I always wanted background noise, no matter what I was doing. I started the long process of cleaning my apartment, and I sweated the liquor out of my system while I cleaned. The sweat coming off my skin smelled like stale liquor. After about four hours of cleaning, my apartment finally smelled clean and fresh again, and I had a feeling of accomplishment.

I sat down on my couch and put *The Last Samurai* in the DVD player. Geno had recommended the movie, saying, "Elements of this movie apply to your journey." As I watched the movie, I recognized that Geno was right: parts of the movie spoke to me. Tom Cruise's character was an alcoholic, and he used alcohol to kill the pain and cover up his nightmares and past transgressions. Another scene that stood out was when Cruise's character detoxed, revealing the absolute terror and struggle of detoxing. The part that stood out to me most was the meaning of "Samurai": be of service. When Cruise's character started being of service, his feelings about himself changed, his sleeping patterns changed, and his life—and what his life meant—changed.

That night I slept all night, something I had not done in years. The next morning I awoke to birds singing outside, and I could hear the lawn sprinklers. I lay in bed for a few more minutes before I realized that I was not sweating or shaking, nor did I feel nauseous. At that moment I realized: *I was not craving alcohol.* The compulsion had been lifted. I jumped out of bed and said, "No way!" Again I got down on my knees and prayed, *Creator, show me how to be of service.* Over the next several months, I went to many recovery meetings, followed the suggestions of the program for recovery, and remained sober. My life began to change for the better. I was becoming part of a community that I had not fully embraced in my previous attempts at sobriety.

I had seen my son Colin and my dog infrequently that summer; I was feeling better now, and I wanted to see them. Jennifer did not trust me to take Colin by myself, but she always kept the option open for me to come to her house to see him. When I called, she said, "Of course." I was nervous and scared because I had not seen them recently and I wondered what to expect. At the house, I was sweating and breathing hard, and I wanted to turn around and head back home.

Jennifer came to the door with nearly three-year-old Colin in her arms. When he saw me, he cracked a huge smile. Nanji realized I was outside, and came running to the door, barking and whining like crazy. Jennifer opened the door, and Colin and my dog showered me with love. Colin reached out his arms and wrapped them around my neck, and Nanji kept jumping up on me, barking. Even though I did not want to, as hard as I tried to hold back the tears, I began to cry.

The days of holding my tears and emotions inside were over.

I walked into Jennifer's house, put Colin down, threw the Frisbee for Nanji, hugged Jennifer, and thanked her for letting me see my son and my dog. Colin and I walked out back in the yard where the dog was playing. Colin looked up at me with a big smile, as if he were in awe of me. I was playing with my dog, and Colin was running in the yard with us. I asked

Colin questions about Nanji and the grass. All of a sudden, he said, "Daddy, be quiet, let's just listen." Colin sat down on the grass Indian-style, and the dog sat next to him. Colin said to both of us, "SHHH, be quiet." Nanji and I settled next to Colin, and we all became quiet. I do not know what he was listening for, but by the look on his face, it had to do with a higher power.

In memory of David

CHAPTER 35

When One Door Closes...

Unemployed from June to November 2004, I did not have my mental faculties in place to be employable, and I had been fired from my last several jobs. I figured that since I was not working, instead of rushing back to a job, I should focus on getting myself right emotionally, mentally, physically, and spiritually. I had income from the severance package, and I was eligible for unemployment when the severance ran out. Money was not my biggest worry.

Being unemployed allowed me to fully embrace a recovery program, and concentrate on changing everything about my life. I started attending recovery meetings daily, and within a three-month period, I went to more than 225 meetings. In the rooms of recovery there is a saying: "Alcoholism is a disease of isolation." I can truly attest to that fact. When I entered into the recovery program this time, I had no family or friends left in my life other than Geno, and my ex-wife, Jennifer.

That fall, I began the process of cleansing myself of many of my former attachments. I could no longer afford the lifestyle I was living. I had to decide how important material things were to me. I was in heavy credit-card debt, and my current income could not support my lavish lifestyle of shopping and food. I defined myself by the car I drove, the clothes I wore, and the jewelry I owned. I thought that my Lexus impressed other people. Later I learned that not many people were all that impressed by a guy driving a Lexus who lived in a one-bedroom apartment. My thinking was especially absurd when I hardly had enough money for gas.

I found out that people were not thinking about me as much as I thought they were. I was *not* the center of the universe. I decided it was best to file for bankruptcy and begin anew.

My awakening from my thirty-eight-year slumber had begun. I spent more and more time with people in recovery programs, and I began to give back to my community by volunteering. As uncomfortable as it was for me to make friends, I felt it was imperative, and I started to develop friendships in my recovery program. Because I was unemployed, I could go to matinee movies, which kept me from over-thinking things. A friend from the program and I went to see *What the Bleep Do We Know?* Both of us were astonished by the information in the movie.

The main character had a belief system that played out in her life many times over. She repeatedly self-destructed. Feeling horrible about herself, she needed medication and alcohol for her anxiety. I could relate to everything this woman was feeling and going through. I had an established belief system about myself. I always wanted to be part of the "in-crowd," but felt I was less than they were. I always thought people would abandon me, and I pushed them out of my life before they had a chance to leave. When I felt rejected, I would unconsciously reject those who loved me most. Because of my feelings of inadequacy, I thought I was unlovable. These belief systems were established in me at a young age. My parents choose their addictions over me; my adoptive grandmother told me I would never be part of the family; teachers said I was stupid; and my adoptive mom hid in her bedroom, abandoning me for months at a time. These events created my belief system. The movie showed me how I had built up my own thoughts and feelings about the world until this point.

The movie's most profound aspect for me was when one of the main characters said, "It is not what you do to your body, but what you do for your mind that counts." I sat stunned, in awe. "It is not what I do to my body, it is what I do for my mind." The answer came in an instant. One of my major loves had always been learning. I have enjoyed reading my whole life, and in spite of where I was in life situations, I never stopped hungering to learn new things. I knew that moment what I was supposed to do with the next two years of my life: continue my education.

By November of 2004, I was emotionally stable enough to return to work and re-enter society. I applied for a job at a local software company, and while going through the interview process, I reached a level of honesty with this employer I had never had with any other employer. The company required background checks and drug testing. For the first time in many years, I had no anxiety about what my employer might find in my background. I told them that I was an alcoholic and a drug addict, and that I was in a recovery program. I told them that I needed to go to meetings every day to remain sober. I discovered that if a person is honest about such details up front, most employers are gracious and accepting. They were fine with my daily meetings, as long as I made up the hours.

In December, I began working on an MBA degree at New York Institute of Technology. I was excited, full of hope, and finally back to work. I had good friends in my life, and a recovery program. I was seeing my son and my dog every few days. Christmas brought a level of anxiety I had not experienced for a while, but I finally had the tools to help me handle the holidays sober.

My old friend Geno suggested that I read *Power vs. Force*, which he felt would give me insight into my behavior. The book was recommended to him on our first trip to Pine Ridge, and this was the second time he had mentioned it. Since on more than one occasion, Geno had pointed me in the right direction, I thought this book must have meaning and relevance at this time in my life. Nearly every book that I read, Geno had suggested, dating all the way back to 1999 when he introduced me to Zecharia Sitchin and William Cooper. At the time, I did not understand that reading each of the books was putting another pieces of the puzzles together, and each book led to another piece. I purchased *Power vs. Force*, and began reading. I was blown away by finding out we are each responsible for our own actions, and that our belief system is what keeps us sick, and makes us repeat the same unhealthy situations.

Everything kept pointing me back to the real issue: It was not what was happening outside of me; instead it was what was going on inside me.

For the first time in a long while I had true hope, and finished the year 2004 without medicating myself. I was excited about the upcoming year, grateful that I was experiencing a re-birth.

CHAPTER 36

Cosmic Surgery

Early in 2005, I was reading *Power vs. Force,* taking part in most exciting conversations. I met many people who had already studied subjects I was starting to explore: quantum physics, Zen Buddhism, meditation, alternative treatments for sleeplessness, depression, and PTSD. I was attending the local Zen Buddhist prayer house where a teacher combined meditation, Zen Buddhist practices, and the recovery program. I could not believe it; people who knew about these topics were willing to sit up all night and talk about them. Synchronicity was everywhere: One person pointed to a book, and another person said, "If you like that book, read this book." I was overjoyed with what I was learning and experiencing.

In 2005, I had the most fascinating dream. As I dozed off reading, a man in surgical scrubs and mask woke me. He said in an Eastern European accent, "Rob, it's time to come with me."

"Where are we going?"

"Please follow me."

I followed him into my living room, where I saw another man sitting in a chair with a white cloth draped over his shoulders. A bright light shone over the man, but I could see no lamps. The man in the white cloth had his head shaved, and was sitting peacefully with his eyes closed. The surgeon asked me to come close and watch. The surgeon pointed his finger at the man in the white cloth, and a bright beam of light, like a laser, began to make an incision in his forehead. The surgeon kept pointing his finger at the man until he had gone all the way around his head. A little bit of blood began to show along the incision.

When the surgeon motioned for the top of the skull to come off, it began to levitate. He started explaining the brain to me. He pointed out the frontal lobe, and explained what its purpose was (hearing, smell, sight, and taste). He pointed out the neocortex, midbrain, pons, pineal gland, hypothalamus, and many other areas of the brain. Each time, he explained what the area was, and its purpose. I took particular interest in the pineal gland and midbrain. He explained that the pineal gland is how we enter and exit our physical bodies, and the midbrain receives and sends energy, but doesn't analyze thought like the frontal lobe. Each time he showed me a different part of the brain, he asked in a booming voice, "Do you understand?"

"I think I do," I said.

He repeated more sternly, "Rob, do you understand?"

"Yes." I said, with more conviction.

The surgeon explained what an atom is, and how atoms are connected to other atoms, and that our thoughts run along a vibrating band or string from one atom to another. He said, "It is important to understand that all of our thoughts are connected, and that nothing is separate."

The surgeon kept asking me each time he explained new concepts whether I understood. I continued to respond, "Yes, I understand." The surgeon motioned for the top of the man's skull to be put back. It came down, centered on the man's head, and sealed itself up perfectly. One last time he asked, "Do you understand?"

"Yes." I looked at the man in the white cloth, and his eyes opened. It was me! Instantly I woke up back in my bed, turned on the light, and wrote down my experience in the dream. The next day I called Geno to explain the dream. Using the Internet, we started looking up what I had learned in the dream, and were amazed at the accuracy.

After that dream, I stopped questioning the power of the Great Spirit. Overnight I had learned about subjects that previously I had no knowledge of or no interest in. In a short time, I raised my vibration from shame and guilt to courage and love. I was experiencing the unfolding world moment-to-moment, and my outside world became a reflection of what was going on inside me.

When I spoke about my experiences, people began to tell me that my life experiences, and my ability to overcome them, were inspirational and gave them hope. I discovered that every time I shared my experiences, I felt better inside, and wounds from my past began to heal.

In February of 2005, I crossed my first significant hurdle in recovery. Because our dog had bitten more than one person, Jennifer and I felt that Colin might be in danger, and we tried to find the dog another home. The home we found was nice, but Nanji did not like it and he bit the homeowner. When we decided we had no choice but to put the dog down, I brought him to the vet, and held him. After he took his last breath, I rested my head on his fur and cried. Nanji was my do-over for what I had done to Nikko. I made every effort to make his life full, healthy, safe, and wonderful. I gave him all I had as if he were my child. Putting our dog to sleep brought Jennifer and me closer in our shared loss.

By March, I tipped the scales at a bulky 237 pounds, and my blood pressure was near 140 over 100. I had left alcohol, but had shifted my addiction to food, and it was driving up my blood pressure. I knew I needed to make a change, but did not know how. I called my old friend, Geno, who had guided me many times before. He was already practicing a technique called "food combining" that was introduced by Herbert Shelton back in the 1950s. He suggested that combining too many types of food creates a digestive nightmare. By eating the same types of food at mealtime, and not combining carbohydrates, proteins, and starches, digestion improves and the colon is cleansed, helping with intestinal problems.

Geno suggested that I first try a detox program before reading the book *Food Combining Made Easy*. Following directions, I did a ten-day detox program, which cleansed my colon and contributed to immediate weight loss. While fasting, I discovered deep meditation, and how much influence the ego has on everyday life. My ego is attached to everything that will stimulate it and make it feel important, and during the fast, my ego fought me all the way. I began to understand that I needed to separate from my ego, but I had no idea how that was going to happen.

In late March, I went on another Native American spiritual retreat with the Lakota shaman who had been instrumental in helping me find my way back to the Native American community. While at the retreat, I talked with the shaman about doing an ancient Lakota ceremony called the Sundance. He felt that we should begin to pray on this idea, and in the fall, decide whether I should do it.

Leaving that retreat feeling refreshed and new, I could hardly wait to get back to Minneapolis to share what I had learned. This time I had many friends, and people I called family, to tell about my experiences and spend time with, which kept away the loneliness. I went right back to work, and to my recovery program, and did not miss a beat, unlike the previous year when I had gone to the retreat, and immediately returned to my old destructive patterns. I was establishing my roots, but still didn't want to let go of my old lavish lifestyle. Even though things in my life were good, it was hard to let go of my belief system.

Terry, my oldest adoptive brother, called in mid-April of 2005 to tell me

Bachelor's degree graduation

MBA graduation

Rob

Colin

Two cowboys

Colin and Nanji

Nanji, Rob, and Colin

Reflecting on the journey

Reflecting on the journey

Standing for today

Return to Mount Shasta

that my adoptive mother had died. I was sad that she was gone, and yet glad she was not suffering anymore. My brother asked me to come to the funeral. I was reluctant at first, but finally agreed. I had not been home to northern California for more than fifteen years. I met with my recovery sponsor, and my spiritual advisor, and we all agreed it would be good for me to go home. This time I would go with integrity, dignity, self-respect, and a willingness to close this chapter of my life.

I had mixed feelings about my adoptive mom's death. I had been away from her for so long that I had forgotten what it was to have a mother. At the same time, I was still angry over various things that had happened in my childhood. I was also sad, because if it had not been for my adoptive mother, I would not have had the opportunities I did.

Back home, I attended Mom's funeral, but I did not stand with the family. Her sisters did not acknowledge me at the funeral, so out of respect to my mom and aunts, I stood in the back. Their reaction did not hurt me or bring up any feelings of guilt, shame, or remorse. I thought, *Holy shit, this recovery thing just may work.*

When everyone left, I burned sage for my mom, made a few Lakota prayer ties for her, and wished her a safe journey. I burned the prayer ties, watching as the smoke rose to the sky, envisioning my prayers rising in the sky with her soul. I felt a sense of relief that I had been able to attend her funeral—sober. Years earlier, I had not attended my adoptive father's funeral because I was caught up in the self-centered, selfish behavior associated with my addiction. That day I burned sage for my adoptive dad, bundled prayer ties, and offered the Great Spirit my sorrow, asking for forgiveness. I was grateful I could stand at their gravesites, and I thanked both of them for their help on this journey.

That week I visited many people I had wronged, and to the best of my ability, offered repayment and restitution. Many of them felt that bygones should be bygones, others did not remember the incident I was apologizing for, and still others thought it was funny. A few could not believe I was alive, as they thought somebody, possibly myself, might have killed me a long time ago. I visited my son, Billy, and was able to mend fences with him as well. I told him I loved him, but he already had a dad in Brad, Lucy's boyfriend. Once we met, we were both able to close that chapter of our lives.

Our outside conditions have nothing to do with whether we drink or not.
I discovered this was true:
I drank when things were good, and I drank when things were bad.

I left northern California feeling like I had shed my old dead self, and unloaded an eight hundred-pound gorilla off my back. Excited about my life, I realized that my recovery was separate from my life situations. I read in the big book of Alcoholics Anonymous that our outside conditions have nothing to do with whether we drink or not. I discovered this was true: I drank when things were good and I drank when things were bad. Now I discovered that I stayed sober through some good things, and stayed sober through some bad things, like death. My outside conditions had nothing to do with my recovery. I had a renewed sense of commitment and strength that I had never known. I had tapped into a power or energy that was giving me infinite love and wisdom.

David, the first man I had met at the recovery meeting back in July 2004, told me that my story was powerful, and that it was a gift that should be given away. Over the next several months, I began speaking to many chemical dependency programs, discovering that I was not the only one who had been hopeless, down and out, and needed inspiration. Still today, every time I tell my story, an audience member comes up and tells me that they, too, had felt the guilt, shame, and fear I had experienced.

I had discovered my tribe and family, and they were in the recovery community.

CHAPTER 37

Graduating From One dream to Another

Education has always been important to me—whether that is book smart, street smart, or just plain experience. At an early age, I began questioning the laws of the universe, the laws of my adult guardians, and the laws of physics. It has seemed to me that people, places, things, and situations had a deeper meaning. The winners throughout history got to tell the story. The possibility that there was an untold story or epic saga in human history was often forgotten or covered up. I never believed that man sprung up out of the primordial ooze, or that we developed from apes. I also questioned all of our religions around the world because they came from the pen of man. Maybe they were the words of God, but man wrote them down, and since the beginning of time, man has been flawed, which for me raised the possibility that his writing may be flawed as well. Not knowing for sure that one or the other was right or wrong, I needed to seek these answers for myself.

I did that seeking, in the form of books, life experience, and listening to other men and women's life experiences and knowledge. I studied some of the greatest teachers in history, contemplated some of the finest art the world has ever known, and went to the depths of the well where I learned about the human condition and my own creation. In that journey, I discovered a love for education. During my whole life, the one constant was learning, learning, and more learning. Many times when I opened a book, I lost myself in the words as if I was teleported to a strange universe, separate from the one I had created for myself in the here and now. I looked at a piece of artwork and immediately wanted to go into the mind and feelings of its creator. My thirst and hunger for knowledge only grew as I aged. Each book I read led me down a path to the next book, and then the next, and so on.

This burning desire to be educated became a reality in 2000, after the world didn't come to an end, which as a child I was told would happen. I enrolled in the University of Phoenix, where I found others like me, men and women who took detours at a younger age, or had life-changing events that had kept them from college. By this point, I had cleaned up the wreckage of my past well enough that my mind wasn't focused on all the bad things that I had done, or had happened to me. It was fabulous learning with people that had professional jobs, families, and careers. I ate this opportunity up, cherished every moment of being in school, finishing near the top of my class in nearly every subject.

My recovery program gave me the tools that enabled me to continue my education. By this time, recovery had set in and I was fully present, thirsting for more knowledge. I was encouraged to continue with school, as it was obviously something important to me. I enrolled at New York Institute of Technology, thus beginning my journey toward an MBA. My recovery program—and specifically steps four, five, eight, and nine had helped me deal with so much baggage that I was clear for the first time. I was fully present, and I felt alive. I had knowledge to share with other students, and experience that was in line with my teachers and classmates. I was truly a contemporary.

I mentioned earlier that my first love was alcohol. Now I can look back and say that wasn't entirely true. I loved education and learning long before I ever took a drink, starting in that little library on my way home from elementary school. My first true love was learning. I became what I had always dreamed about during and after high school. Many times in the past I drank at night while watching commercials about college, thinking, *Well, someday I hope I can do that*. Now my dream became fully realized, and I continued with my education.

I have a tremendous amount of gratitude for every writer, painter, artist, poet, seeker, and risk taker that has given me a little crumb so that I continued to go down the path of education.

Graduating from one dream to another

CHAPTER 38

The Alpha and Omega of Two Native Lives— "Conversations with Dying Mother"

Winter covers the valley, and in the dwelling house, Mother is reclined with her most trusted aide by her side, sipping vanilla grass tea, believed to be a medicine that helps the mother have a safe birth. On that December day an Avansaxiich (boy) is born.

Meanwhile the medicine man is sitting alone in the Ikmahachraam (sweat lodge) in prayer during his three-day fast. At the break of dawn on the third day, the entry to the lodge opens, and steam rises into the cool air. The medicine man stands upright and gazes into the sky. He closes his eyes as this phase of the birthing ceremony is complete. At the dwelling house, the medicine man sits with the mother and son, observing the baby's every move.

It is time for the medicine man to journey to Ikxariyatuuyship (God's Mountain), today called Offield Mountain, which is the most sacred place in the Karuk land, the place where gods come to pray, and men come to pay homage. At the top of the mountain, he will name the child based on the characteristics observed in the dwelling house after birth. He will sit on the ground and ask, Huutthvuuyti (what is your name?). "

We call ourselves "Araar," and our creation stories are "Pikva." It is said that my people have lived here since the beginning of time. In the "old days," the time before this time, which would be the long period before the white man, we knew every origin of plants, animal, and species in this land. We are the Karuk, referred to as the "Upriver People."

We believe Ikxareeyavs (means God) lived on this world before human beings. We Araar believe that nature is alive, possesses both feeling and consciousness, and is capable of seeing and hearing our prayers. Through our oral traditions, we've been told that the earth is a physical manifestation of God's creative spirit, and we are part of that manifestation.

Our wisdom tells us that Ikxareeyavs (God) was alive, which means that our lives were purely creative, and that each moment of existence resulted in some kind of creation.

Our social and legal systems were put into place to sustain life, and to teach us how to live in peace and harmony with the tribal communities with whom we shared the Klamath region.

The shaman cried out, "This boy has been born many times before, and is consciousness in motion. In this time, he will be given the name Shining Fame-Bright Light, otherwise known as Robert."

This was how the birthing ceremony went before the invasion of the white folks. Mine went something like this. Born to divorced parents, both addicted, and the father had a prison roll number. My roll number was different than my father's; his was given by the prison system, and mine by the U.S. Government.

For years, the Native people were not considered citizens, thus were not counted in the U.S. census, and treaties set in the 1800s had moved them off their land to less desirable areas. Some of these treaties allowed for individual Native people to receive an allotment of land. The roll number identified Indian names, English names, age, sex, and date of birth, and determined who received this allotment. Not all tribes have or use roll numbers, but the Karuk tribe did.

Mine is 3743.

Karuk family tree

Since 2002, I had been communicating with my biological mom, Marlene, on a consistent basis. I lived in Minnesota, and she lived in Redding so it was the best way we could communicate. She recited this amazing birthing ceremony story. After my adoptive mom died, Marlene and I began talking more frequently. At first, the communication was more about what was presently happening in our lives. She was amazed at my ability to communicate, saying, "You must be the mailman's son, because none of us communicate like that." She said the way I spoke with her showed intelligence and thought, instead of saying whatever came off the top of my mind. As she put it, I did not "have rez speak." We talked about her bad hip, sore legs, and poor financial situation. She shared her disappointment about my brothers' and sisters' lives, and told me how proud she was of me.

Mom and I spent endless hours talking about our tribe and traditions. When I'd talk about school, she'd tell me how smart I was. She made fun of my style of communication, which went from surfer to corporate, and giggled when I spoke "Minnesotan."

My mom had this great Native American voice, kind of deep and soft. Because she had smoked for years, it was somewhat gruff. I teased her on the phone about that, and she laughed heartily. In nearly every single conversation, I asked her to share things about my dad, but she always responded, "Well, he wasn't around that long, and all I really remember was how violent he was"—before quickly changing the subject.

Mom contracted cancer in 2004 or 2005, and when that happened, she became much more open about her sadness in relation to us, her kids. She told me that she used to prostitute herself at the bars and truck stops to make money. She told me that in the '80s, she killed a person while driving drunk, and ended up in a California jail for nine years.

Mom admitted that because of her experience with men, and the fact that she had met a woman in prison who was very good to her, she was living as a gay woman. She told me that my brother Johnnie had gone to prison, too. She said she felt responsible for all the family ills. Although she talked about a lot of things, she never said much about my brother Ronnie, who had taken his own life, and she never talked about my biological dad.

One day I said, "Come on, Mom. You're sick and going to die someday, and it's not fair to keep the truth from me." I mentioned the gasoline incident when I was four, and she sighed into the phone.

"I'm so sorry I didn't protect you and your brothers and sisters." She verified the gasoline incident, and many more like it, saying, "It's time you know the truth." She apologized repeatedly, sobbing and saying, "Robbie, you're a good boy. I'm so sorry." She said that she regretted everything, including the day she almost killed us when she got drunk and fell asleep with a cigarette in her mouth, burning the house down. That is when she realized she could no longer take care of us kids, and decided to turn us over to child protective services.

Over the next few years of her life, she shared her memories of my early childhood with me. I'm still not sure if I became recovery support for her, or more like a confessional priest, but my mom and I spent many hours on the phone. In an odd way, when we said our good-byes, I could feel her nearly levitating from the conversations. One day my mom said to me, "I can't look you in the eyes out of shame. You have the eyes of the Great Spirit, and I can't face that."

One of the most beautiful gifts my mom gave me was to help me understand my Native American heritage and our Karuk tribal ways. She told me that we had several medicine men in our family who were referred to as "Red Caps," beginning back in the 1800s with Red Cap Johnnie. My mom shared what "Eagle Medicine" meant, and how I should practice it. An eagle is seen by many Native nations as the connection to, or the symbol of, the Great Spirit. It teaches us to release past hurts by embracing our core selves, and to accept our emotions and heal. She told me of "Blue Jay Medicine," which is like Eagle Medicine, but is individual to the Karuk. Blue jays are said to bring healing medicine from the creator. She said that I was born into the traditional ways of our people, and in her mind and in the mind of her spiritual advisor, I was chosen to "break the cycle," which is exactly what had been mentioned before in my life from shamans, and to carry forward the medicine bag of my grandfather, Red Cap Johnnie.

Mom was near the end of her journey when I was on a business trip to Las Vegas in 2007. When I got back home, I had a voicemail from my biological brother, telling me Mom was in the hospital. I called her and told her that I loved her and forgave her. She passed away that evening. I was the last person to speak with her.

I continued to seek the wisdom of tribal elders and traditional teachers. I met a medicine woman I'll call Vivian. She had awareness of the practices of the Incan and Peruvian tribes. Vivian, who was trained in western medicine as a doctor, offered to share her knowledge of tribal medicine and traditions with me. Over the next several months, we spent many hours together reading, studying, and sharing. My spiritual life was growing daily, and whenever possible, I shared all of that awareness during my speaking engagements.

This incredible woman introduced me to the talking feather. This is an eagle feather wrapped with leather at the quill that is used in ceremonies to promote respect, truth, and compassion. The person with the talking feather is the only one in the sacred circle that is able to speak. All others in the circle wait until they have the feather to talk or share their thoughts. Every time we sat together, she pulled out the talking feather, and we then begin to share our experiences.

In the fall, when I attended another one of the shaman's retreats at the treatment center, the shaman and I decided it was time for me to do an ancient Lakota ceremony called the Sundance. The Sundance required me to practice specific disciplines for the year leading up to the Sundance. The Lakota shaman asked me to offer him my grandfather pipe as a token of my commitment to dancing. Over the next year, I spent my weekends in prayer, dancing in a circle as I had been instructed, making prayer ties, and fasting for as long as three days. I felt myself developing deeper feelings, and being more and more connected to nature and other people.

CHAPTER 39

The Sundance

The Sundance is a ceremony practiced differently by several North American Indian nations. Many of the ceremonies have features in common, including dancing, singing, and drumming, the experience of visions, fasting, and often, self-piercing. The Sundance lasts from four to eight days, starting at sunset on the last day of preparation, and ending at sunset of the final day of the ceremony. It shows continuity between life, death, and regeneration. The required dance and preparation show that there is no true end to life, but a cycle of symbolic and true deaths and rebirths. All of nature is intertwined and its parts are dependent on one another.

I was given very specific directions to prepare for my Sundance, and many times over the year, I wanted to quit and go back to my old lifestyle. One phrase kept playing in my head: *Don't deny the miracle.* The preparation showed me how my ego had continued to show up in my life. At times, I felt like I was outside myself, observing my ego, and was able to know and understand the attachments my ego had to people and material things.

I leaned on many people, but mostly on the Great Spirit and on my best friend and teacher, Geno. As I prepared over the course of the year, I became more compassionate to other people's needs and character defects. I discovered I wanted to commit myself to a life of service. All my problems became secondary.

One of the activities needed to prepare for Sundance was to make the wooden pegs that would be used to pierce my skin. While I was carving the pegs with a knife, a voice came to me, saying, *You're doing this for the greater good, and you're the chosen one to break the cycle.* Again, here was another person mentioning the breaking of a cycle—making this cycle language a common theme, not just a coincidence. I had an incredible sense of presence at that moment, and the world was unfolding around me in such a loving, miraculous way.

The closer the Sundance got, the more my ego made its presence known. This year the Sundance was taking place in New Mexico on the Zuni Reservation. By the time I arrived in southern New Mexico, I was in total fear. I could not believe I had committed to dancing in New Mexico's hot sun for three days. It was too late to turn back!

Many of the people at the Sundance grounds were there to separate from the ego, to find themselves, and to sacrifice a part of themselves. I found myself connecting to every ego in the desert that day. People were irritating me, saying things that made me angry. People were being pierced, and staying tied to the tree for hours. I thought, *What incredible egos these guys have.* I had learned a saying in my recovery program—"If you spot it, you got it,"—and that is exactly what happened to me. I was spotting everyone else's ego because mine was very big.

When the dance started, I felt like I didn't have the strength to last the entire three days, since I had been fasting for the two days leading up to the ceremony. The hot sun was sapping my strength, and dancers were allowed only a small amount of water per day. As the days went on, I found myself in a battle. My ego kept telling me to quit, that this whole Sundance thing was silly. My ego was telling me that I was making good money, and I was sober. There was no need to be out in the desert dancing around a decorated tree. The battle between my spirit and ego raged on for another day until I got the call to be pierced. My heart dropped. I thought, *What was I thinking, letting these people put wooden pegs in my chest and tying me to a tree?* Up until the last minute when I was laying on the buffalo robe , which was traditional for this ceremony, waiting to be pierced, I was trying to find a way to quit. A simple, small voice came into my head, saying, *Surrender, Rob, surrender.* I went limp on the buffalo robe and felt my chest being cut open, a slice on one side and then a slice on the other. I felt the blood running down my chest to my armpits. My stomach felt weak, and I was nauseous, and I thought I was going to pass out from the pain.

I climbed off the buffalo robe and was tied to the tree. As the rope tightened and the skin pulled away from my chest, more and more blood ran down my stomach. The more I cringed and tensed up, the more pain I felt. The tenser I became, the more I realized I was attached to my physical body. I learned that pain is born out of attachment. I understood that my mind was attached to the pegs in my chest. When I ignored the ego and relaxed, the skin on my chest became more elastic, and the pegs seemed about to break through my skin. This thought made me tense up again, and it became a battle between the spirit and the ego. My ego did not want to separate from the spirit, even though it was necessary in order to separate from my old belief system. The pain was not physical; it was emotional. As the medicine man passed me on his way around the circle, he said, "Let go now. It's obvious you don't want to surrender."

The medicine man came back to me, asking, "Are you ready to separate?"

I asked myself, *Do you know what you're doing?* The answer was no. I had to have faith. I leaned back, the pegs tore out of my chest, and blood poured down. In letting go, I separated from my ego. In a split second, years of childhood pain and trauma were gone.

After I broke, it became clear to me that through all the years of addiction with my family, my brother's suicide, my other brother's heroin overdose, my belief system, my ability to be a father, and my recovery community, I was part of the greater whole, not the center of the universe. The Sundance was not about a person tied to a tree; it was for my family, tribe, and society as a whole. It was to break that cycle that so many other shamans had spoken about before.

That night I cried like a little baby—not tears of pain, but tears of gratitude and joy. I was humbled by the experience. My body felt as if my cells had completely reorganized, because the vibration that had driven me crazy most of my life—the anxiety, fear, and anger—were all replaced with a much slower vibration, both rhythmic and harmonious.

When I arrived home from the Sundance, I picked up Colin at Jennifer's. The moment he saw me, he asked, "Daddy, what is that big smile for?"

"Because I miss you and love you," I said. That night when five-year-old Colin and I sat outside on my deck, the wind was blowing, and the leaves on the trees were shaking. I was talking to Colin, and he said, "Daddy, be quiet."

"Why?"

"Do you hear that?" he asked.

"What?" I was curious.

"Do you hear that?" he asked again.

"All I hear is the leaves on the trees."

"Yes, the trees are happy, and they are clapping." he said simply.

I sat in awe of his awareness of nature, and thought, *Maybe this is what people mean when they say to look at the world through a child's eyes.*

By the end of 2006, nearly everything about me had changed. I felt like I was reborn into a new life and body.

A few nights later, Colin and I were sitting across from each other. First he looked at me, then at the television, then back at me again. He reached up and pulled my cheeks close to his face. "Daddy, I love you," he said.

I realized at that moment that everything I had been through was worth it.

I spent the next day with my shaman, and she said, "You're breaking the cycle thus living your name, and your son is the beginning of the new cycle, thus living his name."

Colin: Young soul or young pup

Robert: Shining fame or bright awareness

CHAPTER 41

My Name Is Kevin

I set out to be of maximum service to my fellow human beings, my family, my child, and my friends. I created a company that was service-oriented and I dedicated my life to be of service.

And then...

One day at Target, a young man came up to me. "Rob," he said, "my name is Kevin, and I heard you speak. The day I heard you speak, I was on my way to commit suicide. Your story changed my life. I've been sober eighteen months. These are my two girls." Then he said, "Girls, this is the man who saved Daddy's life."

My roll number is 3743; my name is Rob Cabitto...

Epilogue

Amazing transformations can happen to a person when the miracle of recovery is embraced. As I sit here today writing this last chapter, I reflect on all the people who have been in and out of my life over the years. Honestly, I am sincerely humbled by the number of people who have helped me every step of the way.

When my biological parents couldn't take care of me, I was adopted by a family who gave me a warm bed and food, and loved me the best they could. When I needed support while my dad was going through treatment for his brain injury, a baseball coach took over. When I needed a friend, a neighbor invited me into his life, and shared his family. When I was homeless, a friend offered to let me live in his trailer. When I was out of control, a mother (either mine or a friend's) invited me into her house to live and grow. When I was in a car accident, someone picked me up, drove me home, and cared for me. Doctors mended my wounds and nurses gave me food, water, and hope.

Girlfriends' parents gave me a place to stay, guidance, and moral support. When I was partying to excess, several families and friends offered me their couch, food, a shower, and companionship. When I was on the road and homeless, men and women fed me, clothed me, offered me a spot at their campfire, and a drink off their bottle to warm my lonely heart, and gave me a smile. When I was broken and lonely, girlfriends cared for me, were compassionate, and offered companionship.

When I went to jail, officers treated me with kindness, giving me words of encouragement that made me hopeful. While in jail, my cellmate used a warm washcloth to wipe the blood from my face, and the tears from my eyes. When I was lonely in jail, gang members gave me a chance to be of service to them. When I got out of jail, employers offered me a job, in spite of my past. When I needed guidance, wise people shared their experience, strength, and hope in order to help me become a better human being.

When I moved, packers took care of my property and truckers transported my things in perfect order. Apartment complexes rented to me, mortgage companies gave me mortgages, and neighborhoods welcomed me. When I drank, detox centers nursed me back to health, not asking anything of me. When I went into a recovery program, my fellow spiritual travelers gave me a smile, a seat, a cup of coffee, a hug, and love. When I was broke, a friend loaned me money with no expectations. When my car needed gas, a neighbor filled my tank.

I did not understand that I needed all these things, or who would provide them. But that happened by perfect design.

One of the greatest experiences in my entire life came in 2010. While writing this book, I decided to try to work on getting my felony set aside. I contacted the State of Arizona—more specifically, Judge Miller's office. When I called Judge Miller's office, I told her clerk who I was and why I was calling. I explained that I had been on her caseload in the mid '90s and was a raging alcoholic who had many more issues after leaving jail and probation, but that I had eventually embraced recovery. The clerk put me on hold, and the next voice was none other than Judge Miller. I could tell that voice anywhere. I introduced myself and explained that I was calling with gratitude for her work—for knowing more than I did about what was good for my life. The phone was quiet for a minute before she responded in a soft voice. "I remember your case: the dog was shot in the hotel room."

When I told her she was correct, she said, "Thank you; you have no idea how much that means to me." We then spoke for about an hour, talking about my recovery, the book I was writing, my education, my son Colin, and my Native American journey. When my attorney submitted the paperwork to have my felony set aside, the state decided not to fight it, and Judge Miller signed the order.

As this chapter of my life comes to a close, I want to say that over ninety percent of all the people you've read about are currently in my life, or have been in the last several years. Recovery has given me a chance to redeem myself with each person I hurt, when they have been available. If I can do it, anyone can! My hope is that I can continue be of maximum service to my community, family, old friends, as well as the new ones I have not yet met.

I tell my story every chance I get because I do not regret my past, and cannot shut the door on it. I credit recovery for the ability and guidance to transform my weaknesses into assets, and pain into hope.

Education: As early as I can remember, I was asking questions about the building blocks of our universe. I wanted to know everything, and I always had a follow-up question that pursued more information about how something worked. I questioned every theory I came across and turned to the back of each book to read the references so I could then check those books out of the library. From the very beginning, I questioned our history books when it became apparent that the winners were always telling the story. My thought has always been this: *If I can just get my hands on another book, it will unlock another secret of our past, present, or future.* This hunger for education went dormant for many years when I found mind-altering substances that deadened and replaced that interest.

Addiction: I did not wake up one day and say to myself, *I think I will be an addict. I think I will sleep on people's couches, be homeless, go to jail, and step over many people in order to get high.* No, those were not my thoughts, hopes, or dreams. Mind-altering substances offered a way to quiet my mind and emotions, and get rid of the bad dreams of early, early childhood. It also medicated the vibration inside me that I thought I needed to fear. But let me clarify something: Drinking and using brought many interesting people and experiences into my life, and ultimately became a gift or a vessel to bring me home to my spiritual nature at its native roots. This makes me realize how young I was when I first felt and experienced these vibrations, also known as spirituality.

Spirituality: When I use the word spirituality, I loosely mean whatever tools bring me closer to my authentic self. At an early age, I felt my biological mother's sadness and pain. I could see the sadness in her big brown eyes. The first time I recognized an energy field around humans was in my backyard. To me, this is a manifestation of the spiritual forces at work in our corporal world. In this incident, a childhood friend was walking toward me and I suddenly perceived a white light surrounding him. At another time, a different friend sitting with me said, "Cabitto, what's your problem? Are you out in space?"—when in fact I was experiencing a non-chemically induced, heightened sense of consciousness. A further definition of my search for the presence and meaning of spirituality came to me as a child. I was in a religion class when the leader explained that if everyone did not believe in this one particular God, then he or she would perish in hell. I asked him, "What if they live in the jungle and never met your God?" His response was a blank stare, followed by a comment that made no sense to me: "They will not be able to go to heaven." It was then that I began this odyssey. I was either running from a god or trying to find a god that seemed to be lost.

Through my voracious appetite to read and learn, I discovered a universal message in so many of the books I read on a variety of topics, which included Hindu, Sanskrit, Indian, Native American, Celtic, the Torah, the Bible, Buddhism, many forms of Christianity, and the teachings of Allah. Other books about the Norse, Greeks, Romans, Catholics, Native Americans, and aboriginals all had a similar message of love and compassion.

In my journey to find some way to reconcile my insides with my outsides, calm my fears and dreams, I discovered drugs and alcohol. And on that path, I've found so many amazing and creative people with philosophies on life that were, in a word, "different." One thing remained consistent: All these people, philosophies, religions, and spiritual beliefs were meant to lead the human being down a spiritual path.

I had to reconcile this love and compassion for myself before I could have love and compassion for others. The self-learning through books, and my education, kept me interested, while my addiction kept me medicated in order for the spirit to catch up, and ultimately set me free. God was never lost. He was, and has always been, inside me. I was the one who was lost.

I have been able to acquire college degrees from the University of Phoenix, New York Institute of Technology, and many certifications in networking, telephony, storage area networks, and advanced technology. In my twenties, I used to watch commercials about attending a university and dream about what it would be like to go to school. Then I would have a drink and pass out, to live another day. I cherish my education and continue to expand it every chance I get. I read as many books as I can get my hands on, and I never quit learning.

My addictions have brought me to the brink of death, but also to an awakened state. What I used to view as the worst thing that could ever happen to me turned out to be one of the best things that ever happened to me. My worst day in recovery is better than my best day drinking and using. In that time, I have seen friends die, neighbors get sober, and people who had been on the edge of death come and say thank you. I've spoken all over the country. I never thought simply telling my story could change another person's life, but I have seen much direct evidence.

I've discovered that spirituality can be found anywhere at anytime, and can come in an instant to anyone. My journey back to my tribe began many, many years ago and passed through many tribal leaders and traditions. I thought I was separate from the Native community because I was raised in the "white world." What I've learned is that tribal leaders and many tribes welcome anyone; they do not recognize skin color, race, or background.

Most of my life I was seeking something "out there" to resolve the issues "in here." The first medicine man I met led me to the next and the next, and so on. I have sundanced with the Lakota, sweat with the Papago, smoked a pipe with the Navajo, and sung fire songs with the Yaqui. All of these tribes offered me one thing: love. Thank goodness for all the people who loved me when I could not love myself, and who were willing to be there until I discovered the true source. It was never something "out there;" it was always in me, as me, and through me.

I have taken all this knowledge and applied it to my personal and professional life. My professional journey has taken me from the top of Fortune 500 companies to mom-and-pop storefronts, and everywhere in between. I've learned so much from each of them. In April 2009, I was inspired to start my own company. I am the founder and president of Nine Mile Communications, Inc. My company's sole purpose is to be of service. Nine Mile Communications moves, adds, changes, and repairs data communications equipment for other companies all over North America. We are in the business to make the businesses of others better by connecting the world one device at a time.

"Continue to promote the life script."
—Steve Karpman, *The Drama Triangle*.

ADDENDUM

Recovery and Relationships

Recovery doesn't mean cure; it means learning to cope with life, and managing it to the best of one's abilities, without the use of mind-altering chemicals. Even free of chemicals, however, life's scripts continue to play out in our human dramas. Recovery is like peeling layers of an onion back. Right when you think you've peeled back all the layers there are, you find another. The essence of recovery is discovering how addiction involves mental, emotional, moral, and intellectual challenges that are equally as difficult to manage as its physical manifestation. For the addict, abusive thinking leads to abusive drinking; values, principles, morals, and intellectual degradation lead to chemical deviation. Even in the absence of alcohol and drugs, the scripts remain in place until they are edited by the growing knowledge, experience, and wisdom gained through recovery.

Each of us has a life script—a belief system and associated behavior that influences our life and relationships. My life script is "the feeling of being abandoned." Through a series of events and circumstances, some in my control, and some not, a script was set in which I created and sabotaged relationships, no matter whether the circumstances were good, bad, or indifferent.

I was not aware of "life scripts" or "drama triangles" until, while in recovery, I had an utter and complete meltdown. I had a some failed relationships that brought significant pain to those involved in these triangles: my son, others, and me. The emotional bottom, and the damage that came from these failed relationships, was worse than the bottom I hit when I put the bottle down for the last time.

For the addict, abusive thinking leads to abusive drinking.

When recovery took hold of my life, nearly everything changed for the better. I was working fulltime, earned an MBA, did service work, established new friends, and repaired many old relationships. Over the last several years, I've acquired profound and prophetic information about myself. First, even though a person like me might no longer have alcohol in my life, I still have some of the same behavior patterns. Second, this holds true for others as well.

Earlier in this book I alluded to how I manufactured relationships in hopes of having a family and security. Dr. Steve Karpman describes it as a "life script." This artificial way of developing a love interest has the potential to bring pain and heartache to everyone involved. As much damage as I caused before quitting drinking, I caused damage after quitting as well. Take out the alcohol, and you still have an alcoholic. This is me.

In my quest for a family and security, I've come across others who had the same desire and characteristics through "laws of attraction." In setting up these artificial relationships, people like me attract others like me, and that person and the subsequent situation can be described as the "drama triangle." Typically this triangle is made up of three: victim, persecutor and rescuer. And it's important for you, the reader, to understand that when one is "trained" in the drama triangle, he or she can shift roles in an instant—regardless of the situation—depending on his or her life script. When I describe the drama triangle, I will try to describe what role I'm playing, and in which relationship. I fit comfortably in the role of the rescuer, but can and have shifted roles to victim and persecutor.

At times in my life, I became involved with women who were often at the tail end of a relationship, in a troubled relationship, or had recently ended a relationship. What I've discovered is that not all people are aware they are playing out their life script, and have these outstanding characteristics associated with the drama triangle. It's important to say that not everyone in my life has been in the drama triangle to the same magnitude.

In a drama triangle are three roles, and each has its own characteristics. Your role can change, based on the circumstances. I had to learn this the hard way. With the new women in my life I always came in as the "rescuer" to her "victim." I was prime and ready to be the new "You can count on me" guy in her life, and that of her children.

The victim's characteristics can be described as overwhelming, emotionally deprived, helpless, hopeless, and self-pitying. Often this person is scared that he or she won't meet his or her own financial needs, and hasn't had laughter or levity in years because of having to raise the children alone, according to her or him. They want peace, a person to care about them, help them, edify them, and touch them. They want an emotionally available partner, and a good kisser. And the thread that binds this person to the rescuer is the fact that the rescuer will listen to them.

I've discovered that people raised in or with the drama triangle will have characteristics of each role, and will utilize them to have their needs met, changing roles in an instant if necessary.

However, I did not understand the power and sophistication of a life script, and how it played out in my relationships, until I entered recovery—and took out alcohol as a solution.

Over the last several years, I've met many women who fit the drama triangle. It is often said that "we don't arrive in the rooms of a recovery program on a winning streak." Often our marriages are a mess, our work lives are in shambles, our relationships are in pieces, and we have a multitude of other problems.

One woman who showed up at a recovery meeting one day, may as well have had a neon sign on her forehead saying, "Pick me." We made eye contact and talked after the meeting. A week later I went on a business trip, and when I got back, her ring was off her finger. The drama triangle was in motion. She was glad to have found a good listener. Later she shared that she was in a troubled marriage, had no hope, and was lonely, scared, and needy. Well, Mr. Fix It (me) stepped in to rescue my poor victim.

As this relationship evolved, we realized the situation was primed for many of the issues that come with the drama triangle: divorce, legal trouble, hurt feelings, the kids' involvement. Later I discovered she had even more emotional issues. The outgoing persecutor was angry. He did not want his position as a professional and father threatened, and he pulled out all the stops in order to persecute his ex-wife and me. He took every opportunity to bash me to his kids. He made racist comments like "Why is this Indian off the reservation?" "Shouldn't this Indian be drunk or in jail" and "Indians are worthless." He badmouthed me professionally. At first his kids overlooked his ravings, but after a while, they discovered that they, too, could use this language and behavior to victimize or persecute their mother. Soon we had a triangle between her, the kids, and their father—and me.

When the kids came to like me, their father became even angrier. He started persecuting the kids, and as they became the victims, their mother and I began rescuing them. This vicious cycle continued over the course of the entire relationship, each of us changing roles based on the situation, and who was creating the drama.

Co-Dependency Rears Its Head

Out of this insanity came the realization that there were deeper issues than the drama triangle and its players. Another issue, unknown to me, came to light: co-dependency. Co-dependency is a maladaptive behavior that can be derived from abuse or from living with an addict or alcoholics. People with this defect are compulsive, needy, and emotionally unstable.

I qualify for all of these behaviors, as did my drama-triangle partners, which is why we "dysfunctioned" so well together. As my relationship with this woman continued to grow, so did my relationship with her teenage daughters. They were interested in the Native world, appreciated that I helped them with their homework, and loved the fact that I drove them to and from their friends' houses. I became the easy alternative to dealing with Mom and Dad. This relationship was new, and they felt free with me. I was an outsider who taught them, but couldn't discipline them. Their issues pulled on my heartstrings, and I became their mediator. While Mom and Dad were fighting, the kids and I were busy playing games, going somewhere, doing homework, and watching television.

I became the go-to guy, Mr. Fix It. When it came to issues with Mom, Dad, and friends, I offered advice, settled disputes, and mediated when the family was fighting. I became everyone's trusted confidant.

One day a wise man told me, "Rob, you don't know how much power and responsibility comes with the role you're playing in their lives. It can backfire and come back to bite you in the butt." How prophetic that statement was.

For any men or women reading this who are involved with a woman with children—especially teenage children—please don't do what I did. If I had it to do over, I'd go to a parenting class or consult with other fathers as to how to deal with teenage girls. I had absolutely no skills to be a father to teenage girls who were manipulative and full of drama. I thought I needed to fix every situation, take care of everyone's feelings, and wipe away every tear. I had no conception of the wrath that would fall upon me from the child, and later, her mother.

Over the course of our relationship, after the "honeymoon phase," more hidden behaviors started to surface. My girlfriend began to complain that she was having physical pain and needed to get relief with medication. Her daughter began describing anger issues between her and her mother. My girlfriend called me to help her deal with her daughter, or her daughter called me to help her deal with her mother. I was constantly in between them. When I tried to mediate, inevitably both turned on me. Even if I didn't take sides, each said I favored the other.

Increasingly, this relationship was becoming disturbing. What was I doing in the middle? I thought if I doubled my efforts, things would maybe get better: Classic co-dependency. If I could control the teenage daughter's emotions, and her mother's behavior, things would get better. I frowned upon the girl's friendship with her wild friend, and consoled the mother, telling her I would keep everyone safe. I proceeded to try to keep everyone in line, but I had no idea the extent to which this was going to backfire.

One day when I took the teenager to visit her friends, I discovered the friend's brother was using drugs. He and the girls were getting high and watching porn. After I alerted the mother, the teenage daughter said she no longer wanted to be around me. The drama triangle had shifted. After the mother banned her daughter from seeing her friends, she turned to her angry father for support.

One day I spoke to a police officer whose exact words were: "You need to get out of this situation as quickly as possible, or it will get worse."

Therapist Patty Fleener said: "Be very careful of victims in your life. You may find yourself in lawful and legal trouble over lies."

After this relationship came to an end, I thought, *With the new insights gained from my failures, I will do things differently if I'm fortunate enough to have another relationship.*

No, I did it again. I sabotaged another relationship with the same behavior. Many times over the years, I've set up relationships that were doomed to fail. I did not realize I was setting them up to fail, nor did I want them to fail at the same time. My life script was playing, but I just wasn't consciously aware of it.

> *"What we don't redeem from our unconsciousness*
> *comes back to bite us in this state."*
> —Carl Jung

Layers Continue to be Peeled Back

A man in recovery asked me to mentor him, that is, guide him in a recovery program. He asked me to meet with him to explain a few of his issues, which were the same ones I had worked on myself.

This conversation turned from recovery to him asking me to share my experience with his wife. I accepted the invitation with the best intention, thinking, *I can guide this guy and his wife through the pitfalls of recovery and relationships, and share my failures with these issues.*

People who see themselves as victims, can bring all sorts of unwanted emotional and legal pain—as well as turmoil—to a person's life.

Unfortunately this man ended up leaving the recovery program, and he and his wife eventually got divorced. However, I later started a relationship with his former wife. Let's call our damsel in distress "Amber."

Amber had all the characteristics that appealed to my life script, and more importantly, my association with the drama triangle. Amber was a victim and needed a rescuer, and I was available and willing to rescue because I had new information gained from a previous relationship that had gone bad. I knew I could incorporate all this, and make things better this time.

Our life scripts play subconsciously. We do not consciously turn them on and move forward in life and relationships. The life script is a way of creating relationships based on our past experiences and our belief system. We attract those who can fit a role or help us carry out our life script. Mine is abandonment.

As Amber and I continued to move forward in our relationship, little things began to pop up that made me think, *Hmmm.*

Amber asked me to give advice in several areas of her life: her divorce, communication with her ex-husband, physical problems, and emotional issues with her mother, children, and friends. My opinion mattered. I became her trusted confidant for legal matters—plus, I could fix anything electrical. Again, I was Mr. Fix It, performing all my duties well. My responsibilities in her life began to grow and grow, and soon I was helping and participating in nearly every decision in her life. Wow, I felt wanted, needed, important, and a part of something special. In my eyes, we were developing the kind of give-and-take relationship or partnership that I'd always wanted.

My whole day was dedicated to Amber. That's the way she wanted it, and I was most willing to buy into her need. I woke up thinking about

Amber, showed up late for meetings at work and in recovery in order to help Amber with the current or perceived crisis. She texted and checked her phone constantly, anticipating issues that didn't come to fruition. I thought some things were odd, but I really wanted this family thing to work, so I thought maybe if I helped more, some day soon Amber would be present for me. I thought, *If only I had tried harder…* so I worked my schedule around Amber in order to support her in every possible way. I became the perfect helper: Amber's sidekick and Mr. Fix It. If I missed a call or showed up late, Amber would scold me and punish me by not talking to me for two or three days at a time.

I tried desperately not to misstep or make a mistake.

One day Amber reminded me of my shortcomings, and told me I was like her ex-husband, and that I needed to get help with my issues. I was stupefied and asked myself, *What issues? What is she talking about? I've done everything for her, remained sober, put my life on hold, and cared for her in ways I've never cared for a woman!* I doubled my efforts and, of course, told Amber that I would do more.

Professional Help Turned On "the Light"
At the advice of a wise old friend, I went to counseling. Sitting with my therapist and explaining my dilemma, he handed me Melody Beattie's *Codependent No More*. He shared a plan that could bring a bit of relief to my current situation. I was desperate and willing to do anything. I wanted the relationship to work, and to nurture this beautiful family unit we were building. Amber, her kids, and her family had become paramount to me, and I loved them with all my heart. I was willing to work on myself the same way as the day I put down my last drink.

My therapist asked me to complete a homework assignment before seeing him again: Create a responsibility list outlining my responsibilities, Amber's responsibilities, and our shared responsibilities. this assignment, I was shocked. I was actively involved in so many of Amber's day-to-day affairs that it was surprising that my company and my life was even running. Her responsibility to me, on the other hand? None.

What the heck happened here? I thought Amber and I were in this thing together, working toward the same goal, had great synergy, and were committed to the same cause. All that is true, but the "cause" was Amber, and nothing else. At my next appointment, I read this spreadsheet to my therapist. He asked, "Rob, do we need to go any further?"

I responded, "NO."

Reality hit me in the face. My life script was playing, but this time it included the drama triangle *and* co-dependency issues. Many of the symptoms that had been very subtle at first, were now glaring: control, blaming, self-pity, hyper-vigilance, emotional unavailability, perfectionism, intimacy problems, avoidance of feelings, and physical illness. Amber rotated between needing to get everything done immediately and lethargy because she was exhausted from trying to get everything done.

Amber and I were on the same page, which meant we were both committed to Amber's issues and worked on them day and night, leaving no time to develop a relationship, have balance, or nurture a loving family environment. At that moment, I began disengaging from all of Amber's responsibilities. She found other men to mow the lawn, fix the electronics, help her with legal troubles, watch the kids, indulge her texting, tell her how pretty she was, and help her with her daily issues like how to articulate an email or whether or not to respond to a request. It was amazing how many people she had working for her on a daily basis, as if she was running a little company. When any one of the individuals bucked the system, Amber cut him or her off, and found another person to fill that role.

I knew I had entered into another relationship with an emotionally unavailable woman. What I discovered in my own personal experience with this person, and through my counselor, was that this person was a user. Melanie Beattie explains this behavior so eloquently in *Codependent No More*.

I equipped myself about the drama triangle, and my part in it. I discovered my life script, and began working on my co-dependency and that thought process. I entered the most intensive therapy I had ever undertaken in my life. In the end, I realized all I've ever wanted was a family.

WE INVITE YOU TO CONTINUE YOUR JOURNEY WITH US.

Visit us at
www.robcabitto.com

If you would like to book Rob as a speaker please contact us at 952.767.3743 or by contacting Rachel Anderson at 952-240-2513

WE INVITE YOU TO CONTINUE
YOUR JOURNEY WITH US.

*Share your insights and discuss the
book with other on our blog*

Buy the book

If you would like to book Rob as a speaker please contact us at 952.767.3743
or by contacting Rachel Anderson at 952-240-2513

WE INVITE YOU TO CONTINUE YOUR JOURNEY WITH US.

Become a facebook friend

Follow us on Twitter

If you would like to book Rob as a speaker please contact us at 952.767.3743 or by contacting Rachel Anderson at 952-240-2513